THE EARTH ADVENTURE

Your Soul's Journey Through Physical Reality

The Wisdom of the Guides Through

Ron Scolastico, Ph.D.

UNIVERSAL GUIDANCE PRESS

THE EARTH ADVENTURE
Your Soul's Journey Through Physical Reality

Copyright © 2019 by Susan Scolastico
Copyright © 1988 by Ron Scolastico, Ph.D.

UNIVERSAL GUIDANCE PRESS
www.ronscolastico.com

First Hardback Edition, 1988 Universal Guidance Press
First Trade Paper Edition, 1991 Hay House, Inc.
Kindle Edition, 2011 Universal Guidance Press
Second Paperback Edition, 2019 Universal Guidance Press

ISBN 978-0-943833-30-9

Cover Art by Kathy Hasenberg

Prepared for Kindle Direct Publishing by Susan Scolastico

This book is dedicated to
My beautiful wife, Susan,
To our family,
And to all of the people
Who have encouraged my work
with The Guides.

CONTENTS

INTRODUCTION

The Making Of A Trance Medium

This book has come into being in a rather unusual and exciting way that, for me, a scientifically trained and academically oriented person, has been quite mystifying at times. It grows out of a long series of extraordinary experiences spanning a period of several years.

These experiences have led me from the calm and peaceful campus life of a Midwestern university into my present-day profession, in which I find myself to be, not the sedate university professor that I might have been, but a professional "trance medium" who is able to enter at will into vast unlimited psychic realms of wisdom and truth. Instead of teaching in the college classroom, I am now giving lectures, workshops, and "life readings" for thousands of people throughout the United States, helping them live more meaningful lives by providing them with profound knowledge that is spoken through me by non-physical "spiritual guides."

I have written this introduction to share with you my process of discovery of the Guides, as well as the surprising unfoldment of my ability to allow the Guides to speak through me. The rest of this book has been "written" by the

Guides. Chapters one through nine present the speakings of the Guides that describe the vast journey our souls have undertaken in their creation of human life on earth.

THE FIRST DOOR OPENS

My transformation from an academician to a trance medium was initially set into motion by a strange experience that occurred more than ten years ago as I sat in my office at the University of Iowa. It was a warm spring day and I was contemplating a bright blue sky outside my window while I savored the luxurious feeling of having just completed my Ph.D. degree. I was eagerly looking forward to the offers of employment that I expected to come flooding in from the universities to which I had sent my resume.

On that day, I was intent on launching my career as a university professor. Had someone suggested that I might eventually be publishing a book of knowledge gained from spiritual guides, I would have laughed as loud as my sophisticated and cynical, sharp-tongued academic colleagues. Even though I was quite knowledgeable in the area of human consciousness, having studied for many years everything I could find on the subject—from ancient mystical teachings, through humanistic and transpersonal psychology—and even though I had practiced meditation for more than ten years, I was not at all interested in "psychic" explorations. I was totally convinced that all meaningful knowledge came through the disciplined use of the *intellect* and the rational mind.

On that sunny day in May, my incredible transformation began quite simply with the ringing of the telephone. When I answered it and the caller identified himself as Bill ____, head of the faculty search committee of a large western university with plenty of funding in my field, I was intensely interested. At that time I was practically penniless, and I desperately needed to generate some income to pay back more than twenty thousand dollars in educational loans.

Bill began by telling me that they had carefully studied the material I sent them on my experience and qualifications, and that they were very interested in me. As he talked on in a warm and friendly way, he sounded like he thought I was exactly the man for their department. The salary was generous, the location excellent, and the reputation of the department was good.

Bill said he wanted me to fly out the *next day* for an interview. By then, I was excited about the possibility of being hired by Bill's department.

We talked for a few more minutes, then Bill said, "Well, Ron, what do you say?"

I opened my mouth and began to speak, fully *intending* to accept his invitation. I was a hungry graduate in dire need of a steady paycheck.

However, instead of saying what I *thought* I was thinking—"Wonderful, Bill, I'm very interested, and I'll fly out right away"—in horror, I heard myself saying into the phone: "I want to thank you very much for your interest, but I'm seriously considering another offer, and I'm just not able to respond to yours right now."

After Bill expressed his regret and asked me to keep his department in mind, I mumbled goodbye, numbly replaced the phone, then sat there, stunned by what I had done. I found it hard to believe what had just happened.

A strange feeling of calmness had come over me as I had responded to Bill. It was as if someone else had spoken the words that turned down his offer. But, I needed that job. And it was *not* true that I had another offer. This was the first one.

For a long while, I sat puzzling over how such a thing could have happened. How could I have said what was exactly *opposite* to my intentions?

Thinking about my pile of debts, I kept having to control the urge to grab the phone to call Bill back and tell him that I had changed my mind.

I sat and pondered the situation for a long time. Gradually, through my fog of confusion, there began to emerge the beginning of an understanding of the complex things stirring within me.

First, I recalled that for years, in order to put myself through school—starting with the Bachelor's degree, then the Master's, then the Doctorate—I had worked at jobs that I had disliked. All of the things that I really loved to do were done in my spare time, like teaching classes in human consciousness, mysticism, and spiritual teachings. I had never really "worked" at anything important to me. That was always squeezed in around the job that put the bread on the table.

Also, even though I thought I was ready to embark on a new university teaching career, I suddenly had the realization that I did *not* want to teach what my new Ph.D. qualified me to teach (an interdisciplinary study of humanistic psychology and human communication theory).

Sitting there, carefully sorting it all out, I gradually began to see that it had been this unconscious dislike of my chosen academic field, and my reluctance to spend my life doing another job just to make money, that had prompted an inner voice in me to refuse Bill's invitation. That voice was saying that I now refused to spend any more years doing work that was not fulfilling. Even though at the conscious level I thought I was ready to take it on, my inner wisdom knew better, and it had come to my rescue just in time.

Then I felt a mad, swift rush of determination and I suddenly decided that, for the first time, I was going to do the kind of work that I *wanted*, not what I needed to do just to pay the bills. So on that fresh spring morning, with no job, and with my twenty thousand dollars of debt hanging over my head, I asked myself: "Well, what do you *really* want to do?" Instantly, in a rare burst of clarity and certainty, the response came from deep within me: "I want to teach spiritual truths."

On that day, some form of inner wisdom and guidance had spoken to Bill for me, and it resulted in a decision that radically altered the course of my life, opening the door to the most fascinating, exciting, and fulfilling life's work that I can imagine. However, the path was not an easy one.

SEEDS OF INSPIRATION ARE PLANTED

With my new Ph.D. and my debts, along with much concern about how I would pay the debts, I turned my back on an academic career and settled down to figuring out how to make a living as a teacher of spiritual truths. Following my new decision to work only at things that were meaningful to me, I took a job in an art frame shop at minimum wage because I am an artist and I love art. At the same time, taking my first step toward my new career, I organized an evening class in which I was paid a token fee to teach principles of spiritual growth, as I then understood them from my intellectual studies.

However, even though I felt good about my decision to give up academia, and although I liked my new job at the frame shop, I was confused about my life and the many things that I had studied about human consciousness over the years. None of the truths that I had absorbed from my intellectual study seemed to help ease the feeling of emptiness that had been growing in my own life for a number of years. In spite of the fact that I had now set off in a direction of my own choosing, I still did not feel that there was any meaningful purpose to that direction or to my life in general. Also, I had studied so many different versions of "truth" that I was left with a feeling that, when it came right down to it, I didn't really know anything about truth. So, I was struggling intensely to understand myself and my life.

During the winter of that year, I happened to meet two women with unusual abilities who were to help me in my struggle. Both of these women, Lina and Cora, were involved in giving what they called "psychic trance readings." These readings were to lead me into the next intriguing steps of my transformation.

At the point at which I met Lina and Cora, I was interested in "cosmic" philosophical issues. As a result of my many years of study in the academic area of human consciousness, I considered an intellectual study of the *spiritual* aspects of life to be the only serious pathway to truth. As far as the *psychic* area was concerned, even though I had read widely in this field, and in spite of a respect for the work of people like Edgar Cayce and Jane Roberts, before I began having readings with Lina and Cora, I believed that people involved in psychic pursuits were lacking in intellectual discrimination. I considered such people to be the "cheap thrill seekers" of the human consciousness area.

With this rather arrogant attitude, late on a cold, clear November evening, with a brilliant full moon lighting our snowy town, I set out on foot toward Lina's house to have my first psychic reading. Although I felt foolish about wasting my time on such nonsense, my curiosity had been peaked by Lina's description of readings she had done for other people.

As I walked through the cold, still night, huddled into my down jacket, listening to the snow crunch beneath my feet, I was inwardly smiling to myself as I puzzled over why an intelligent man like myself was wasting time on a psychic reading. Still wondering about this, I stopped and looked up at the bright moon against the blackness of the sky.

While I stood staring at that brilliant moon, something strange began to happen to me. I started to feel a deep sense of expanded awareness. All at once I was feeling acutely vital and alive. This was accompanied by an intense thrill of joy and exuberance that shot through my entire being. This feeling seemed to be a kind of vibrant "energy" that coursed through me and around me. It felt like this energy was actually warming the air that surrounded me.

Then I began to feel deeply moved, as if something of tremendous importance was about to happen. Everything seemed to be standing still. There was no sound. No movement. I was enveloped in a warm cocoon of the extraordinary energy, and it was filling me with a profound sense of love. It was a strange, unearthly moment. It seemed like time had stopped, and, in the space created, I was literally being infused with love.

Then, suddenly, a thought flashed brilliantly through my mind. The thought was so out of tune with my own conscious thoughts of the moment that it seemed almost as if this strange idea had been placed there by someone other than myself—just as the words had been put into my mouth when I turned down Bill's invitation. The thought was: "This is a night that will change your life."

Even as I became aware of this inner statement, I smiled skeptically to myself. My conscious mind immediately began to ridicule the whole experience. It was nonsense. In spite of the extraordinary *feelings* I was having, my intellect was so powerful that I was able to completely ignore those feelings and shrug them off as imagination.

By the time I arrived at Lina's house, I had completely dismissed the unusual experience. I was busy feeling foolish about involving myself in a psychic reading. I walked up to Lina's door encouraging myself to make the best of an embarrassing situation. I decided that I would leave as soon as I could make a polite exit.

Lina was an attractive, intelligent woman in her late twenties. I had met her socially several times. During our last meeting she had told me about the readings that she was doing, and she said she wanted to do one for me. On that cold November night, when she opened the door and politely invited me into her cozy upstairs apartment, I was irritated with myself for having let her get me into such a ridiculous situation.

Lina explained briefly that she would be tuning in to spiritual guides, and she told me that I could ask questions at a certain point. Then she stretched out on the bed, gave me a reassuring smile, closed her eyes, said a little prayer, and lapsed into silence.

I sat quietly, trying to contain my amusement at the situation: an attractive woman laid out before me on the bed with her hands folded corpse-like on her chest, while I sat beside her, waiting for spirits to speak to me.

The silence lasted a long time. Becoming impatient, I idly stared out the window at the full moon. Suddenly, I was startled by a strange sounding voice.

The voice did not sound like Lina's voice, yet it was coming out of her mouth. There was an unusual accent, difficult to place. The voice was strong and spoke with a confident sense of authority.

The sound of the voice had a curiously soothing effect on me as it spoke in detail about intimate aspects of my personal life. The comfortable feeling was vaguely similar to what I had experienced on my way to Lina's house.

My patronizing sense of amusement was gone, replaced by an astonished curiosity. The things being said about me were amazingly accurate, and they were things that I was certain Lina did not know.

As the strange voice continued to speak, I was given information that offered deep insights into some of my negative personality traits. This was followed by wise suggestions for changing those patterns.

By the time that the voice coming from Lina told me to

ask questions, I was taking the whole process quite seriously. I cleared my throat, gathered myself up, and boldly
asked what my most pressing question at that time was:
"What is my purpose in this life, and why is it that even
though I have studied so many teachings, right now, I feel
totally confused about life?"

The voice immediately responded with: "You have followed many pathways with your *mind*, but you have followed none with your *heart*." The voice went on to describe how I had used the power of my intellect to build a
wall around my heart, my deep feelings, because I was
afraid of being hurt. Because I had trained myself not to
feel too deeply, I was unable to grasp the inner, intuitive
promptings that could lead me to find my own purpose and
to *feel* truth.

As the voice described this process of closing off my
emotions, I had the clear realization that everything that
was being said was absolutely true. Even though I had not
previously been aware of it, now that it was being pointed
out to me, it became obvious. I could see that my feeling of
emptiness was due to the fact that I wasn't allowing myself
to truly love, or to be loved, and that my confusion about
truth was due to the fact that all of the many truths I had
studied were permeated with the dry, detached quality of
intellect. I had absorbed the *words* of the teachings, had
analyzed and compared them, and had remembered them.
But, I had never *lived* them. I had not brought the truths to
life in my own intimate experience. In essence, my heart
knew no *real* love, and it knew no truth.

I went home that night with a new sense of excitement
about myself and my life. I hadn't been told my purpose

straight out, but I now had an understanding of the causes of my confusion about it, and I knew I was on the right track.

THE BARRIERS FALL

During the following months, I became good friends with Lina. She gave me several more readings that helped me begin a profound opening of my heart.

Lina also introduced me to Cora, a friend of hers who had a psychic ability similar to Lina's. I had several readings with Cora that led me deeper into an understanding of my life.

Working with the knowledge that I gained from these two sources, I literally transformed my life in a few months. I opened stimulating new areas of friendship and love with the people around me. I also came closer to what I felt was my own personal vision of life. I learned to distinguish my *personal truth* from the mass of intellectual material that I had absorbed during years of study. I really began to live the higher ideals of love and joy that I had only *thought* about in the past.

A real shocker came about six months after I began my work with Lina and Cora. In the middle of a reading with Cora, I suddenly heard these words being spoken: *"You have promised to be a trance medium in this lifetime."*

I sat and stared at Cora. My immediate thought was, "Wait a minute, you've got the wrong person."

The information coming through Cora continued to describe certain abilities that I was supposed to have—the ability to "reach into the heart of others and draw forth their pain" so that it could be healed; the ability to show them their purpose in life; and many more unusual and amazing things. Then I was given some strange information about having developed these abilities in some past time in Egypt.

When the reading was over, I felt troubled that this otherwise accurate source of information had suddenly come out with total nonsense. I believed that I knew myself quite well, and I was sure that I had no abilities in the psychic area.

At that time, even though I had had several experiences of expanded consciousness, along with a few deeply spiritual experiences during meditation—as well as a bizarre experience that had occurred when I was eight years old, during which I literally began expanding until I became a huge sphere of awareness filling my whole room—I felt that I had never had what I would consider to be a *psychic* experience, nor did I expect to have one in the near future. I had become convinced that in this lifetime I would probably not manifest any psychic abilities.

However, even though I doubted that I had the abilities described in Cora's reading, I decided, out of curiosity, that I would test myself. I believe now that I actually wanted to test Cora's accuracy because I was disturbed that the reading had made such a gross error in calling me a trance medium.

I had been meditating for several years, so I decided to combine my meditation with a test of these so-called trance abilities. I devised a simple plan to carry out after my meditation each day. I would have a tape recorder standing by, and, at the end of the meditation, I would turn on the tape recorder and try to talk from the deep meditation state.

Afterwards, I could evaluate what was said to see if it expanded upon my own knowledge, or if it brought through something that I didn't consciously know.

Several days later, with a sense of amusement and a slight feeling of foolishness, along with a complete lack of belief in my ability to bring through anything, I sat down for my first attempt.

My meditation was peaceful and calming. When it was finished, with my eyes closed, I groped for the recorder and switched it on.

Out loud, I said a brief affirmation that stated my intention of attuning to love and truth, and then I settled into silence. I decided to help myself along by imagining that I was tuning in to spiritual guides. Even though I had no idea what guides look like or feel like, at that point the *concept* of guides was not difficult for me to accept because much of my study, especially my work with Lina and Cora, allowed me to develop a fairly strong sense of the possibility of such guides. So I tried to "think" guides. But I had no belief that I could tune in to guides.

Sure enough, true to my expectation, during my first attempt I felt no sense of guides. In fact, I didn't feel anything but my normal self—just as I expected. I had *never* felt anything but my normal self all of my life, even during my few consciousness-expanding experiences in the past. The single exception was the bizarre experience that had occurred when I was eight, when I had expanded and filled up my room. During that, I definitely was not my normal self. But I had completely put that experience out of my mind. I had not thought of it again.

During this first attempt, I *was* able to speak from my

deep state of consciousness, but nothing out of the ordinary occurred. I spoke for about ten or fifteen minutes. I was perfectly aware of what I said. It *felt* like me, and when I listened to the tape later, it was clearly nothing but my own thoughts spoken aloud in my normal voice. They were ordinary statements about how we all need to love one another and work toward peace in the world.

The same thing happened the next day; and the next; and on and on. For more than two months, the results were the same: I would say my brief affirmation, sit in silence for a few minutes until I felt like starting to talk, then I would speak about general ideas that were mundane and obvious, with me feeling normal as I spoke. It was exactly what I had anticipated. I certainly didn't feel disappointed, for I had never really expected anything else. Yet, surprisingly, I continued to do these speakings consistently, day after day, without fail, seven days a week. I was enjoying them.

One morning, several months after the beginning of my test, I sat down and did my meditation as usual. Then I reached over and turned on the recorder, said my affirmation, and settled down into the now familiar sense of deep relaxation that always came before I started speaking. When I felt ready, I opened my mouth and began to speak. What I then heard nearly shocked me out of my deep state of attunement. Instead of my normal voice, a thick Irish brogue had popped out of my mouth!

I stopped speaking and sat there with my eyes closed, inwardly examining myself, trying to objectively figure out what was going on. I felt normal, except for my sense of deep relaxation. There certainly wasn't any feeling of guides or anyone else making my words sound like an Irish brogue. Clearly, there wasn't anyone there but me. But I wasn't causing the Irish accent.

Finally, I decided to start speaking again. This time, I willed my voice to stay normal, and it did. However, I immediately began to feel an intense nervousness and tension in my body. It felt like an instant case of bad coffee nerves. I stopped speaking again. I was very puzzled.

Something in me seemed to offer the idea of letting the Irish accent come back again. I felt silly at the thought of doing it, but I decided that since no one would hear me, I might as well give it a try. Again, I started to speak. There it was. The accent was back. They were my words, but it was *not* my voice. It was a perfect, extremely thick Irish brogue.

As I continued to speak, although I still felt like my normal self, the strange accent kept coming out of my mouth. I allowed it to continue and began to feel a wonderful sense of peace and joy filling my experience of the moment. I decided to relax and enjoy the nice feelings. I let the Irish voice ramble on. It felt pleasant, but what the Irish voice was saying was no more interesting than what my own voice had said during earlier speakings. Even though I allowed the accent to continue, I finally decided that the Irish accent and the good feeling had nothing to do with guides. I concluded that everything was being caused by some strange influence of my own unconscious mind.

During the next few days, I experimented with allowing the Irish accent to occur and then willing my normal voice to speak. Each time I "forced" myself to speak normally, I felt the tension and nervousness. When I allowed the Irish accent to occur, I felt the deep sense of peace and joy. I let the Irish accent come freely after that. Every day it was there.

Yet, I was still unimpressed with the content of what was being said. It was simply a rehash of my own spiritual and philosophical ideas. And I still felt relatively normal during the speaking, even though the unusual voice was coming out of my mouth. Certainly, nothing "psychic" was happening.

The next experience of noteworthiness occurred several weeks later. By that time I was used to the Irish accent and took it for granted. It was beginning to convey a very deep sense of warmth and love, and I was enjoying the pleasant feeling that came along with the accent. On this particular day, after my meditation, as I started to prepare for the speaking, I suddenly thought of a friend of mine named Martha. She was going through a period of emotional turmoil over a broken relationship and I began to wonder if the speaking could be about Martha and her situation. I mentally suggested this to myself before I began to say my affirmation.

When the Irish voice came through, it immediately began to talk about Martha, discussing the causes of her turmoil and offering suggestions about ways she could change the situation. Again, I felt fairly normal during this, and all of the things that were said about Martha were things that I knew. It seemed to me that the advice given was the same advice that I would probably have given in my normal conscious state. Once more, I wrote it all off as the influence of my unconscious mind.

The next day, it just so happened that Martha stopped

by my house to see me. I was impressed by this coincidence and thought that perhaps this was a "sign" that I was supposed to give her the tape of my speaking. I told Martha about my little experiment and said that I would let her hear the tape, after I got her to promise not to laugh at me when she heard the strange Irish voice. Then, with embarrassment, I handed over the tape.

The following day, I had forgotten about Martha's tape. The morning speaking was back to the mundane truths about life in general. Business as usual. I went off to work at the frame shop.

Later that evening, Martha called. She was very excited. She said, "Your tape was the most amazing thing that I have ever heard in my life. It told me exactly what is causing all of my sadness and depression, and it told me how to get rid of it. I feel great."

I was happy for Martha, but I told her not to take the reading too seriously. I said that it was general advice that could apply to anybody. She insisted that it was just perfect for her, and she also said she wanted me to do a reading for a friend of hers. I tried to refuse, but Martha was quite insistent. The friend was a man I knew, so I finally agreed to do the session if she would be certain to tell him that I was just experimenting, and that the information was probably coming from my unconscious mind.

The next morning as I sat alone preparing for my speaking, I gave myself the mental suggestion that the information would be for Ted, Martha's friend. The experience was a repeat of Martha's "reading." I felt normal as it happened, and the information given seemed quite ordinary to me.

When Ted came by that evening to pick up the tape, I carefully explained that I considered the information to be nothing more than my unconscious ramblings. However, it turned out that Ted also thought that the information on the tape was extremely helpful, and he made it a point to call me later that night to say so.

After that, somehow word of what I was doing got out, and suddenly all my friends were calling me, asking me to do readings for them. Although I still believed that the readings were my own unconscious train of thought somehow translated into an Irish brogue, I decided to do the tapes for these friends, since the messages seemed to be helpful and the speakings were always positive, reassuring, and loving. Still, I was cautious about the process, and I never felt that anything psychic was happening during the readings.

Finally, after several months of doing these readings in private, Lina decided that I needed to do a "live" reading for someone. She volunteered to be the first someone.

I was skeptical and reluctant. Lina kept pushing me. Finally, with complete doubt about my ability to do such a reading, I agreed to try it.

We met at Lina's apartment on a Sunday afternoon. By then it was summer. The day was warm and sunny. There was a gentle breeze drifting through her living room as we placed two comfortable chairs face to face by the open window. Thank goodness I had practiced my speaking sitting in a chair. At least I wouldn't have to lie down and look ridiculous like I thought Lina had during her early readings.

As we sat facing one another, the breeze stirred the

sweet smell of the colorful flowers that she had placed on a table near us. But I hardly noticed that. I was too nervous. It was one thing to sit in the privacy of my own room verbalizing my unconscious stream of thought. But the idea of having someone ask me direct questions, expecting answers in areas that I knew nothing about, and believing that all of this was supposed to happen through a psychic attunement that I did not believe existed—this was too much for me. I wanted to call off the experiment.

Lina playfully coaxed me on, promising not to tell anyone if I made a fool of myself. I told her I felt like an impostor. She laughed and said that was fine. I argued some more. She wouldn't take no for an answer. Reluctantly, I agreed to try to do the reading.

Lina turned on the tape recorder as I closed my eyes and tried to relax. I said my beginning affirmation and then sat waiting for something psychic to happen. I suddenly thought about the straight-laced chairman of my department at the university and I inwardly cringed at the idea of him somehow finding out what I was doing. Many other confusing thoughts came and went as I struggled to release my nervousness.

Finally, I managed to relax a bit. But nothing seemed to be happening. I just sat there in silence. Stubbornly, I did nothing. I was determined that I would not open my mouth unless something psychic happened. I sat there for perhaps twenty minutes. Nothing unusual was occurring, and I was not about to pretend that it was.

All of a sudden, I heard Lina's trance voice. Evidently she had slipped into her altered state, and her "guides" were now speaking to me. The voice said that it understood my inward struggle and recognized that, in effect, I was waiting for someone to *make* my mouth move. It said that I would have to cooperate a bit. If I would agree to open my mouth and start the speaking, then my guides would help me say the right words.

That seemed fair enough. So, putting aside my Libran sense of decorum and dignity, I took a deep breath, opened my mouth, and plunged in. I consciously willed the speaking to start, and the Irish accent came out, just like it did when I sat alone. But I wasn't alone. Lina was sitting there listening and I felt silly. But I kept talking, waiting for something or somebody to help me out.

Nothing different happened as I talked. The Irish voice was making an opening statement, talking in general terms about Lina's life. It seemed the same as during the morning speakings. I consciously knew everything that was being said about Lina. I felt relatively normal, although I was getting very relaxed and that deep sense of peace was coming again.

Finally, the opening statement came to an end. Then the Irish voice coming from me instructed Lina to begin asking questions. She asked something about her current love relationship. I felt cornered, with nowhere to go. My conscious mind thought, "I don't know anything about that." There was nothing to do but open my mouth and let the Irish voice talk.

The answer seemed intelligent enough as I listened to it coming through. After answering the question, the Irish voice asked, "Do you understand?" Amazingly, I heard Lina say that she did understand.

She asked another question, and there was another answer. She said that she also understood that answer.

As I listened to the exchange that was taking place, I was greatly relieved that answers were coming through. However, I was not impressed with the *quality* of the answers. They did not seem to be particularly profound. They sounded more like my own thoughts than the wisdom of spiritual guides. I was also troubled by the fact that I still felt relatively normal, and still, nothing psychic was happening.

The questions and answers went back and forth for what seemed to be thirty minutes or so. I had pretty much settled into the process and was feeling relaxed when, all of a sudden, I began to notice a strange sensation spreading through my body. It was as if the normal feeling of my body's weight was beginning to *dissolve*. Suddenly I began to feel very light, as if I had no weight. I was feeling like my body was made of air instead of flesh.

Then, an extremely intense feeling of *expansion* began to happen by *itself* within me. I had nothing to do with it. I was not creating the feeling. *It was being done to me by something other than myself.* I was gradually being expanded outward, growing larger. What I ordinarily experience as my conscious self, confined within the limits of my physical body, was now becoming a huge sphere of intense awareness that was beginning to fill the room. It was amazing. *I was soon clearly experiencing myself as actually filling the entire space of that room.* In addition, this expanded feeling brought with it an incredible feeling of love that was more profound than anything I had ever experienced.

I was stunned. I was astonished. It was totally apparent

and clearly obvious to my skeptical intellect that the experience was *real*. It was not my imagination. There was no doubt about it. I was definitely expanded beyond my body. I was literally filling that entire room. At the same time, I was being filled with a love so intense that I wanted to laugh and cry at the same time.

"My God," I thought, "this is real." I grew very excited, realizing that I was somehow being taken *out* of my normal self. I was being projected into a totally foreign mode of perception that was extremely beautiful. How amazing! I was truly *beyond* ordinary reality.

I was completely caught up in the deep sense of love and joy that was permeating the same "space" that I was expanding into. It was a wonderful experience. I kept marveling at the fact that it was being given to me. I wasn't doing it. I couldn't tell *who* was doing it, but it was beautiful and real and true, and the experience was totally free of all doubt.

I have no idea how long this amazing state of expansion and love lasted. It seemed to be a long time, but time had no meaning to me. I had lost all points of reference. The Irish voice had ceased speaking when the experience had begun, and I had lapsed into silence. My physical body no longer existed. I was awareness only, totally infused with the wonderful, completely fulfilling love.

After a long time, still immersed in this expanded state of existence, I felt a surge of energy flow through me, and instantly the Irish voice was speaking again. Only this time it felt very different. For the first time since I had begun practicing the speaking, it felt as if I had nothing to do with what was being said. The words did not feel as if they were originating within me. They were somehow being spoken *through* me, without me having any part in choosing the words or in speaking them.

In my beautiful, expanded state, I listened with extreme interest to what the strange Irish voice was saying. Since I was not involved in creating the words, I had no idea what was going to be said. I heard only one word at a time as it was being spoken.

This new surge of speaking began by explaining to Lina that the long silence that had just occurred had been due to the fact that *I had left my physical body*. The voice described the expanded state of existence that I was now experiencing and said that this expansion beyond the physical reality was necessary in order for me to attune to a vast realm of truth that I was now drawing upon. It talked about how I was being infused with a great energy of universal love that would help me in many ways in my personal life and in making these deep attunements in the future. Then, even though I had no idea where my body was or what was happening to it, I heard the voice say something that made me feel like the hairs on my head were standing up. The voice said: *"The experience of expansion that Ron is now having was first implanted in him when he was eight years old so that it could be returned at this time so that he would believe."*

The voice went on to tell Lina more about what was happening to me, but I didn't hear it. Within my expanded state, my still-alert conscious mind was reeling. The statement about my experience as an eight-year-old boy had instantly brought that forgotten event back to me, and that past moment now seemed to leap across time, mysteriously fusing past and present into a remarkably clear instant of truth: the past experience of the eight-year-old boy and my present experience of expansion *were the same*. They were both given to me by something outside of myself, and they were the only times I had ever consciously broken through the boundaries of physical reality.

For the first time since I had begun my experiment, my conscious mind was forced to seriously consider the possibility that perhaps I *was* a trance medium. Perhaps the readings were really guided by a higher source of knowledge. Perhaps these strange speakings could actually help people.

I don't remember the rest of the reading with Lina. I was totally caught up in the expanded awareness and the amazing intensity of love.

After it was over, I sat with my eyes closed for a long while, savoring the lingering effects of the wonderful experience. When I opened my eyes, I saw that Lina had a big smile on her face.

"It was a beautiful reading," she said.

I nodded in agreement. "I'm amazed."

GAINING TRUST

I knew that something important had happened during that first reading, even though I wasn't quite sure what it was. All I knew for certain was that somehow I had left my ordinary reality behind and had entered into a brilliant new kind of *experiential* world of intense fulfillment where I was filled with a love I had never known before. I had theories about such experiences, developed from my study of accounts in the literature, but this was *my* experience, and it was unique to me, and it was real. The theories did not fit my *feelings* about the experience, so the meaning of the experience was not clear to me. However, the events that had transpired during my reading for Lina strongly indicated that perhaps there was some validity to the attunement that I had attained during the reading. It was enough to give me a sense of confidence about continuing to pursue the experiment.

A few days after the experience with Lina, I received a call from a friend of mine who had talked with Lina. He wanted a reading like I had done for her. After reminding him that the process was very experimental, and clearly explaining that it needed to be studied further, I agreed to do the reading.

Again, just as with Lina's session, I began the second live reading with my affirmation and then sat silently for a few minutes. After a while I felt a gentle "push" of energy in my chest and throat, and I knew it was time to begin speaking. As the Irish voice gave the opening statement about my friend's life, I once again experienced the unusual expanding sensation, although it was not as intense as before. However, the feeling of love and deep caring was even stronger.

After the opening statement, the voice told my friend to ask questions. The questions and answers went on for fifteen or twenty minutes. As my conscious mind listened and observed the process, I had no idea whether the answers were true or not, but I was fully aware of the depth of gentleness and love being communicated from the source of the reading. I was permeated by that love, and I could *feel* the truth of it, no matter what the words were saying.

After the reading, when I opened my eyes and looked at my friend, I saw that he had tears in his eyes. He told me that he had been deeply touched by the reading. He said that he couldn't remember when he had felt so loved and so understood.

After that, I gradually began to experiment with in-person readings for my friends. I was still quite cautious and avoided making any rash assumptions about where the knowledge was coming from. I carefully reminded all of the people who came for a reading that it was an experiment, and I asked them to check out the information and decide on its validity for themselves.

Soon, total strangers began to come to me for readings. My rational mind was impressed by the fact that, without me having any conscious knowledge about these people, the readings could give them information that reflected a deep understanding of their personalities and their lives. I was continually amazed by the profound insights and wisdom contained in these readings. It was knowledge that went far beyond my own conscious understanding. Many people would tell me that the information they received was quite accurate, and, most importantly, that the readings were very helpful to them in their lives.

At the end of each reading, there would always be a closing statement by the Irish voice. Even though I was aware of a deep love being expressed throughout the reading, I noticed that during this closing statement the intensity of the love would always increase appreciably. It would literally become an uplifting atmosphere, surrounding and permeating myself and the other person. After the reading, many people would be moved to tears, and many would comment on the intensity of the love that they could feel during this concluding portion of the reading. Some would tell me that they could even re-experience this love later when listening to the tape of the reading.

On a rare occasion, a person would remain skeptical throughout the reading, would experience nothing important, and would go away feeling that the reading was of no value. After such readings, I would fall into periods of uncertainty and doubt. If this was supposed to be a source of universal wisdom, why couldn't it help *everyone*? During such periods of discouragement, I would consider abandoning the whole experiment. Usually such experiences would be closely followed by a powerful and profound reading that would inspire the person receiving the reading, thereby encouraging me to continue the project.

At this point, I still did not have an awareness of spiritual guides being involved with the speaking that was coming through me. During the speaking, I was aware of the expanded state of love, and the words seemed to come by themselves. Yet I perceived nothing that would indicate the presence of spiritual guides.

As word of the readings continued to spread, it wasn't long before I found myself busy doing many readings in my spare time. People were continually calling and asking for a session with me. This began a flood of interest in my work that has not ceased since those early days.

I began to receive calls from people in other states who had heard about the readings. They would drive in to have an appointment with me. Eventually, people began to invite me to various places around the country to do readings, to lecture, and to give workshops. I soon found myself traveling extensively, having to struggle to work this in with my regular job.

As all of this activity increased, I carefully monitored the readings to continue to assess their validity and their usefulness. They seemed to be growing stronger in the love expressed, and in their effectiveness in inspiring people to expand their lives in creative ways. However, I still cautioned people to use their own intelligence and to evaluate the material carefully. I reminded each person (as I continue to do now) that even if the knowledge did come from spiritual guides or some other source of universal wisdom (which is always an open question), since the knowledge was being expressed through my own personality, then it was necessary to consider the possibility of confusion or error being caused by my own mind, conscious or unconscious, or by unconscious interference in the complex process of translating *experiences* of truth into spoken words.

After about a year of intense work with the readings and with my teaching and workshop activities, the demands of this work became so great that my "regular" job began to suffer. I had begun to charge a fee for my readings, and I was paid for teaching, lectures, and workshops, yet, the income was irregular and undependable. As I considered the situation, I realized that what I needed to do was to let go of my full-time job and trust that I would not starve doing the work that I loved. It was time for another leap of faith

I made it boldly, with only a small amount of fear. I resigned my job and held a celebration with my friends. As I joyfully embarked on my new career, I realized that I had actually fulfilled the desire I had expressed on that spring day almost two years earlier when I was guided to turn down a career as a university professor. I had become a teacher of spiritual truths. In addition, to my amazement, I had also become a professional trance medium.

THE GUIDES

Since I still had no direct perception of the *source* of the knowledge, I decided to conduct some research readings with friends in order to obtain an explanation from the source itself. During these readings, we were told that the knowledge was coming from spiritual guides to myself who would tune in to the guides of the person having the reading. These guides were described as advanced souls who had already evolved through a series of earth incarnations, and who now exist in a nonphysical realm of beauty and love that lies beyond the physical world.

It was explained that each human being has his or her own spiritual guides, and in the course of the readings that I was doing, my guides could bring forth knowledge from anyone's guides. Thus, it appears that the non-physical realm where the guides exist stands as a vast pool of knowledge that we can tap in to by attuning to our own spiritual guides.

Of course, this is just one of many possible ways of conceptualizing the belief that extra-conscious knowledge is available to human beings. I always give this explanation as a simple theory, reminding those who come for readings to use whatever concept they believe to be true.

SHARING LOVE AND WISDOM

After launching myself as a full-time trance medium and teacher of spiritual truths, I did readings day after day, year after year, bringing fulfilling and inspiring experiences into my life and into the lives of others. This work accelerated my own personal growth, which in turn led me to a greater trust in my ability to attune more deeply during the readings. As my level of trust rose, the knowledge brought forth during the readings became more profound and more beneficial to people. Also, as the helpfulness of the readings increased, I seemed to be guided to more and more people in need.

Curiously, as the work began to spread, somewhere along the way the friendly Irish accent gradually faded away. The voice of the readings now has only a very slight unrecognizable accent that sounds almost like my normal speaking voice.

Even with the widespread experience I have gained in sharing the wisdom of the readings, I still have not had direct perception of the *source* of the knowledge. I still cannot positively confirm that it is spiritual guides, since I have not directly perceived guides. During the readings, I continue to experience the most beautiful feeling of love and truth that I can imagine, and the intensity of my experience grows with each passing year. Yet, the words spoken during the readings still appear as if by magic, without any perception of the source of the knowledge. I only *feel* the source. I feel it as a deep, unlimited love. I think of the source of the readings as *The Guides* because I believe that such guides exist, even though I have not directly perceived them.

REACHING OUT TO MANY

I woke up one morning several years ago and thought about all of the knowledge that was available on the tapes of personal readings that I had done, yet those thousands of tapes were sitting in people's desk and dresser drawers all over the country. I needed to find a way to make the information more widely available so that it could be of benefit to more people.

The solution was quite simple: do recorded readings on general subject areas for *everyone*; then the tapes of these sessions could be made available to people everywhere. Working with several close friends, twelve initial subject areas were chosen. Questions were prepared that covered a broad range of issues in each subject area. Then we took our questions into the recording studio and did the readings.

Over a period of weeks, twelve comprehensive "Guides" tapes were created. In a short time, copies of these tapes were being ordered by people across the United States and in foreign countries. Readings on many subject areas have followed over the years.

Listening to these recorded readings by the Guides is a unique experience. In a deeply loving way, the spoken words of the Guides create an intense focus of spiritual attunement that helps the listener penetrate deeper levels of truth. The knowledge that the Guides present in spoken form has an inspiring quality that lifts people into new realms of inner experience. I have found that listening to these tapes is quite a different experience than reading the Guides' words in print.

(Publisher's note: information about current available books and audio recordings can be found at www.ronscolastico.com)

ABOUT THIS BOOK

In order to make the wisdom of the Guides more readily accessible to even more people, *The Earth Adventure* was created. For this book, my beautiful wife, Susan, and I planned a sequence of questions for the Guides that would bring out the kind of knowledge that would help us all understand where we come from, what we're doing here on earth, and where we go from here. Then, over a period of several weeks, we conducted many hours of readings during which Susan directed the questioning and organized the knowledge that poured out from the Guides. As you can see from the contents of this book, the teachings cover many areas that are important to all of us, such as the purpose of our life on earth, knowledge about our spiritual nature, ways of understanding and expressing our human personalities, and, an understanding of what happens to us after we leave this earth life.

The following chapters present the wisdom of The Guides as given in the special readings done for this book. I have edited the typed transcripts of the readings in order to bring clarity to the material.

The teachings of The Guides that are presented in this book reflect what The Guides have taught in the thousands of personal readings that I have done. Working with these teachings, I have made incredible growth in my own life, and I have watched many people use the teachings to bring about beautiful changes in their lives.

As you read this book, you will decide for yourself whether there is "truth" in the teachings of The Guides. Each of us is quite unique, and what rings true for me may not inspire another person. I certainly can't claim that The Guides are speaking truth through me. I only know that the material has been very beneficial for myself and for many people that I have worked with.

A FINAL WORD

Over the years, during the thousands of readings that I have done, questions have been answered by The Guides in just about every conceivable area of concern to human beings. However, the subject that remains the most fascinating to me is the area of *spiritual truth*—the knowledge about our souls and their place in the universe. Time and time again, I have found that powerful experiences occur, for myself and for the person receiving the reading, when the questioning is directed toward an understanding of the deeper purposes of life. For those who have come seeking truth and spiritual guidance, the readings have provided an apparently unlimited source of knowledge and inspiration.

Throughout the years of doing readings, I have had the opportunity of entering a wondrous, joyful realm of existence during each reading. In each session I am enlivened, loved, and inspired by the "energy" or "force" that sustains that realm. During such experiences it becomes quite clear to me that I am—we all are—also sustained by that force in daily life, even though we are not always consciously aware of it.

As I slowly return to my ordinary state of consciousness after a reading, I occasionally feel my own personality challenges and problems descend upon me like a heavy, dark cloak. At that time, fresh from my experiences of truth, it is clear to me that the thing that causes these subjective feelings of darkness within me is my self-generated fear, and the personal negativity that arises from my fear. During such experiences, I can clearly feel myself again taking up my cloak of personal fears, doubts, and pains as I come floating back from my magnificent expanded self into my sometimes tight-fitting Ron Scolastico personality.

Of course, like most of us, I sometimes struggle against my personality self, usually trying to browbeat it into becoming the perfect ideal that I experience during the readings. At other times, I am more loving and understanding and I can rejoice in being my Ron-self. But always, the profound and extraordinary beauty of the *true self,* of the *source,* that I experience during the readings lures me on. To fully manifest *that* every day as the Ron-self would be truly fulfilling.

The message of The Guides is that we can all learn to create such ideal experiences for ourselves. They say that eventually such an unfoldment can become a reality for all of us in this lifetime. We *can* fully and completely manifest the magnificence of our soul in the everyday reality of our lives.

It is my hope that, as you read the wisdom of The Guides in the following chapters, you will be able to *feel* the truth being expressed. If you can feel it, and then act on it every day, I believe that you will gain a beautiful new understanding of your whole life, from birth, to death, and beyond. This will help you actually live all of the ideals that are important to you in your present life.

The Wisdom

Of The Guides

CHAPTER ONE

Where The Earth Adventure Begins

As you now begin to explore with us how it is that you as a human being have come to be standing upon earth in this particular moment, and how it is that you have come to exist in your present form as a thinking, feeling, self-aware human being, you will first need to understand that the beginnings of your earth adventure lie in areas of reality that are very different in nature than your present earth life. Your beginnings as a human being lie in vast realms that are the eternal realities of a *soul*.

Your present personality is imbued with earth capacities and sensitivities with which you are quite familiar: mind, emotion, and bodily perceptions. These are perfect for living as a human being in earth. However, they are not so beneficial for comprehending the eternal realities, from which your present personality springs,

What is needed to comprehend the larger realities of yourself is a different kind of perception, a new *creative* functioning within your inner life. We could say that this new kind of perceiving is similar to *imagination*, imbued with *feeling*, or *emotion*.

To help you feel inside yourself the quality of this kind of perception, imagine that we would say to you: "Make up a drama. Create a story." If you followed this request, you would have a rush of imagination imbued with feeling as you engaged in this process of creating your story inside yourself. Let us say that you work with this story for a long time, and with great passion you elaborate upon it and refine it in many ways. Then, imagine that you discover that the story that you made up *actually exists*. You discover that you *have created reality* with your inner work.

In the same way, in these teachings, we are asking you to create a story with us as we guide you. We will help you to use your imagination and your feelings to create a close approximation of that which is the reality of your beginning of this earth adventure.

This expansion that you will do with your imagination and feeling is necessary because the earth words are not yet large enough, the human understanding of the word symbols not yet great enough for us to clearly bring to you through words the realities of the beginnings of your present personality. Yet, the earth words are potent enough to stimulate new imaginings and intuitive sensings within your thoughts and feelings. These new inner creations can eventually bring you very close to a *direct perception* of your true nature as an eternal soul embarked upon a vast adventure in the realms of earth life.

By working with our words with imagination and feeling, you will be engaging in an opening process that will not only feed your mind and heart with understanding, but it will help you actually trigger within your present human personality a new sensitivity. You will activate an *inner sensing capacity* within you that eventually can enable you to intuitively and directly experience more of your true nature as a soul, and your beginning of this earth adventure.

YOUR ORIGIN AS A SOUL

You have many *possibilities* within yourself now as a human being. In this moment, we ask that you focus your abilities of thought, imagining, and feeling with us to unfold some of your possibilities for *understanding* as we turn now to look at where your earth reality first began.

Let us start in a simple way. You can begin by holding in your mind a vision of a large room. In this room there is such beauty, such magnificence. There is a perfect artistic expression. The colors and forms are of a radiant, unending beauty. But, in this room, although there is quite a magnificence that thrills you, there is no *companionship*. There are no other beings loving you.

Your awareness of yourself in this beautiful room includes the awareness that *you have created this room.* Although you have created magnificently, you now notice a new desire arising within you that is not satisfied by your creation. This new desire is for companionship and love.

Imagine now that you also have a capacity to create beings, beings of perfection and magnificence, just like yourself. To satisfy your desire for companionship, you begin to create those beings.

To avoid philosophical or metaphysical complexities, let us state the truth of your origins in a very simple way:

you were created by a vast, unlimited, perfect force that did have a feeling similar to the feeling of standing in that magnificent room desiring companionship. This is not to imply a sense of *lack* in that creative force, for there would be in that force only love and perfection. The desire for companionship that arose in that perfect force was a beautiful, creative desire filled with love.

For purposes of clear understanding in presently accepted human words, you could speak of this magnificent force that created you as the *God force*. This God force created you, and many other companion beings, as independent, self-aware, eternal beings that can be spoken of as *souls*.

In using this simple image, those of you who now have certain understandings that you would consider to be knowledge of God, whether you have drawn this knowledge from your own thoughts and feelings, from religious training, or from philosophical study, you can use your present beliefs to expand this simple vision that we have suggested. You could say to yourself:

"Let me feel, in my own unique personal way, that God itself, desiring companionship, did somehow create my soul and the souls of all human beings so that we could rejoice together in the various dimensions of reality."

In your day-to-day life, you can use your imagination in silent periods of privacy to form in your mind, images of that beginning reality in which you were created as a soul. You can imagine vast universes and worlds of beauty, manifesting in unlimited creative forms. You can imagine how you as a soul, with many other souls, did share the joy of creation with this magnificent force of God. And, if you wish, you can create images of, and feelings about this God force that now lives within you, and that infuses you with love moment by moment. Imagining these vast realities in your own unique way will be more effective in bringing you an understanding of your beginnings than any earth words that we would use to try to approximate realities that are so different than your present human experience.

PERCEIVING YOUR ORIGIN

You will need to hold these kinds of images and feelings in your heart in order to come closer to perceiving the truth of the beginning of your earth adventure. If you experiment with such inner creations, eventually you will be able to *feel* that you began as a soul force of love and creativity, and you will know that this reality of you as a soul has continued without interruption. You will come to understand that since your very beginning, there has never been a separation between yourself and that magnificent God force that created you.

These areas of reality that are your beginning as a soul are quite difficult for your human personality to comprehend if you attempt to explore them with *logic* alone. If you begin to seek a logical understanding by asking yourself, "If I was created by this magnificent God force at some time in the past, then what was I before that creation?" then you could begin to confuse yourself. By creating many logical questions to ask, you would most likely discover contradictions and limits in the answers that you found. You could become caught in many twistings and turnings, *all of them created by your mind as you attempt to use logic without intuitive feeling.* The result can be much discouragement and frustration.

You would need to ask yourself: "Why should I choose such a course?" For many the answer would be: "Because I desire truth." We can assure you that by attempting to comprehend the eternal realities of your beginning by logic alone, you will not find truth. *You will find the projections of your own human mind.*

The capacity to categorize and question logically is highly developed in the human mind. This capacity is magnificent for resolving earth dilemmas, for creating earth results, and for fulfilling earth desires. *It is hardly useful at all for direct perception of your soul and your eternal nature.* That is why we have begun with a focus upon feeling and imagination. We would desire to help you train yourself in a new way of learning, a way that involves the intuitive imagining of hidden realities imbued with deep feelings of love, leading eventually to direct intuitive perceptions that come from seldom-used sensing capacities that are woven with your emotions.

TWO CHANNELS OF PERCEPTION

To help you to refine your perception of your soul, and to increase your sense of how, where, and why your earth adventure began, we will elaborate a bit upon our quite simple image of the God force creating souls. This will take you a step deeper into the new kind of perception that we have suggested. For this, we must ask your cooperation.

First, we would ask that after you have read what we will now say, that you would set aside this book and make a moment of silence with yourself. We would ask you to pretend to be your soul, in the following manner:

Sit in silence for a moment and feel that you are not simply a small human being limited to one lifetime. Use your imagination to create a feeling that you are your soul. You are the creator of the force that has come forth through human procreation to create your body, your mind, your feelings—all of your personality. In a very simple way, attempt to imagine how you have created the forces of awareness that exist in your present personality. Feel the love and the beauty that you as a soul placed into your human personality as you created it.

Do this now as a very simple way to begin to understand the origins of your present earth adventure.

Now that you have experimented, in a small way, with a feeling of being your soul, we ask you to use the same process of inner attunement to attempt to become aware of two separate kinds of feelings that you can have. First, recall how it felt to imagine that you are the eternal force that has created the personality that you presently experience as yourself. Take a moment to do this now.

Next, enter into yourself and recall feelings from times in the past in which you were deeply preoccupied with concerns for your earth affairs. Do this for a moment.

Now, in this moment, bring these two different feelings into your awareness simultaneously. Hold the feeling of being your unlimited soul side by side with the feeling of intense personality concerns. By doing this, you can begin to feel that, in a certain sense, *there are two separate "channels" in your awareness.* One channel is your *ordinary human awareness* that is saturated with earth concerns. The other is a unique kind of awareness that gives you the ability to feel beauty and love in any moment, no matter what kind of earth concerns may be filling your ordinary channel of awareness. In other words, *you have an extraordinary second awareness that can transcend any limits that you may experience in your first-channel awareness of your ordinary personality experience.*

Throughout these teachings, we shall help you understand these two channels of awareness as they apply to all areas of your life. But, for this moment, in a simple way, we wish to focus on a beginning understanding of the second channel, which is your *eternal perceptive capacity.*

Even as a temporal physical human being, you have the capacity to deepen your awareness in such a way that you can come closer and closer to directly perceiving that which lies beneath, and beyond, the physical reality of earth life. Through this second channel of awareness, you have the capacity to feel the eternal forces that have created you, and that have set you out upon this earth adventure.

Throughout these teachings, we will help you develop

your second channel of awareness. By working in the ways that we will suggest, you can learn to heighten your eternal perceptive capacity. But, for now, we would hope that this preliminary understanding will help you sense more clearly the nature of the origins of your earth adventure, and give you confidence that you can learn about your beginnings through your own heart.

Your origins lie in a realm of reality that ordinarily cannot be directly perceived by human beings who walk in physical form. Yet, under certain conditions, and given certain personality adjustments toward love and inner sensitivity, you can increase your perceptions of these eternal realities through developing your second awareness that is tied to *intuitive* perception.

REMEMBERING A GREATER YOU

Rather than giving you many words to attempt to describe, in terms of form and shape and human understanding, the forces of God and your soul that have created your personality through great evolutionary periods, we would ask your patience and your willingness to work with these intuitive feelings that we are suggesting. As we take you further into an exploration of the earth adventure in this book, if you read our words and respond to them with the gradual opening of your imagination woven with your feelings (and we shall guide you throughout this book in the process of this opening) you will find that you can eventually come to have a profound new understanding of your origin as a human being. You can develop a clear sense of the eternal reality from which you spring, and in which, even in this moment, you have your true existence. Not only will you learn more about your origins, but this inner work will illuminate your present existence as a human being in a way that will bring you a greater capacity to love, to create, and to fulfill the purposes for which you have come into earth.

As you merge knowledge of your origins with your present personality experience in this new intuitive way, you will discover that the eternal magnificence of all of life that existed in your beginnings also lives within you in this present earth moment. You will come to understand that these eternal realities will live within you in all *future* moments, whether they are lived in earth or beyond earth.

Thus, as you now begin with us this study of the earth adventure in which you are presently participating, you are setting out to discover *yourself.* You will discover yourself as you existed in the *beginning* creation of all souls, of all life, and of all universes; as you exist now as a physical human being walking upon a physical earth; and, as you will exist in the *future* as an illumined being, having created, through many earth lifetimes, a portion of reality that is your unique expression of the force of God.

These are areas of knowledge that we will help you discover for yourself through your own sensitivity. We will also help you align your knowledge of these areas with your present earth personality in ways that can bring greater meaning and purpose to you as you strive to fulfill your personality desires. And, you will find that as you work with us in these areas, you will begin to establish a great feeling of mastery over your human life. You will find that this earth adventure is not a dangerous, threatening experience, but an *exciting, fulfilling journey through unlimited realities that will be created by you.*

We would say to you, as you prepare now for that which we will share in these teachings, that you can spark a greater brilliance in your understanding by reminding yourself continually as you read our teachings:

"The truth lies within me, not within these words that I am now reading in this book. These words are given to me by guiding-ones out of their love and wisdom. The purpose of the words of the guiding-ones is to spark love and wisdom that live within me, in the deep portions of my personality, in the vast magnificent qualities of my soul that continually feeds my personality, and in the even greater forces of God with which I am eternally woven in love."

These are the kinds of inspiring thoughts and feelings that will help you use your imagination and emotion in the profound new way that we are suggesting. By working with these kinds of inner creations as you read these teachings day after day, you can bring ideal realities alive within your thoughts and feelings. This will move you toward direct perception of those realities as they exist in the eternal realms of existence that sustain your physical world.

So, as you read these teachings, and as you study them, also *respond* within yourself. Create feelings of love. Create vast, magnificent realities within your thoughts and your feelings. You will find that by so doing, you are opening an inner sensitivity to perceive, to feel, and to *live* the eternal portions of you. This will help you understand that the adventure of earth is a pathway that *you have created*. And, just as you *as an eternal soul* have created the path, you *as a human being* shall create your own personal *fulfillment* as you walk that path.

CHAPTER TWO

Creating The Earth Reality

A s we take you deeper into the teachings concerning your soul's expression in earth reality, we remind you that our primary purpose in giving you the knowledge contained within this book is to bring forth an understanding that will help you to live a more joyful and fulfilling life as a human being. And, to help with this, in later portions of this book, we will directly address the important cycles of your day-to-day earth life.

However, for you to attain complete fulfillment in the physical world, it will be necessary for you to understand the *eternal* portions of you that now live in your human personality, but that will be released from the limits of that personality at your physical death. Your happiness as a physical human being can be enhanced by an understanding of that part of you that is not physical. Thus, to help you feel the truth of your eternal self, we will now describe the process whereby the souls of you ones of earth did come forth independently from the God source as self-aware beings. Then, we will show you how your *souls* eventually came to be involved in the creation of the physical reality that has culminated in earth life.

Again, we shall be speaking of realities that are difficult for your human capacities to grasp. Thus, we will
gradually build an understanding of these complex areas,
step by step. This will help you bring your creativity and
imagination to bear upon the picture of eternal life that we
shall create together. This picture will help you feel eternal
realities within your present experience of this temporary
earth life.

THE SOULS' FIRST REALITY

As souls, you ones first existed in an energy matrix that
included many realities that you would speak of as universes. But these universes are realms of *experience*, not physical matter. These universes of experience have to do with
realities that existed in the "beginning" of life, and that
continue to exist now. Although these magnificent realities
are invisible to human beings, they can be clearly perceived
when you stand *outside* of earth perceptions and are not
limited by narrow earth understandings.

We would say then that the true beginning of the creation of earth life took place in these vast universes of
experience. Within these eternal realities, your souls first
created the non-physical *forces*, or energies that would
eventually become physical matter. These new creative
forces grew out of the souls themselves, but they were
variations of the God forces that originally created the
souls

To clarify this for you, we will again return to the simplified vision of the original God force that created the

souls. For now, we will symbolize this God force as a magnificent eternal being, existing in realms of unlimited beauty, desiring companionship, and creating souls as independent beings such as itself. These "new" beings included the souls of all ones who would eventually choose to come into human form.

In the realms in which this God force exists, there are realities that are different than the souls of human beings. You could consider these other realities to be *beings* of a different nature who have existences that are *unhampered by any limits.* Your souls themselves are also unhampered by limits, but souls are drawn, by their own interest and fascination, to "specialize" in one particular kind of expression, and in so doing they temporarily cease to occupy themselves with all of the other realities that these other beings are concerned with. This area that the souls of earth have chosen to focus upon is an aspect of eternal reality that you could understand as forces and energies of *love.*

There are, as you would imagine, *unlimited* expressions within all of the universes, some of them dominated by *creativity,* or potency of *will,* or other kinds of creative energies. So, you would understand then, that all beings in all universes have the capacities for all expressions. But, just as you ones of earth would be drawn to a certain restaurant because of your taste and desires, so it is that we could say that beings of all universes are attracted to certain kinds of expressions through taste and desires.

Thus, we could say that all of the souls that occupy themselves with expressing in *earth* form are attracted to the expression of *love* that is intensified in the earth reality. We speak of love here in its broadest sense: a feeling of caring, to a very great extent, for all of life; a deep desire to nurture, and to encourage goodness in all ones, and to uplift that good and expand it. These areas of love that we attempt to describe here are difficult to convey in words of earth because the earth words have to do with *emotions*. These realities that we attempt to describe for you have to do with much larger forces of love that are presently not within the grasp of human intellectual understanding. However, your heart is capable of *feeling* these larger forces of love.

Before the souls became involved in the creation of the new forces that would later become the physical universes, they experienced (from the earth point of view of *time*) many eons of expression in *non-physical* universes of love that were created by the God force. Thus, the souls were involved in a certain pristine, perfect existence that continued endlessly, and that was constantly expanding, in terms of greater fulfillment and greater love.

Here, again, we remind you that you must read these words with imagination and an active heart. For the words themselves are quite flat. They do not have the power to even approximate these vast realities of which we speak. But your imagination and your heart *do* have that power. Thus, we ask you to imagine this pristine realm of existence of your soul as an unlimited vastness of experience that is beautiful, magnificent, all good, completely permeated with feelings of love, and, in which all souls have total freedom to create as they desire.

THE FIRST STAGE OF EARTH CREATION

This pristine, perfect existence of the souls that we have just described was the "breeding ground" of the new soul forces that later became the earth reality. Keep in mind that even as these souls became involved in the creation of physical reality, including earth, their pristine eternal existence continued uninterrupted and unimpeded. Even in this moment, all souls still exist and fulfill themselves within these eternal realms of beauty and magnificent love.

Now, if you would hold these preliminary understandings in mind, we will summarize the process of the *beginning stage* of the creation of earth. The present earth reality has grown out of the independent creation of a new, non-physical energy that was created by a large grouping of souls who were themselves created by the God force for the loving companionship of itself. These souls became preoccupied with and attracted to the eternal forces of *love*, and they desired to expand those love forces in new ways by combining them with the new energies that the souls had created. The first stage of earth creation began when the souls created their new forces out of their desire to expand the *eternal love forces.*

Let your own inner understanding of this stage of creation begin with a vision of all of the souls living in their perfect, pristine non-physical existence, and see them beginning to desire a creation of love for which *they* were responsible. Out of the souls' great desire for creativity, and the intensity of their desire for *authorship* or mastery over their lives and their experience of self-awareness, many of the souls who existed in the pristine beginning reality were able to bring forth a new energy that had never before existed. This new energy was a *desire*, a longing to create in a way that was *totally independent* from the force of God.

The souls' new desire to create independently of the God force grew out of a sense of *love*, not out of rebellion, or out of human motives that you would understand as negative. The souls' desire was to propagate the joy and magnificence of the God force that they experienced within their pristine realm, and to project that magnificence into *new* forms and creations.

Thus, the souls began to communicate this new desire to one another in a communication that was totally shared in the depths of their beings. This vast *desire energy* of many souls grew over eons of "time," gathering momentum until it became a great surging force within a vast number of souls. This new energy was deeply shared by them, and it was clearly recognized by them for what it was: a desire to create new realities of love for which *they* would be responsible, and of which *they* would be masters.

In this rising tide of new desire energy being communicated between the souls, there came "ideas" and "suggestions" (there are no earth words for the inner feelings of the souls) for how these forces of creative desire could be fulfilled. Gradually, these many individual creative suggestions of the souls became one huge force, and the various ideas became *individual energy patterns* within the large force. These new energy patterns could be spoken of as *the primary causative forces of the physical universes*.

In all of this, the force of God itself was influencing the souls, loving them, teaching them, nurturing them, and *encouraging them to create freely and independently.* The God force imbued the souls with the *will* to create freely with no restrictions. Also, as the souls began the creation of the causative patterns for the new physical reality, the forces of God were woven with the souls' choices in the new creation. Thus, in a very real sense, as many human beings have believed and taught one another, the forces of God led to the creation of earth and all physical reality. But these forces were modulated and overseen by the souls that were created by that God.

Within the soul patterns that were the causative forces that began physical reality, there were many different kinds of unique expressions. There were non-physical energies that would eventually evolve into the physical atoms and molecules, the early gases and liquids of primal creation, and later, would become the mineral, plant, and animal worlds of earth. We could say that each of these variations and permutations of physical reality, and all new expressions that will appear in the future, began as energy patterns in those early periods when all of the souls were uniting around the impulse to create a new reality. To capture the feeling of this, you can imagine these *energy patterns* as a vast, infinite orchestra with many instruments playing different beautiful individual sounds, but all of it harmonized into a perfect, magnificent symphony.

We could say then, that these beginning causative forces of the souls were like *sounds*, and forces of *light*, and all of the kinds of vibrational energies that you are presently familiar with. But, all of these causative forces were imbued with a depth of love and with other realities that were like the *feelings* of the souls.

MAKING A PLACE FOR A NEW REALITY

The souls then brought forth all of these new causative forces into their pristine non-physical reality, seeking a "place" to manifest their new creation. They needed to create a new dimension for their independent reality. Yet, the dimension that they created would exist *within* the eternal realities in which the souls existed.

We will now give you a simple vision to help you understand the complexities of the creation of the new physical reality. Imagine the souls placing their new creative forces in the "middle" of the eternal dimensions of reality. Then, the souls use the eternal power of creation to bring these forces into a new *wavelength*, or a new vibration *that has never before existed*. Using these new vibrations, they begin to transform their creative causative patterns into the new reality. This is an infinitely complex process. To simplify, we would say that the souls bring about a *slowing down* of the vibration of the eternal divine forces of reality. And, as these forces are slowed, the *first intentions* of the souls come into *tangible* existence. These first intentions are: to make a *place* within the vastness of divine eternal realities in which this new reality can unfold.

Now, this place, from your point of view, can be called *physical space*. In all of the existences that are eternal, *there is no space*. There is not a need for empty space. There are only the overlapping experiences of beauty and magnificence that happen in many realms of non-physical reality, and all of these realms are interwoven with one another. For the moment, do not be concerned with attempting to imagine these complicated realities. Simply know that, from your point of view, your earth adventure begins with the creation of this new *space* that did not previously exist within the eternal realities.

This physical space becomes the first reality created by the souls of you ones of earth that is not totally woven inescapably into the fabric of the divine realities. In other words, this is the first "breaking away" from the divine patterns; the first creation that is not directed and mastered entirely by the God force. This is the first independent creation by souls who were given free will by the love of that God force. This is the first *temporal* reality in all creations-the first reality having a temporary existence within *time*.

So, if you wish to simplify in earth terms, you could see the God force as the eternal teacher of the universes that the souls inhabit. Then you could see the souls as the *students*. The space that you can now perceive with your physical senses is the first *project* of those students, created in total perfection as a reflection of the God force, and in total harmony with all other universes. But, this new space is unique and different, set apart by its own new *physical* reality that exists within a context of time, or *period of duration*. All realities before this were, and are, eternal, having no beginning and having no end.

THE FIRST SEPARATION

The souls who have created this new space are now able to *inhabit* it. They are able to perceive it, and to fully live within it. Those divine beings who were *not* involved with the souls who created this space will now view the souls' new creation of space from a slight *distance*. (This is a *subjective* distance of *experience*.) In the process of creating this new space in the middle of eternal realities, the souls are fulfilling their desire for a unique expression. The souls who created this new space are the only eternal beings who can *directly* experience this space by inhabiting it. It is their own unique reality. All other eternal beings can perceive this new reality, understand it, and rejoice in its beauty. But these other beings do not choose to directly experience the new reality by inhabiting it.

Thus, in the creation of this new space, there comes about an entirely new event in reality. There is the creation of the first *separation* in the entire universes of all of life and eternity. This separation is a necessary part of the new reality of the souls because it is this separation that eventually will make possible the creation of the physical earth. However, this separation is not negative. Negativity is a *human* experience. This new separation is a portion of the divine realities and the eternal magnificence, and it occurs in the "middle" of other realities, so it is imbued with eternal love and perfection. But, nevertheless, it is a separation or "distance," from the point of view of the conscious awareness of the eternal beings.

This new distance between eternal beings is necessary so that the souls involved in creating the new space can be aware that they are slightly separate, temporarily, from all other beings, as a result of their own creation. This separation is very slight, and in all other ways, the souls are still woven and united with all other eternal realities.

It would be as though you are standing in a field. You can see all of the flowers in that field that are so beautiful.

You can look about at will and enjoy all of them. But you have found one flower that is of particularly great beauty and magnificence. And you have become so captivated by this one flower that you now stand and stare at it. If you choose to change your focus of attention, you can again see all of the flowers. They are still there for you. But, for that moment in time, you have chosen, out of fascination and love, to keep your attention focused on the one special flower. You have not lost a thing. But, *you have gained the intensity of a narrower focus.*

So it is with the souls who have decided to create the physical space, the new reality. They are standing in the midst of all of the eternal realities, and, in any instant when they choose, they can perceive the other realities and rejoice in them. But, the souls have become so fascinated and intrigued with their new reality, the physical space, that they desire to focus upon it in order to gain a greater *intensity* in their subjective experience of it.

FILLING IN THE SPACE

Next, you would see the souls bringing forth all of the original causative patterns into which they have implanted their ideas and suggestions for what the new reality can be, and you would see them infusing these patterns into the newly created space. All of the forces of these patterns begin to arise as energies within that space. Through vast periods of time, all of these individual unique forces, which are of a type of energy not explainable in human words, come into that space as invisible forces. But, to the perceptions of the souls, these energies come into the space as great beautiful symphonies, with meanings and purposes woven into them. These energies are the seeds of what will later become physical reality. These seeds are the magnificences of the eternal realities *transformed into a new type of energy that can inhabit the space created by the souls.*

So we would say then, to simplify, (and we shall accelerate the description for you now) that these new energy forces began a process of *solidification*. This resulted in the creation of the first *physical matter* in the universes. In the new space that you now consider to be your entire physical universe, this physical matter took the form of vapors and gases. Yet, there was a depth of love, beauty, and magnificence of soul forces woven into these vaporous forms.

These magnificent, beautiful vapor forces eventually coalesced into what you would speak of as *liquids*, and *waters*, and the many earth *chemicals*. Your science has not done justice to these forces to simply label them as inanimate, nonliving, unaware chemicals. But, for this moment, you could align our explanation with your scientific earth understanding.

Eventually, the souls brought about the solidification of certain chemical forces into *solid matter*. To simplify, you could use your scientific understanding of the evolution of earth, and we could say that eventually there came the appearance, over vast periods of time, of hard physical manifestations within that space, becoming living stars, and eventually planets. All of your scientific understandings are approximately accurate here. You could expand that understanding by seeing all of the souls rejoicing in the magnificence of this, over-watching this evolution in love.

THE BEGINNING OF EARTH LIFE

To bring you then to the earth itself, we could say that all of the areas that now exist, from your earth scientific point of view, as galaxies, stars, suns and planets are permutations of one another—variations on a theme. They are an expression of the unlimited variety of the souls' choices reproduced endlessly to reflect the infinite nature of the souls' true eternal existence.

This new reality created by the souls, which is your present physical universe, is quite accurately a reflection of the eternal reality in which the souls have their being. There is no end to this physical universe, from your point of view, even though in a larger sense it is contained *within* the eternal reality, and, the *physical* nature of this new universe will have a beginning and ending. Yet, the forces *within* the physical realities are eternal, and they will simply be transmuted into eternal forces again.

In the vast new *physical* universe, the souls rejoiced in their creation, while at the same time they began to desire a more intense focal point for their subjective experience. Following this impulse, the souls desired to see if they could create self-aware life forms, or beings, within this new physical system. To manifest this desire for life forms within the physical realms, the souls began a process of solidification in one particular area of the physical universe. You could understand, for your purposes, that your present earth was the first of these areas of expression of the new, solidified life forms.

Here, we would ask, for the sake of simplicity, that you would limit your thoughts for now to the earth as a unique expression of the life forms that would become physical human beings. Your earth mental capacities and curiosity could lead you to extrapolate and imagine many other such earths throughout the physical universes. To think in this way can confuse you. We assure you, there are many forms of livingness. But the form of *physical* life as you now experience it is an expression of souls that occurs only in the earth. All of the other expressions of souls in the physical systems of stars and planets are *non*-physical. These non-physical forces serve to remind the human beings that live in earth of the infinite nature of the eternal life. But, the souls do not desire to propagate *human* life forms in other areas of the physical systems.

Remember that there are certain forms of existence created by eternal souls that do not overlap your present physical world. These forms cannot be perceived by physical senses. They are expressions of the souls in *non-physical* forms, and in certain complex ways they *do* exist throughout the universes that are physical. But, we would say, for the purposes of this teaching, that the only *physical* self-aware beings living in the physical universes live on this planet that you speak of as earth. The intent of the souls in this is to continually demonstrate the vast generosity of God to human beings. *You ones are so important to the souls and the God force that this entire physical universe has been displayed and built about your physical existence as a reminder of the eternal magnificence of your true beings.*

For the time being, let us consider that the earth is the focus, the center of attention of the souls who have created the physical universes. And it is to earth human lives that the souls direct their attention now.

Next, the physical earth received the impregnating forces of the souls, woven with the forces of God, to influence the beginning of the first simple cellular life forms that some of you ones have postulated as the beginning of the physical existence of life on earth. Again, for simplicity, you could assume that there is accuracy in your scientific understanding of evolution if you would add to it the feeling that it was the souls themselves, in their creativity, who *caused* all of the permutations and all of the changes that led from the beginning cellular life forms to all of the many present forms of the minerals, the plants, the animals, and the human forms. In this evolutionary creation of the physical earth, there were large groups of souls hovering "above" earth, overseeing the gradual development of all of these earth forms.

In this evolutionary process, the souls were drawn to various aspects of evolution by *desire* and *interest*. Certain groupings of souls would "specialize," rejoicing more in certain of the life forms of earth than others. For example, there was a large grouping of souls fascinated with the various *mineral* forms who were overseeing the creation of those forms. Most likely, in later periods, a human being created by one of the souls of this grouping would have a particular fondness for the mineral forms of earth. There would be another grouping of souls fascinated and preoccupied with the development of the fishes, and with the sea itself. Thus, you could have, later, a human being with a magnetic pulling toward those interests.

These early interests of the souls in different streams of earth evolution were the beginnings of *individuality*. In the creation of the overall earth reality, the souls were all united. But there came to be large groupings of souls with these individual desires and fascinations. As a result of this, there came about another slight *separation*. It was very slight, and not negative in any way. The process was imbued with love. But, those souls who were preoccupied with one particular earth form, such as the mineral form, became less interested in the other forms. Returning again to the vision of standing in a field of flowers, the souls' interests caused them to begin to stare at one flower, rather than to focus on the entire field. Thus, you have another slight sense of distance, or division created in the physical universe.

Eventually, the souls brought about the creation of all of the animal forms that you would understand as the beginning animal forms, including what you would speak of as the ape forms. You have then, a physical earth as you would imagine it in ancient prehistoric times.

THE FIRST HUMAN BEINGS

Again, you could assume accuracy in your scientific understandings, and, building upon that, we would say that next, the ape forms began to evolve toward man. But know that this evolution of the ape animals was guided by the souls over watching earth, who chose, through interest and desire, to become preoccupied with the ape animal form.

There would be other groups of souls who were not interested in ape forms, but continued their interest in maintaining the other animal forms. You could speak of the energies of this group of souls collectively as the ones who over watched *animal nature*.

Still other groups of souls continued to focus their attention on the plants, while others continued to over watch the mineral forms. The forces that you understand as *nature* are created and orchestrated by souls who essentially had no desire to focus upon the final stream of differentiation which we will speak of as human evolution.

There were large numbers of souls interested in this final physical permutation which is the evolution of the human body. There were also large numbers of souls *not* interested. But still, there was not a sense of negativity in this difference in interest since all of those souls who occupied themselves with the forces of nature, instead of with human beings, were still joined in their *eternal* existence to all of the souls who occupied themselves with the stream called human evolution. So, in the eternal sense, all of the souls were sharing earth. But, in the sense of bringing the forces of God into *individual* creations, there would be a large grouping of souls intensely focused on the evolution of the ape form into the beautiful, magnificent, perfectly functioning form that you now understand as the human body.

We would summarize *human* evolution in this way: there would be the ancient periods during which the souls over watched those early animal forms and first implanted within them a cleverness of mind, causing the growth of the *brain* within the race of the small ape forms. Next, there was the implantation of *imagination* and *creativity* into those animal forms. All of this was done over many years of earth time.

After that came the extremely important implantation

of *feeling* into the evolving animal forms that would become human. There were feelings of love and beauty, reflecting the perfection of God itself; feelings of kindness, and feelings of belonging together, so that the race of early human beings would accurately reflect the divine patterns of the souls by existing together in harmony and understanding of one another. All of the individuals would experience a feeling belonging together, feeling themselves as the *entire wholeness of the group*. In this, there was absent the feeling of being one separate, individual human being, which is such a normal feeling for you at this time.

In the beginnings of human life then, there were human societies in which love, kindness, and harmony manifested. But, for many generations, the most intense subjective awareness of each human being was a feeling of belonging to the group. Thus, in the earliest stages of human life, there were the full human capacities of creativity, inventiveness, intelligence, and feeling, but not yet that sense of each person being one unique individual. Early human beings did not have that unique awareness of *self* that was the reality of the souls.

We shall attempt to describe further the early human societies, and here the earth words will be quite weak in their power to communicate a difficult area for you ones to understand. In those early human societies, with the souls rejoicing in their creation of human beings, and with all of this creation permeated with such love, beauty, and perfection, *there was no negativity at all*. Even though there was a physical birth and death of the animal forms that were the early human bodies, there were no subjective feelings of negativity. The animal-human forms were imbued with such a totality of love, and such a sense of perfection, that the early human societies lived in a kind of perfection that mirrored the true nature of the souls.

SOULS CREATE A NEW HUMAN EXPERIENCE

In this beginning period, the souls had only *created* the physical animal forms imbued with all of the human characteristics; they did not *inhabit* them. The souls used these animal-human forms as patterns, and from these patterns they began to create new "versions" of those early human forms that would eventually become refined enough so that the souls could *enter into*, and subjectively experience through human beings.

The new versions of human forms that the souls created and first inhabited would not be considered entirely physical from your present point of view. These new forms were made of the eternal non-physical forces so that the souls could place a portion of their own self-awareness into these non-physical bodies. These bodies that existed alongside the physical animal-human forms, if seen with present human eyes of earth would appear to be rather vaporous and etheric. The existing animal-human forms of the time were able to perceive these new bodies in ways that you would now speak of as "seeing spirits."

For many generations of earth life, the souls rejoiced in projecting a portion of their self-awareness into these etheric human forms. The etheric bodies were *refined* versions of the animal-human forms that continued to exist side by side with the new forms.

Now, as the souls began to desire more and more intensity of subjective experience inside of these etheric human forms, in a very complex way, they began to make changes in the non-physical forms that eventually, over vast periods of time, resulted in these etheric human forms becoming more solid, more *physical.*

To simplify, we would say that eventually, from this process, these etheric forms evolved into human beings who were quite physical and solid, and, they contained *within* themselves projections of the *consciousness* of the souls. They had a divine *self-awareness.* In some earth teachings, these new humans have been called "the sons of God." At the same time, there simultaneously existed the other stream of animal forms raised to human capacities. The animal-humans were able now to make communications in words and in inner projections of thought and emotion, but they did not have a portion of soul consciousness living within them. In some earth teachings, these beings are spoken of as "the sons of man."

The sons of God can be seen as a race of physical human beings containing the projection of self-awareness and the creating the divine spark of the souls. As the souls who created human evolution concentrated on the development of the sons of God, the animal-human beings gradually came to be infused with the forces of the souls who had chosen to over watch earth nature and the other animal forms. If these "nature forces" that grew within the sons of man had not been altered, then within each of the individual humans in this group there would have simply been physical life, and then death, and that would have been the end of the existence of those human forms. So, the sons of man formed a race of human beings that was *not* eternal.

The life and death of the sons of man were rooted in earth cycles, and these cycles are quite temporal.

THE TRANSFORMATION OF ANIMAL-HUMANS

All of the souls who were then over watching earth, in concert decided that the human form was a thing of great beauty. They began to rejoice in it as their most magnificent creation. And they began to say: "Here we have come to create what is closest to our God, what is closest to ourselves as eternal beings. This is the creation we most rejoice in—the human beings that we are able to infuse with a portion of our eternal awareness. This is the creation about which we will build all of physical evolution. This is the jewel in our crown."

So the souls began then to build all of the earth evolutionary forces about this particular refined race of human beings called the sons of God. And, for long periods they worked to transmute and transform the other race of humans that was the sons of man. Eventually, there came a point in time in earth when all of the sons of man were finally infused with a portion of a soul expressing in the way of the sons of God. All human beings then were transformed into this new jewel in the crown of creation— the sons of God. Thus, there came a time, in the ancient past, when all human beings physically existed as humans now appear, and all of them were imbued with a portion of soul awareness that brings the eternal force into human form.

These evolutionary changes took place long before what you would think of as recorded human history. In most cultures of today, this ancient period is reflected only in myth and legend.

There were ancient ape forms that did *not* become a part of the human evolution. These ape creatures were watched over by a certain group of souls who were more fascinated by the evolution of the animal forms. These souls could be understood *as the forces of nature.* The animal forms that they guided have come to be the present apes, and all of the other animal forms. Although they are not infused with a soul awareness of the "human" type, all animals have *reflections* of qualities of soul that human beings are able to identify with. There is a certain warmth, love, and caring in animal lives. However, the *awareness of self,* and the eternal soul spark are not *inside* of these animal forms. They are hovering *outside* of the bodies. In a similar way, the souls who animate the plants and minerals hover outside of them, not investing their awareness inside of the physical forms.

The large grouping of souls that chose to work with human life were the souls that created the sons of God. The animal-human forms that were the sons of man, and that were eventually transformed into the sons of God, were then relinquished by the souls who over watch the animal forms. The sons of man were given into the trust of the souls who over-watch the human forms. To put this in a simple way, we could say that the transition human beings who were the sons of man were transferred to a new kind of reality: to an energy force that now comes under the watchful eye of the souls who direct the human evolution.

As a result of the transformation of all humans, there was a further *separation.* The animal forms and the nature forms continued on the path of evolution limited to the cycles of physical life and death. Although the human forms *physically* followed the cycles of life and death, the human beings themselves were quite consciously aware of the blending together of the eternal portions of themselves with their temporary physical bodies. They understood quite clearly that they were only *borrowing* the physical forms that were ruled by life and death. They understood quite consciously and clearly their own *eternal* nature. Those human beings were set apart from the rest of nature by the portion of soul awareness projected into their human personality. That awareness, that sense of eternal self, brought those human beings conscious knowledge of all truth in the early stages of earth. Those early human beings were aware of the eternal realities, and they were able to manipulate matter at will, with the mind, the heart, and the powers of God. The ancient legends and stories have been created to remind yourselves of the abilities of human beings in those early periods.

INTENSIFYING THE HUMAN EXPERIENCE

Gradually the souls realized that because of the vastness of the conscious awareness of eternal realities that was living inside each human being, there was a certain impediment to experiencing the *intensity* of earth life. It would be as though you are having a dream in your present reality. And in that dream you are having a great love affair. Your heart is so full. The beloved one is so brilliant to you. And then, suddenly, in the dream, you remember: "This is only a dream. This is not real." Because of this memory, the intensity of your joy is diminished.

In those early periods of human life on earth, the portion of the soul that was projected into the early human
forms as self-awareness was so conscious of its eternal
existence as a soul, and its larger eternal reality was always
so present that the human person found this vast awareness
inhibiting to the enjoyment of physical earth. The clear
memory of eternal reality made it difficult for the person to
experience the great intensity of earth life that the personality portion of soul consciousness desired. So, among the
souls, there was an agreement that there would be certain
manipulations done to the minds of the human beings, and
to their eyes, their ears, their feelings, their intuitive abilities, and other human capacities.

These manipulations brought about an evolutionary
process in which human beings gradually developed the
capacity to: focus clearly upon themselves as *physical*
beings; to experience themselves as *one unique ego*; and, to
temporarily, while living in physical form, dim their *conscious* awareness of the eternal realities. All of this took
place over many generations of human beings, and thousands of earth years.

As the human ego developed through generations of
human beings, there were human teaching-ones, guided by
souls, who taught human beings to focus on earth life as the
most important aspect of their existence. Of course there
was no negativity or loss of goodness in this new focus
upon earth. This was the implementation of the great love
of the souls for their human creations that helped them
experience themselves as *individuals*. And, in the early
portions of this "individualizing" process, there was still

harmony, love, and a feeling of belonging in all of the human social groupings of earth.

Next, there came a major turning point in human life. In the creation of the individual ego within each human being, the souls instilled *free will* into the human personality patterns, just as the God forces had infused free will into the souls. Into the human beings the souls planted total freedom for the human personalities to do as they pleased, and to create what pleased them. The souls understood that in all universes there is only good. So they knew that human beings could never do other than good. This implantation of free will was the great turning point. Human beings began to feel more and more: "I am *myself.* I am not my entire tribal grouping. I am not my entire family. Even though I feel the love between ourselves, I am quite independent and unique." This feeling of independence *intensified* the experience of earth many times over. And, the joy and love and beauty of the human experience was even greater than at any other stage in the process of the evolution of human life.

Thus, there came to be, for many generations, human beings feeling themselves uniquely as themselves, expressing creatively, freely, without restraint, in great love, feeling their own *will*, and aligning it with their own unique desires. Included in their inner subjectivity was a feeling of love for all other human beings. All of this was accompanied by a diminishing awareness of the eternal portions of reality.

During this long period of human evolution, the gradually dimming eternal realities became *personified* in the human societies as what you would now speak of as *God.*

In other words, it was not desired that human beings would entirely forget the eternal portions. These portions were only to be dimmed a bit, while the personality portion of soul consciousness walked in human form.

In these early periods, life on earth resembled what some human beings have come to write about in terms of "the Garden of Eden." Here were individual, unique human beings with the power to create and express, walking in a physical perfection of love that they shared with all other human beings. There was a subjective feeling of belonging to an earth that was created by God.

In a certain sense, we could say that this existence was the perfect pattern that the souls desired for earth when they first began their physical creation. This was the new physical reality that they had set out to create.

THE BEGINNING OF NEGATIVITY

When the souls said, "Go forth human personality and create what *you* desire," this marked the beginning of a new cycle of creation. This cycle is very important in terms of bringing the God forces more *physically* into human life. The souls could create the physical bodies, they could prepare them with divine forces, and they could live within them through a projection of a portion of soul awareness. But, it was the free, independent human beings who could create physically in earth, in terms of thoughts, feelings, and physical actions. So, to accomplish the physical creation and evolution of earth from *within* the earth, the human beings, feeling themselves to be independent egos, had to go forth into earth and *choose* what they would make of earth. The human beings went forth as the actors upon the stage created by the souls.

Now, here we must simplify again for you, so we would say that, in a certain sense, in the early portions of this new independent human creation, human beings gradually came to look about with a new attitude that began to emphasize their own *personal desires* more and more. Confusion arose from this overbalance toward personal desire, and the first area that the confusion settled over was human *possessions,* physical objects. The human beings began to be more enamored with a possession than they were with the love of their fellow human beings. And soon (we are condensing a long process that occurred over many generations of human beings) there were human beings who would desire a brilliant jeweled cloak more than they would desire the well-being and happiness of their brother. They would say to their brother: "You cannot wear this cloak, it is *mine*."

From this preoccupation with possessions and ownership of physical things, there came about the beginning of human *fear*. This was the beginning of human subjective feelings that you would speak of as negative. That brother who was denied the use of the cloak began to have a strange new feeling that you would call *sadness*. Along with this came a feeling of separation from the one who owned the cloak. In the person feeling sadness, there came about another new feeling that you would understand as *resentment*. Gradually, over many generations of human beings, there were many kinds of interactions where those who had been deprived of the prized possessions began to desire the possessions more than those who had them. From this, there came about what you would understand as *thieving* and *stealing*. The development of all of these kinds of negative feeling patterns was part of a complex social process involving many generations of human beings in many societies spread across the face of the earth.

By understanding this process that brought about negativity in human affairs, you can see quite clearly that negativity is most certainly a *human* creation. It is only an *inner subjective experience* that exists nowhere in eternal existences except in human feelings, in human personality experience. *Negativity comes about when the subjective experience of personality is squeezed into one single ego without a conscious awareness of the love that joins one human being to another.*

It is very important for you now in your present life to understand that negativity is a human creation, so that never would you be tempted to blame life, or nature, or evolution, or God for the negativity that you perceive in life. All of you ones walking the face of the earth in this time were participants in those early human changes that created this negativity. All of you were involved in the creation of what you would speak of as *selfishness*, and the lack of sensitivity to others. All of the fears, angers, resentments, and painful experiences that are now a portion of the present human experiences were all first created by you ones as individuals living through many early lifetimes.

HELP FROM HUMAN TEACHERS

During these early periods in which human beings were

living in ways that created negativity, there were teaching-ones who were attempting to remind human beings of the eternal love of their *true* beings. These teaching-ones were physical human beings who had retained a vital, clear, and distinct inner knowing of the eternal beginnings, and of the generations of love and beauty that had preceded the long period of growing negativity. In other words, these were ones that you would now speak of as enlightened beings. Physically, they appeared to be ordinary human beings, but inwardly, in their subjectivity, they were able to expand their conscious awareness to directly perceive their own soul and the union with all other souls. They understood all of the reasons why earth was created, and they were able to attune to all of the creative impulses and forces that the souls set into motion to create earth. They were able to understand these forces intuitively, to align with them, and then to translate them, *within their own human subjectivity*, into teachings for other human beings; to translate them into thoughts, feelings, and ideas that ordinary human beings could understand. In those early periods, all human beings were in close proximity to one of these teaching human beings, either through direct contact, or through students of the teaching-ones.

Thus, there were teaching human beings giving "divine" teachings that came to them as intuitive impulses and inner experiences that were not understandable to other human beings. These teaching-ones, in sensitivity, love, and wisdom, evaluated the capacity of understanding of the ordinary human beings around them, and then they translated their inner intuitive knowings into human words and deeds that they believed were the most understandable to the ordinary human beings of the day. Since these "translations" of truth were made in different places in earth, and in different times in human history, there came about different spiritual teachings that were given over centuries, in quickly evolving cultures. These differences in spiritual teachings came about because the teaching-ones of each period needed to communicate as human beings of their day in order to be understood, in order to be of benefit to those around them.

In those early periods, even as you ones of the human race were guided by the enlightened human beings, you were still able to vaguely perceive a portion of your soul, although your capacity to perceive eternal realities had been diminished (in order to intensify your experience of earth). Thus, the early human beings were guided both by unconscious impulses directly from their own souls, and by human teaching-ones walking in physical form.

HELP FROM SPIRITUAL GUIDES

As the centuries passed, and human life became more intensely focused upon physical fulfillments and earth creations, there needed to be another adjustment because human beings had begun to ignore the guidance from their own souls and from the human teaching-ones. This adjustment was needed to amplify and intensify the guidance from soul. Thus, the souls amongst themselves did say: "We did establish earth so that I, as one soul, would be all that would guide and influence my personality in that one human form in one earth lifetime. But the human ones have become quite rigid and tight in their feelings, and they can no longer hear the inner truth. We will need to speak to them with a louder voice." The human personality would no longer listen to the soul that was animating it. The physical patterns were becoming rebellious, over-focused upon fear, doubt, and negativity. (We are simplifying and condensing for you here, putting these areas into human words which do not quite capture the reality, but they will suffice for this time.)

There was a new decision made by the souls over watching the human evolution of earth (and this decision was a *possibility* inherent in the original impulses of earth creation). The decision was to amplify the voice of one soul guiding its one human being by bringing forth other souls into the process of guidance. These others souls who were called upon to help were souls who had, in the past, projected portions of themselves into human beings, but who, at this point, had "completed" their earth projections; they felt satisfied with their earth experiences.

Thus, certain souls who had completed earth joined with a soul who was still guiding a human being in order to augment the force of love and wisdom flowing into that one human being. For all humans then, there came to be new souls helping to guide and inspire. These new helping souls became *guiding-ones* to the human beings walking in earth.

You ones who stand in your present earth form and personality are now guided by the continuing inflowing of your own soul's forces, as well as the forces of guiding souls who have walked with you as physical human beings in past times of earth, and who no longer express through their own human personalities. These guiding souls unite with your soul in order to fill your present personality with wisdom and love.

THE NEGATIVITY GROWS

Even though there was new "spiritual guidance" from the guiding-ones, the expansion of human negativity continued. After the individual differences between human beings arose, gradually *families* began uniting against others to protect their possessions, or to hold their mating-ones so they would not be "stolen" by others. Soon, there were *tribal groupings* protecting against one another, and then larger groupings, and then nations.

You can see here that *all of the earth competition and struggle that have led to all of the wars, and all of the human pain and suffering, began with an unwillingness to care for other human beings more than you care for things of this earth.* There is not a badness in this, except from the human subjective point of view. From the soul point of view, the soul continues to pour forth love for *all* human beings, even as it pours forth a portion of its conscious awareness into that one individual human being that it animates in any given lifetime. The soul does not love you as *its* personality more than it loves all other human per-sonalities. It loves *all*. The soul would not make a separa-tion or a distance. It is human awareness without love, human thought and feeling colored by fear, and human action growing out of fear that create the differences and the separations between human beings.

The negativity that human beings inadvertently created brought about a pattern that the souls did not intend to create. The souls understood quite clearly in the beginning creation of earth that human negativity was a possibility. But they certainly did not view this negativity as a *bad* possibility. The souls understood the early strife of human beings, even all of the war and death and violence, as temporary adjustments being made by human beings, for the souls are rooted in the perfection of all of life. They can even see the perfection of your challenges as human beings. They can see beauty in those experiences. They can see the perfection of God in all of human life. Most of you ones have not yet learned this, but as you continue to grow, you will also see the extraordinary goodness in all experience.

To summarize all of this for you, we would say that the physical earth was created by the souls in perfection. The freedom to create was given to human beings by the souls. The human beings created many magnificent areas. They also created one thread of human experience that you could understand as fear—the feeling of *badness*, the feeling of *wrongness* that begins to cause human beings to squeeze in upon themselves and to make a wall between themselves and others. *That fear that temporarily squeezes out the awareness of love is the underlying cause of all human suffering and pain through all of earth life.*

In terms of creating earth and knowing where your earth adventure has begun, and how you have arrived at your present point in earth, what we have given here will serve as a simple beginning. We ask that you expand upon this understanding and intensify it with your own thoughts and feelings, your own beliefs, and attitudes, and ideas. Understand that you have total freedom to create your life as you desire it to be. And you have total freedom to create your understanding of where you began, and why you have come into this earth adventure.

CHAPTER THREE

Civilization: A Human Creation

As generation after generation of human beings lived on the earth that was created by the souls, there came forth a reality that was the creation of human beings alone. This was what you would understand as the *civilizations* of human beings created by large groupings of individuals. There are several stages of human civilization that could be of interest and enlightenment to you in the present time. Knowledge of these areas can help you understand yourself in a way that will enhance the joy and happiness that you will create in your lifetime.

First of all, before looking at these stages, you would need to remember that you as a human being, along with most humans upon the face of the earth at this present time, were living in the past as human beings during the time of those early beginnings of ancient civilizations. Thus, the story of human civilization is your own personal history as a human being.

You would understand here that in the beginning periods of human civilization there were a greater number of human beings alive than most ones presently believe. Those ancient periods preceded recorded human history by thousands of generations, and after those beginning times there were many periods of change in the earth that drastically reduced the number of living human beings; it was as though there came about a new beginning for the human race.

CIVILIZATION BEGINS

The first significant stages of human civilization came about during that ancient period that we have described during which all human beings upon the face of the earth were finally infused with portions of a soul. All of them had become the sons of God.

This period is quite ancient, occurring before what you would understand as the "Atlantis" period, which would be hundreds of thousands of years ago in terms of present earth years. From that time onward, the earth would be a place in which all human beings would be infused by eternal soul forces.

This early stage of human civilization, as we have previously indicated, was quite *ideal*, in the sense that so many individual human beings were able to live together in love, in mutual cooperation, and in perfection of social interaction. Human beings were living as the souls intended them to live. The purpose of earth life was being fulfilled, just as the souls had desired when they first created earth. And these ideal human habitations took place in many different physical locations about the earth. Thus, there would be, throughout earth, many groupings of human beings expressing freely in joy and in love, just as the souls intended for earth life.

After these ideal periods of human civilization, there came the stages of unfoldment that we have referred to earlier as the beginning of the confusion growing out of human *self-preoccupation.* During these periods of personal strife between individual human beings, there were created the forces of misunderstanding that later became conflicts throughout earth. In a relatively short period of time, perhaps ten to ninety generations of human beings (varying with the physical location in earth), beginning with strife between small groupings, there were conflicts between social and tribal groupings occurring in all of the various large concentrations of human beings all about the face of the earth. These differences and struggles between groups of human beings became widespread over subsequent generations of human life. From these generations of conflict came the disturbing influences that are the present energies of human misunderstanding and fear—human negativity.

During this period of accumulating human negativity, there existed different "racial" characteristics of human bodies. These different racial characteristics were created by the souls in the beginning of human life as an expression of the unique differences of the souls' ideas for what human life should be. Any of the races of human bodies chosen by the souls would be equal to any other. Subjective responses to differences in race are *humanly* created. From the soul point of view, the reason for different races was simply to create *variety* through different kinds of expressions of the human forms.

No matter what racial grouping was involved, no matter in what location human beings were concentrated, during this particular period of the beginning of human strife, there came about the separation of human beings into different groups. These kinds of separations were not intended by the souls. The souls desired all human beings to live as one family upon the face of the earth. The various divisions between the new groups of human beings were created by the human beings themselves. They were primarily motivated by the conflict growing out of human fear.

During these periods of human strife, the creativity, the beauty, and the magnificence of human beings also continued to unfold. And, essentially, the love and the cooperation did continue. But, in many ways, the strife and conflict grew stronger as large groupings of human beings began to concentrate into the physical locations of earth that were most popular, due to climate, and due to ancient wisdom that would prompt groupings of ones to align themselves with different locations in earth because of spiritual beliefs.

TURNING TOWARD THE PAST

At the present time, there is much interest in various ancient human civilizations, particularly the early Egyptian period. Some are drawn to ancient China or India, while others are fascinated with human expression through the Indian tribal groupings of the American and South American lands. Interest in the past is being aroused in many human beings. We would say that in letting your desires to study these past civilizations grow, you are blessing your present personality. Many of you are stirring up intuitive unconscious memories of past times in which you did physically live in some of those places. Often, such interest will stir up personality patterns that you created in those physical places of the past. These patterns can be quite beautiful and magnificent. They can be important for your present personality to feel and to understand.

As you become interested in past human civilizations, you will need to look at them with a sense of enthusiasm, curiosity, and passion to know. It will not benefit you to look to the past with a sense of comparison and say: "It was so much more beautiful in the time of Egypt when there was not a nuclear bomb capable of destroying the entire earth. It was so much more beautiful in ancient Rome when so many were of great artistic sensitivity and understanding. It was so much more beautiful in the time of India when those ones who walked earth in God-like understanding of truth could come forth and teach us and take us by the hand." If you compare what you imagine to be the beauty of the past to a feeling that the present is cold and lonely and frightening, this indeed will not benefit you, and, such a comparison certainly is not truth. Remind yourself: in those beautiful times of the past, you also had your cycles of fear and suffering. You also had your habits of judgment and confusion that caused pain.

So, we suggest that you follow your desires to study the past if they are strong, but understand that you have chosen to live in the *present*. You have completed your lives in those past periods. Physically they are ended, even though emotionally and spiritually they are alive in the heart of your present personality. All of the areas of magnificence of those past times are infused into you now. Your soul has poured forth the great capacities that you have developed as a human being in the past, and has woven them into your present personality us *potentials* of magnificence and beauty.

If you find yourself longing for a beauty that you believe existed in the past, remind yourself: "What I am longing for is the beauty of my own being, the majesty of my own soul, and the perfection of the forces of God. These are all living in me now, in this present moment. My personality life in this moment is more important to me than the past."

CREATIVE FORCES BRING CHALLENGES

In the ancient periods of human civilization, there gradually came to be a great deal of human confusion and negativity in the major human living centers occupying most of the land masses of the time. As the negativity grew, the souls that watched over earth began to see that the human beings had become so confused that they would respond only to *physical* realities. Thus, there was a need for a dramatic event in earth life that would help human beings return their focus to the love that joined them. These over watching souls that would create the dramatic earth event included the souls who were animating human beings, aligned with many different kinds of eternal forces, and interacting with the souls whose energies would be spoken of as the forces of nature.

As there came to be extremely deep confusion of negativity in a large grouping of human beings living in a particular place in earth, members of the grouping began to create very rigid beliefs that were deeply rooted in fear and in self-preoccupation. When it appeared that the human beings were about to become hopelessly overbalanced in the area of pre-occupation with their own desires, all of the over-watching souls decided that a challenge in the physical earth life would be the dramatic event that would influence the human beings to again see the truth. Thus, in certain times and in certain places, for particular groupings of human beings who were beginning to find it more and more difficult to know the true purpose of life, a certain "permission" was given, by the souls expressing through those human beings, to the souls over watching the nature forces: a permission to create physical catastrophe through nature—through storm, flood, volcanic activity, and, at times, through the impacting on earth of portions of physical debris from the space surrounding earth.

Understand that in these physical events, there was never a sense of *punishment* for the human beings (punishment is a human creation). It was the eternal wisdom of the souls that could see that if human beings were led to grapple with the challenge of catastrophic earth events, they would come to see that they needed to care for one another; they needed to help and stand by one another if their own personalities were to survive. (All of this is quite generalized for your understanding.) As a result of the human beings needing to struggle with the challenge of such difficult earth situations, there would come an appreciation of one another.

In these ways then, there were set into motion, in the early portions of human civilization in earth, factors that could be considered to be the first disturbances by nature to drastically affect human life. Over many generations, these disturbances gradually changed the physical appearance of earth—the structure of the outer layer of land masses, and the relationship between the land masses and the water masses, or the seas. So, as many are now beginning to understand, there came to be, over long periods of human existence, shifting and changing of the physical structure of the earth, brought about from the earth challenges that served as teachings to human beings.

These earth changes were similar to those that had taken place in the earth's evolution before human development, but in this new period of human occupation of the earth's land masses, the natural forces were controlled not only by the souls preoccupied with such forces, but the nature forces were also correlated with the desires and needs of the souls who were expressing through human form. From these kinds of understandings, you can begin to see that the earth is not an enemy in which the forces of nature rise up without purpose or meaning to indiscriminately cause death to human beings, or destruction to different lands. Rather, the forces of nature can be seen as a portion of the *creative forces* of earth, brought forth through the wisdom of all souls, and aligned with the souls expressing through human form.

All that you human ones do in the present (as it has always been throughout human existence) feeds back into the wisdom and the experience of the souls. At certain points in human history, when what human beings chose to do became quite confused and frightening and painful for one another because of the distortion caused by human fear, then human beings created forces that led the souls to bring forth teaching experiences for the personalities. These experiences were brought about in many ways, including natural disaster.

To put this another way: by choosing to create negative attitudes in themselves, human beings have fed back into their souls certain experiences that prompted the souls to begin to make adjustments in the earth experience that would affect the human personalities in ways that they would notice that their fearful attitudes and actions were causing pain to other human beings. This would lead the human beings to reexamine their lives, and eventually to deepen their understanding. So, the souls' "intervention" is a portion of the natural unfoldment of the human personalities, and is a direct consequence of the choices made by those personalities. In a certain sense then, we could say that human beings were *creating* natural disasters or other challenging earth situations in order to learn from them.

CHALLENGES FROM HUMAN FEAR

Prior to the periods that you ones now understand as the "Atlantean" period, and other periods of ancient existence, there came about a certain lack of ability of many human beings to attune to the needs of others, just as there had come earlier the inability to attune to their guiding-ones and their souls. Thus, we could say that human *choice* (choosing to focus on self-preoccupation and fear) caused the diminishing of the ability to love other human beings.

The self-created fear and negativity of these early societies also diminished the human beings' ability to express

through their personalities the eternal forces of love and
magnificence that maintain the perfection of earth life.
When these forces are not maintained properly, then there
comes a weakening of human life, in terms of a loss of
idealism. Thus, from the beginning earth expressions of
civilized human groupings that were quite ideal, there came
about many challenges, created by human fear, that led to
what appears to be, from an earth point of view, a "worsen-
ing" of human life. There was an increase in human pain
and suffering in all ways. There came about what appears
to be, from an earth point of view, a *degeneration* of what
in the earlier portions of human life was quite magnificent
and perfect.

We assure you that such an observation is a *human* observation. That which *appears* in earth life to be a loss of
the perfection of God, is seen from the souls' point of view
as simply another expression of human freedom and
choice. The souls were able to see, within those human
choices, the forces of God that were being utilized by the
human beings. The souls knew that there could only be
goodness in those human unfoldments, even though the
experiences were painful and at times very discouraging for
the human beings who lived through them.

You can see then, that in the history of civilized human
groupings, even though there has been the unfolding of
great capacities of creativity, love, and awareness of God in
the personal lives of human beings, this has been mingled
with the negativity, pain, and suffering caused by human
fear and over-preoccupation with the human self. From this
negativity there has come misunderstanding, conflict, and
war in human societies. Although these challenging experi-

ences appeared throughout the physical reality of earth life, *all of this negativity began in the subjective personal reality of human beings.* The negative interactions between individual human beings eventually became strong negative social forces. This negativity gradually became woven with the human choices made in social groupings that would subsequently influence the unfoldment of human civilization.

HUMAN CHOICE CREATES EARTH

In the historical descriptions of the unfoldment of human civilization that are now available to you, you have a chronicle of *human choice.* In the civilizations of great artistic creativity, beauty, and justice, there are examples of human beings choosing in *love.* In those civilizations where you find war, struggle, and a lack of understanding of one group for another, you have examples of the unfoldment of human life through choices made in *fear.* You can look for yourself at the historical record of human life in earth, and by observing the harmony and beauty created in certain periods, you can identify the periods of love. You will understand that in the periods in which human beings were not able to achieve these heights, they were confused and trapped in their own fear, often to the extent that they were willing to lie and cheat and steal from one another. At times, they were even willing to cause death to other human beings.

Negative interactions between societies that result in

international struggle and war began in many of the ancient civilizations, and they have extended into the present. Throughout the unfoldment of human civilization there has been a thread of negativity, caused by human choice. There has also been a longing for truth in large numbers of human beings. There have always been feelings of kindness, love, and creativity. In the weaving of these different threads of human subjective experience, both fulfilling and painful, *there has come about the creation of earth through human participation and freedom of choice.* In other words, the souls did not create the earth to unfold in a rigid way, predetermined by the souls. The purpose was to give to the human personalities the opportunity to create the earth realities according to human choice, and human will. This has been accomplished, even though the human choices have resulted at times in what you now consider to be negativity.

GOODNESS AND "BADNESS" IN CIVILIZATION

In the history of human civilization, and also in periods for which you have no history, there have been two general streams of human choosing. From the present viewpoint, you could look backward to all human civilizations and see that in the first stream of choosing were those human beings in past periods of time who were able to open their hearts to love; they were able to understand one another and thereby create a civilization marked by fairness, creativity, honor, idealism, and all of the other qualities that are the truth of you ones as human beings and as eternal souls.

The second stream of human choosing is the stream of

personal fear and doubt, of preoccupation with self, and the inability to trust others. This brought about a fear of others that was so great that even in the face of the unending forces of love that were being poured forth into earth, some human beings chose to strike out against others.

Of these two streams of human choice, the most important thing to understand is that the currents that are the creativity and love are aligned with the eternal truth, and they will continue throughout *all* of human existence on earth. They will never be diminished. They have come from the ancient past to the present. In any moment of human society, and in any moment of the evolution of human civilization, no matter how much negativity human beings have created, there has always been, and will always be streams and forces of love living within the human hearts of all ones who are existing in physical form.

Now, whether human beings would heed these forces, and rejoice in them, and take them into their hearts as love, is a matter of *choice.* You ones have been free to ignore such eternal impulses in the past; indeed, many times you have chosen to do so. Yet, even when you find it difficult to *feel* the truth, you can use your mind to remind yourself that the love and goodness that have been expressed through human choice throughout all human civilization is an expression of your eternal nature—the perfection of your soul which has its existence in a matrix of forces of God itself.

On the other hand, the stream of negativity running through human civilization is caused by *temporary* human fear. The negative human expressions in earth are confused human choices that eventually will be healed.

Understanding this, you can see how it is that *all* of human civilization is an expression of God, brought forth as energies expressed through the souls, into the human personalities, and then freely manifested into the physical reality as human choice. Eventually, you will come to understand in your own heart that in all of human civilization, in the many thousands of generations of human beings following one upon the other, through all of the many human lifetimes, there has only been good. There has only been the unfoldment of the forces of God, for that is all that exists in all of human life. *Within* this eternal good, human beings have at times chosen to act in ways that have caused pain, and *temporarily* there has been the appearance of "badness" many times throughout human history.

You could ask yourself: "Where are the bad human beings from the past?" They no longer exist. Perhaps there are stories remaining of their deeds, but these stories are kept alive by living human beings in the present. The only badness is being created in the present, and it is an inner feeling being created by human beings. The more fearful the present beings are, the more strongly are they attracted to negativity, past and present.

So, we could summarize human civilization in a simple way: In any moment, there lies within earth civilization the potential for all human beings to express, to the fullest degree, the perfection of God that lives within them. *Human civilization has the potential to transform itself instantaneously, as soon as all of the human beings that comprise that civilization are willing to love themselves and all those about themselves.*

As you attempt to understand human civilizations,

past, present, or future, and you look from your own personal point of view, if you find yourself drawing conclusions that are essentially negative, feeling that a certain period was a period of badness or wrongness, you must understand that *the negativity that you feel is a creation of yourself.* The subjective feeling within you that there was badness in the past is a function of your own personality. It arises from your inability to understand that in all human civilizations, no matter how confused the individuals did become, there have always been the eternal forces of love living within those human beings.

To gain a deeper understanding of this, you could ask yourself: "Why am I drawn to this particular attitude toward human civilization that focuses so much upon what appears to be negativity? Why am I seeing through eyes of fear and judgment and condemnation? Why is it that I am attracted to this negative way of describing entire generations of human beings who were essentially quite loving, honest, courageous, and idealistic? Why can I not understand that the pain and suffering that perhaps did exist at that time were caused by the fear of those people who were attempting to manifest the love that is their true nature?"

We can assure you, given our vision of all that has occurred in human life throughout all of human civilization (and our vision is clearer than your present one, for we do not have the necessity of limiting ourselves in this moment to one human personality and the vision of that personality), we can assure you that the choices of most human beings through all of their lifetimes have been made in ways that do reflect goodness and the perfection of God. You must remind yourself that in this particular period of earth life, it is quite popular and fashionable to cleverly point out flaws in all of life, to find fault, and to criticize. Understand that this affects not only your present vision of the history of human civilization, but it also affects your interpretation of that history. With such a critical focus, you ones of earth continue, by your negative subjective responses, to re-create those streams of fear that began in the past. Yet, even in this confused response, you human ones in the present, just as in the past, are essentially choosing in magnificence and beauty, even though at times you cannot see it.

If, on the other hand, you believe that in the past there was goodness, but now in the present world there is too much strife, war, and badness, it would not benefit you to say to yourself: "I long for those periods of human existence when human beings only chose in love. I long for those periods when there was the absence of human-created negativity." For if you believe that those ancient periods were good and the present is bad, you will continue to make a gap between goodness and your subjective feelings, and you will frighten yourself. You will feel that you are in a hostile world that eventually will destroy you. You will feel there is not enough goodness, there is not enough love; there is only badness. If these feelings grow too large, you will create feelings of hostility, fear, doubt, confusion, and resentment within your personality.

In this particular period of civilization, as we have said, many of you ones are quite fond of finding flaw and criticizing. Often, you place these criticisms before one another in the vastness of your electronic communication networks, and you give human beings more reasons to judge other human beings, to judge life as being of badness, of being not good, of being untrustworthy. Together, you fall so deeply into your fears that it is as though you ones are standing in the midst of a great nightmare and you are saying to one another: "This is reality. We must guard ourselves from badness. It is right to be frightened."

You will soon come to understand that these kinds of feelings are passing cycles. They are *dying* patterns. More and more human beings in this period are beginning to see the part that their own individual personal fear plays in the collective sense of negativity that you ones presently create as a civilization. More people are beginning to see that if they can love in their own human path, day to day, in the simple ways, then their feelings about life will be transformed. This will enable them to see areas of goodness and beauty in life that were previously hidden. Soon they will be able to see through the illusions of badness to the underlying fear in human beings that causes them to strike out against one another. And, as a result of this expanded understanding, they will become a portion of the *healing* of that fear, first by healing *their own* fear, and then by loving others and helping them to heal their fear.

To move toward this kind of evolution, you could ask yourself each day:

"How do I choose to view human life? What is my feeling about the goodness or badness of life in general, from the past to the present? What are my beliefs and attitudes and feelings about human civilization? Do they come from fear, or do they come from love?"

We can assure you that if you can train yourself to consciously love and to see with eyes of love, then you too can
look back into the history of human civilization as it has
unfolded in this great earth adventure, and you can see
beauty and good. Eventually, you can see the manifestation
of the forces of God itself through all of human civilizations, throughout all of human earth time.

TODAY'S CIVILIZATION AND A CHANGING EARTH

We will now look at a confused understanding about earth
life and human civilization that is becoming more common
in the present time. This concerns the area of *natural
disasters* and *earth changes*. There are many in this period
of time who feel that the quickened evolution of human
unfoldment will be signaled by new dramatic changes in
the physical structure of earth—changes that could be quite
disastrous for some human beings. This kind of attitude is
caused by different factors in each person, depending on
their personality structures.

To look at these kinds of attitudes, we will first speak
of an overall general attitude that is held by many. This is a
great sense of *discontent* that many feel with the present
earth life. This grows out of a feeling of frustration that
comes from their belief that there is badness in earth;
badness from wars and from the many struggles between
people that are taking place about the earth. For many, this
feeling of badness is so intense, and the earth challenges
seem so out of control, that they come to believe that it will
take a very dramatic destruction to shake human beings

enough to turn them toward idealism, kindness, generosity, and love of one another.

Now those who have such a belief are misjudging and misunderstanding the earth and its evolution. This is caused by seeing earth through a screen of their own frustration. The frustration is caused by their inability to find any way to change what they consider to be the rigid negativity that they now see in human civilization.

For those who have such feelings, we can assure you that the earth forces are not going to rise up and destroy earth. We can assure you that there are many changes that human beings can make in the present time to bring peace and harmony and love throughout the earth. Human civilization in this time does not require the shock of widespread natural disaster in order to find truth. These are *past* realities. They will not unfold in the present.

If you can work in the ways that we will suggest in these teachings to deepen your love and understanding, you can come to know with certainty, within your own heart, that the present human civilization will be healed by *love*, not by widespread upheaval. You will learn to see beneath the illusion of turmoil and to feel the great strides that so many human beings are making in their own personal lives toward generosity, sensitivity, and love. The growing kindness, altruism, and idealism are the new signals being sent from human beings to the souls who express through human form. These are the experiences the souls are reaping from you, even when you are temporarily caught up in some of your negative beliefs. The souls can see clearly the human desire to find truth, and certainly the challenge of natural disaster is not needed as a prod to human civilization as a whole.

It is possible that decisions will be made by groups of souls who watch over portions of earth that could result in minor changes, such as earthquakes or volcanic eruptions that will be confined to small areas of earth. The reasons for such events in human life are quite complex, and we would not enter into them at this point. Attempting to explain them in the present words of earth often makes them seem quite ridiculous. For example, if we would say in earth words, "This group of human beings has chosen, with their souls, to learn about life by dying in an earthquake," there is not satisfaction for the human mind and heart in such explanations. So, we would caution you not to overemphasize the *intellect* in a search for reasons for such events. It requires patience and a diligent search within your own heart to come to a satisfactory understanding of the kind of earth events that bring about human suffering.

SEEING THE GOOD IN CHANGE

The understanding that is most important to gain concerning the changing earth is that the earth is unfolding in ways that are quite magnificent. It is tempting for human beings to believe that the wars and violence that manifest here and there are the true reality of earth. Many people have already come to have feelings about civilization that are quite negative. Thus, when they think in terms of the changing earth and the future, it is expected that they will think in terms of disaster and catastrophe.

If you should find yourself thinking in these negative terms, ask of yourself: "Am I seeing truth, or is my own fear coloring all that I see in earth?" We can promise you that love, magnificence, and good are being created by human beings. Love is also being poured forth into earth by the souls, by guiding-ones, and by the forces of God. From all of these areas working together, you can expect goodness, beauty, and harmony to unfold within the earth itself. And most certainly it does.

When you look to the future, to the present, or to the past, we suggest that you strive to see goodness. This is not to say that you must pretend that there are not areas of life that do not please you. It is not to say that you will ignore the challenges and hardships of earth, such as hunger, war, and so forth. Rush to those situations if you believe you can be of service. Help human beings in your love, with a sense of confidence that there is good in you to be shared with others. You will not need to ignore the negative circumstances of life that you find about you in order to see the goodness of life. The negativity must be seen, lived, and understood, and, if you desire, changed. But while you are working to change what you believe needs to be changed, you need not judge the entire nature of life and all of the universes simply on the appearances of earth struggles that seem negative to your subjective personality. You can still see goodness in yourself, in others, and in life itself.

NEW DIRECTIONS FOR CIVILIZATION

In this present period of civilization, there are so many human beings who are learning to see the goodness in life that there is actually a change taking place in the evolutionary forces of the earth. We will use a simple vision here to help you understand this more clearly.

Imagine that you are on a large mountain, standing on the very peak of it. You can see clearly that all of the mountain beneath the peak is at a lower elevation than where you are standing on the peak. But you would not say: "The peak is *good*, and the rest of the mountain is *bad*." In the same way, imagine that you are looking back with clear vision at all of the human civilizations that have gone before this present time. First, you would notice that *you* have participated in many of those civilizations as a living human being. Next, you would see clearly that all of those previous civilizations were less elevated by forces of love than is the human civilization of the present time. But you would not say that the present is better than the past. They are simply at different levels of existence.

In a certain sense, we could say that this present period of human existence is a culmination of all that has gone before for all human beings who have ever expressed in earth. All of the qualities of magnificence, beauty, and good that you have built in the past have continued to grow and expand. In this present time then, these qualities are much stronger, much more potent, and more fertile as possibilities than they ever have been in any period of human life. *In this period, there are more living human beings with a great capacity to love than there have ever been in all of human history,* in the physical sense. Thus, there is most certainly a quickening in the evolution of earth, due to a greater potency and power of love living within human beings. These forces of human love are infused with forces of wisdom and strength from your souls, and they are all amplified by the perfect, pristine forces of God that have never ceased to flow into this earth reality since its beginning.

What you ones do with these potent forces will depend upon the choices that you make, individually and collectively. The earth reality will continue to expand. Whether this leads to subjective experiences of joy for you, or to periods of confusion, will depend upon whether you choose to become consciously aware of the vast goodness that is now unfolding in this changing earth, or whether you ignore it. You could say to yourself: "I am standing on a mountain peak, and that mountain grows beneath my feet. It becomes larger and I rise higher. If I can understand that this is good, and that it moves me toward greater love, then I will rejoice in the growing of this mountain."

Each human being now alive has a capacity to *think* in much more brilliant ways, to *feel* in deeper ways, to *love* and *create* with more power, and to experience human life in more magnificence than has ever been possible throughout all of human history. Whether these possibilities become the earth reality in this present period of time, or in the future, will depend upon whether the present human beings choose to draw forth a deep enough love for their own personalities, as well as for the human beings living around them.

UNDERSTANDING THE PRESENT AND THE FUTURE

We would look now at the present civilization and project for you, in general ways, what you might expect in the coming periods of earth. We will also relate this to the past of human civilization.

Let us begin by returning in thought to the initial unintentional separation caused by yourselves when you ones existed as those early human beings who began to hold to possessions and to create fears, and then gradually began to make divisions between yourself and others. You understand that those early separations have grown and have become intense through various periods of earth life. Thus, you can see that there is a certain force of separation that you ones as human beings, living many times in earth through many periods, have unintentionally kept alive through fear.

Now, you must understand that this force is a *small* stream in the overall evolution of human civilization. And, as we have attempted to show you, the largest stream has been the continual loving among generation after generation of families and mating-ones and social groupings. The large forces of creativity and love that are the expression of God have also been kept alive and have continued to grow within civilization. So, the present is most definitely an extension of good and love created by human beings in the past, even though the present is also woven with the small thread of human-created negativity.

This present period of earth life which you ones now create is also marked by an intensification of communication between human beings. You ones have created, scientifically and technically, the tangible means for *participating in the lives of one another*. In a certain sense, through your vast communication systems, you are closing the circle again. *You are dissolving the force of separation; you are healing that human tendency to overbalance toward self-preoccupation.* You are choosing, as a race, to return your conscious awareness to the streams of love that join you to other human beings by becoming consciously aware, through your communication systems, of the personal lives of people around the earth. You are learning to again care for their struggles and accomplishments as you care for your own. This was the intention of the souls in creating earth life, and, as we have mentioned, it was the original experience of human beings. But, in the present time, just as you ones were the ones who chose in the past to veer away from the love, you must now be the ones to will into being a return to the love by making changes in your conscious life. You must feel the desire to love others as your own desire, and then align it with your own will if it is to become real in your life.

These new desires to love other human beings in all parts of the earth have woven themselves with the ordinary personal desires for creativity, inventiveness, profit, and all of the other kinds of human desires that have led to the invention and creation of electronic communication systems about the earth. Divine forces of wisdom from your souls have been woven with your personal desires, and some of you ones have consciously or unconsciously accepted these divine impulses freely as your own choice. You have come to say: "I will participate in this great electronic communication with all human beings about the earth. I will let my conscious mind be impregnated with knowledge of the challenges and the situations that face ones in the far corners of the earth at great distances physically from me. I will allow myself to be filled with knowledge of the lives of other human beings."

Now, *un*consciously, all of you understand that participating in this communication will eventually return you to the great experience of love that unites all human beings. And you know that you will come to this universal love in future times with a fully developed sense of *your own individuality*. So, at a certain point in the future, you will merge individuality with the eternal in ways that will bring about a self-conscious, personal participation in the lives of all beings in all universes.

You could view the present explosion of communication from an earth point of view and say: "Most of these communication systems exist for profit, for influencing others, and for the many human motives that are not rooted in idealism or love of others." But, if you wish to know truth, you must also be willing to understand and feel the deep *unconscious* impulses that we have described that are woven with these ordinary human motives.

In a certain sense then, we could say that unconsciously the present human civilization is using the vast electronic communications systems to move toward that future re-sparking of love for all human beings in all places. At the same time, you ones are having the opportunity to consciously fulfill your individual human desires for entertainment, for education, for power, for wealth, and for all of the particular human experiences that many individuals seek in relation to the vast communication between people that is now taking place.

For you personally, as you look to your own life, it is a question of, what will you focus your attention upon? What do you notice about this present situation in earth? Are you one who would come forth with cynicism and skepticism? Are you one who would say: "I see primarily negativity in these communications of earth. I see disasters, crime, violence, and war being communicated to all people. I see ones manipulating others through advertisements and entertainments in order to draw money to their own hands. I see ones manipulating for political gain, or to gain social power, prestige, and force. I see only negativity in this communication."

If this is what you see, we would say to you most lovingly, perhaps you may wish to look to your own heart, for you are seeing through a screen of misunderstanding and self-created negativity. We are not suggesting that these negative circumstances do not exist. They certainly do take place in human affairs, and they are part of the temporary reality that you must learn from, that is presently being communicated to all ones. But, we are suggesting that your focus upon the painful events and your inner decision to interpret all of life based upon your negative reactions to those earth events will eventually distort the truth for you. Until you are willing to see *beneath* your own negative subjective experiences, until you are willing to let your heart feel the beauty and majesty within the new communications between human beings, it will be very difficult for you to know the truth of the magnificent unfoldment that is taking place in human civilization at this very moment in time in which you are now drawing a breath.

We would say now, in bringing to a close our look at human civilizations, that you can gain a new perspective if you can come to understand that, even though from the earth point of view you see vast periods of *time* involved in the unfoldment of life after life, civilization after civilization, in truth, from the point of view of your own *eternal* subjectivity, there is only *the present moment of experience* that you are now having. Through many human lifetimes, you have lived continually with the feeling: "*This* is the moment in which my life is unfolding." You have lived all those many past lifetimes of earth with the same feeling of continually experiencing the *present* moment of reality. You have also had the same experience of living in the present when you have left behind your human form to stand beyond earth, between earth lives. In the future, your experience will be of living in the present. Always, your subjective experience will be: "I live *now*, and *now* is what is important in my existence."

As you learn to feel the vastness of life in a more intense way, and as you attempt to understand that which has occurred in human civilization, feel that it is all contained within you *now*. It is all contained within you as potential, as love, as strength, and as beauty. This kind of feeling will help you eventually understand how it is that all of the forces of God can be contained within you in each moment of existence, even though you are now consciously aware of only your own personal subjective experience.

If you will take time each day of your life to practice feeling the vastness of human civilization existing within you as potential and possibility, you will move closer to that time in which you will be able to stand in your present human personality and consciously experience the vastness of God itself, living within you in perfection and love. Each day, as you live your life, in your own thoughts, in your own feelings, in your own personal concerns, take many opportunities to remind yourself:

"I am fulfilling myself, and I am also living for all of human civilization. Humanity lives within me, now. And I am willing to share my life and my love with those human beings who are all about me now."

If you live each day with this sense of the vastness of the eternal love that expresses within you, and that joins you to all of human civilization, then you will create for yourself the great fulfillment that you desire throughout this lifetime

CHAPTER FOUR

Creating Human Personality

Now we will look at how your human personality has come into existence in earth. By gaining an understanding of the deeper realities that make up your personality, you open the door to a complete fulfillment of all of the desires that live within you.

In approaching the area of your human personality as it comes forth from your soul, there are several factors that are important to understand. First, there would be the forces, or energies that enable your soul to create your personality. Next, there is the relationship between your personality and your soul. And finally, the autonomy and the freedom of your personality as it exists in human form.

ETERNAL FORCES AND YOUR SOUL

We will look first at the forces that the souls used to create human personalities. You can understand these energies as *the original causative forces of all life*, or, more simply stated, the forces of God. Thus, in the deepest sense, your present human personality, and all of your personalities through your many past lifetimes, have been created by the forces of God. Those God energies have flowed through the individuality of your own soul. The energies were modulated and adjusted by your soul in its own unique ways. Then, those energies, as they became your human personality, came to exist *temporarily* as a separate entity from your soul.

To give you an example that will help you understand the way in which the forces of God, the souls, and human beings can be understood as separate, even though they all exist within the same whole, we would use a very simple vision of an *onion*. As you hold an onion in your hand, it is quite obvious that this onion is all of one piece. In the same way, all of reality, in all dimensions, can be understood as one whole sphere of life energies. It is oneness. It is God.

Now, if you begin to peel the onion, you will notice that it comes apart in different *layers*. So, as you peel off the outer layer of the onion, we could say that this layer represents the God forces that create *inwardly* to the center of the universes. Although this outer layer is the onion, you could not say that it is *all* of the onion. Even though you have identified the outer layer, you do not yet know the whole onion. Thus, as you peel off the next layers that represent the souls, and then the layers farther in that represent human beings, you are discovering different realities with each layer, but still, none of these layers is the whole.

To know the whole, you must use your imagination to hold simultaneously a vision of each layer of forces that we describe for you (the forces of God, souls, and human beings), while at the same time you will attempt to imagine the whole of reality as all of the different layers interacting and interwoven in the overall unity of life; imagining all of the different realities of all universes woven together in love. At the same time, you can hold a vision of a vast sphere of reality that is the God sphere *within which all realities unfold.*

To clarify this vision, you could imagine that the layers of the different realities of life do not sit on top of one another, but their energy particles and waves intermingle with one another. The layer that is the forces of God mixes with the next layer of soul energy, which all then weave with the next layer inward that is the physical universe of human beings. And within that layer of physical reality are the projections of soul energy woven with the earth, and upon the earth; those soul forces are infused into personality matrices, which are woven into physical bodies. All of the various realities interact with one another.

Thus, you could see the God energies that become human beings as a knife stuck into the onion. These energies penetrate through all of the layers to the very core. The God forces that have become your personality energies, after being modulated through your soul, penetrate through all of physical reality. Developing the awareness of *yourself* as these forces of God is important so that you can know that you are not constricted and limited by the heavy energy structures that were necessary to create a physical earth. *You* are the direct expression of God in earth. To remind human beings that this is true, spiritual teachings and writings have been brought forth throughout all periods of human civilization.

YOUR SOUL AND YOUR PERSONALITY

This brings us to the second area of focus—the relationship between your personality and your soul. As you now exist in your present human personality, with your own subjective awareness of yourself as one human being, it is difficult for you to experience the truth of you due to the temporary illusion of being separate from your soul. Thus, as you work in your life to experience the unity between your personality, your soul, and the God force, one of your most challenging tasks may be the transformation of the illusion of separation. Yet, at the same time, the temporary feeling of separation between your personality and your soul must be understood as a necessary quality of your earth experience. Without the feeling of being a separate human personality, it would be difficult for you to maintain interest in your earth life as you are now living it.

In the deepest sense, the separation between you and your soul is not real. It is a subjective experience that *feels* as if it is real. Yet, the experience of separation is so strong that in this present moment, feeling the truth—that you and your soul are the same—is not a direct tangible experience that you can easily draw forth. If you accept the subjective experience of separation and aloneness as reality, then you will confuse yourself. If you can *imagine* the truth that you and your soul are one, then you can begin to move toward *experiencing* that truth.

As we have pointed out earlier, you have a great power

in your ability to imagine. You can use your imagination to create a truth inside of you, whether you can feel it or not. If you can begin by imagining each day that there is no separation between your personality and your soul, that imagining will bring about an unfolding of the energies within your being that will eventually enable you to re-member your soul. Your soul is continually pouring forth those energies of love into your personality, and by bring-ing the creative power of imagination into those energies, you begin to move them toward your *conscious* mind and emotions.

You can also use your imagination in working with all of the temporary separations that appear in earth life—the separations between people, societies, or nations. As you daily unfold your own life, remind yourself that your heart can feel that all earth beings and realities are woven togeth-er in a fabric of love. Use your imagination to create a life for yourself in which there is *no* separation

CREATING YOUR PERSONALITY ENERGIES

To help you understand *how* your present personality has evolved from your soul, we would ask you to use your imagination as we begin with a vision that will simplify this area for you. First, imagine a large sphere of light. This will represent all realities. You can understand this simply as God. Within this sphere is a "smaller" sphere of light that is the energy of all of the souls who are now projecting portions of themselves into earth as personalities. See all of these different soul energies woven together into one sphere of light which represents all of the souls in their natural, eternal state of magnificence.

Now, imagine the souls beginning to shoot forth the energies that are the soul forces that will eventually create human personalities. They project these forces inward into the center of their large sphere of light energy. And, in the center of this sphere of light, you find the whole physical universe. We could say that in the center of this physical universe, within time and space, there exists the earth. Upon this earth are the bodies that the souls created by projecting their forces from the sphere of light that surrounds all of the physical universe into the energies of the earth. The *personality* energies are projected through all of the levels of the physical universe and they are implanted into the physical human bodies. To summarize this simple vision of complex realities: the largest sphere of light represents God. Within that is the sphere of the souls' energy. Within that soul sphere lies the physical universe. Within the sphere of the physical universe lies the earth. Upon the earth is found your human body. And within your body is the personality sphere of energy that is temporarily you.

Although we have symbolized all of these energies as being separate and contained inside of one another, in reality they are all interwoven. Their energies mix and mingle, and they are always interacting in love. Thus, even though we have symbolized the forces of God as the vast outer realities of light and love energy, those God forces are woven into all of the other spheres, and they exist as intensely within the sphere of your human personality as they do in the great outer realities.

Imagine now that through the generations of human

beings evolving upon the face of the earth, there comes a spreading throughout earth of the energies of the souls that have come into the human personalities. This energy, this love, this magnificent reality of non-physical energy from the souls is carried forth in human personalities and is infused *into* the physical reality by the thoughts, emotions, and actions of human beings. Thus, the human personalities become *centers of light*, or centers of love energy that exist in the middle of the large sphere of light from which the souls have sent forth their forces. From these personality centers within earth, all human beings project out into the physical earth the same light and love energies that exist in the outer eternal sphere.

In a certain sense, the reality within the earth sphere that has been created by the souls is quite rigid in relation to the souls' sphere of existence. This is due to the fact that in the earth experience, *time* and *change* are necessary to manifest physical evolution. In the sphere of the soul, there is instantaneous manifestation. The soul standing beyond earth manifests its desires immediately, in a kind of reality that does not require *growth*, and in which there is no time and space. This is not possible in the earth reality where human and animal forms are born, grow, and die within a context of time and space. The earth reality changes the nature of the soul forces that operate within human personalities.

When the soul energies were first projected forth to create space and the physical universe, those original energies had to be modulated and transformed to different "frequencies." These new frequencies formed what you would consider the subatomic energies or particles, the atomic forces, and the other energies that you ones have identified scientifically. As the soul energies become these non-physical earth forces, they align themselves with growth and with physical evolution. When the non-physical energies pass through the threshold of physical matter, they become minerals, plants, animals, and human bodies. They become the forces of earth life that are restricted in certain ways by time and space.

If the energies restricted by time and space were the only energies projected into earth by the souls, then all of earth would be subject to the slow process of birth and growth and death that is the nature of physical reality. You would have then a world which would be *dominated* by physical laws within time and space.

After the souls infused their forces into the early animal forms and brought them to the stage of human beings, there came the need in those ancient times for forces of a kind that were not dominated by the earth cycles of birth, life, and death. There came a need for forces that were more like the eternal forces of the soul. Thus, the souls had to make many brilliant creative manipulations of the energies streaming into them from the God force in order to create a new kind of energy that could enter into the physical reality system without being dominated by the laws of that system; an energy that would be free from the death forces of physical reality. This new energy had to be able to exist *inside* of human bodies and function along with the natural disintegrating forces of physical earth that unfolded within the bodies. But the new energy also had to be able to continue in an *eternal* reality, once the physical disintegration process had claimed the physical body.

We could describe this brilliant new energy in its first stage as a force of *self-awareness*. This force of self-awareness could live within a physical body, yet the self-awareness would not die and disintegrate like the physical body. The self-awareness would live on in the eternal realities after the death of the physical body.

To help you feel this, we will use an example. Imagine that you are sitting in a park and you see a bird on a tree. This bird is so beautiful that it sparks in you a love for the bird. You then send forth the projection of your feelings of love toward that small animal. These projections of your feelings of love are *energies* that are not limited by time and space. They are not limited by the skin and the bones that are the body of that bird. Your love energies can penetrate entirely through the physical matter. And they can touch a life force within that bird. You can do the same for human beings. You can do the same thing for any physical earth reality. You can project a force from you that is love; a force that is a deep *eternal* energy that is not dominated by the laws of physical reality.

This is what the souls accomplished in the creation of the new self-awareness force. They projected a portion of themselves, from their own eternal bosom. This was a force that came forth as an intense ray of love, imbued with *an awareness of itself*. You could understand this as the first ray of personality force. This ray of love was aware of itself as a living stream of energy, and it could also feel itself to be the same as the soul that projected it. Thus, it had the dual awareness of itself and the soul that we have described for you as the awareness of the early human beings that were the Sons of God.

This new personality force was imbued with a different kind of energy that could literally *cut through the laws of physical reality*. It was not limited by those laws. It could transcend them. As a consequence, the early human beings could live in a physical body that was bound by the laws of physical nature and reality, but their *awareness* could rise out of that body, out of those laws, and transcend the limits inherent in the physical reality system.

Now, here is something that is very important for you to feel in the present moment. This same quality, *this same potential to transcend the limits of the physical system exists now as a quality of your present personality energies*. The energies that form your personality have the potential to cut through the physical laws of the universe. This is not to say that you are presently *manifesting* that potential in your life. But, you have the latent ability within you. The energy that makes up your present self-aware human personality is not imbued with the limits of physical reality. It is your *body* that is imbued with those limits.

With this as a base, now we can begin to help you understand the creation of your own present personality, and all of the human personalities that you have lived through in so many past times of earth.

CREATING HUMAN PERSONALITY

In light of what we have discussed, that which you ones of earth would speak of as "reincarnation" can now be understood by you as the process of your soul transforming rays of love energy from itself into personality forces, and then projecting those personality forces into a physical human body. First into one human period of life, then into another later period, then into another, and another, and another. Thousands of times, from the earth point of view. This coming and going into human form was made necessary by the physical laws of earth that were established by the souls, dictating birth, life, and death in rather short cycles for human existence.

The *purpose* for which the souls projected personalities into earth, in the broadest sense, would be the same for all souls: to experience the *intensity* of earth life in love, joy, and fulfillment. In each individual soul, as with each individual human being, there is a slightly different idea of *how* that intensity of earth can best be experienced. In each soul, these unique differences lead to different interests and desires. These form impulses of attraction to particular ways of living earth life. Over many lifetimes, as one soul projects different personalities one after another, some of the soul's impulses of desire do change, and the soul will focus on different earth fulfillments.

For example, in the early portions of earth, many souls projecting personalities into earth were quite fascinated with the physical domination of nature by early man. It was extremely satisfying for those souls to experience, through the personalities of early man, the beginning of hunting, farming, and the building of human communities. Now the souls have shifted their interest and fascination to the domination of nature through *scientific and technological mastery*.

The souls are quite flexible in their earth purposes. They have a certain broad "plan," and the overall objective remains the same-to experience earth intensely in love, joy, and fulfillment—but the souls' ideas about how this is best done are constantly changing.

As we continue now to explore the relationship between your personality and your soul, you would need to understand that when we speak of your soul, we are speaking of *you*, for you are that soul. In your present personality, that ray of awareness from you-as-the-soul is temporarily experiencing itself as one human being, one awareness, one personality. But in truth, you are the soul in this moment, and in all moments. While you are temporarily being your one present personality, you have agreed to put your soul experience out of your conscious awareness.

Now we would ask that you turn your thoughts and imagination to the period of time in which your soul infused personality forces into a physical body for the first time—your first human lifetime. For most human beings now alive, you would understand that your first lifetime took place in very ancient periods of earth. During that first lifetime, and indeed during several subsequent lifetimes after that, you as a human being did have total *conscious* awareness of your soul while you lived in a physical body. You had the dual awareness of the Sons of God.

The human experience of the ancient past was quite different than the present human experience. If human beings with the sensitivities of the past were transported into the present, they would find it extremely difficult to function. Their full conscious awareness of themselves as eternal souls would make it difficult for them to be interested in the many physical realities that are so important to present human beings, such as money and physical possessions. Thus, you would understand that full conscious awareness of the forces coming into the personality from the soul is a thing of the past; the present kind of human awareness is more suited to fulfilling yourself now.

In future lifetimes of earth, and perhaps for some in this lifetime, human beings will again clearly experience the dual awareness of personality and soul. For the time being, it would be of greater benefit to you to focus upon your present personality as you naturally experience it—a personality rooted in thoughts, feelings, and desires of the earth life. Yet, at the same time, you can open your heart in love to move toward a greater awareness of the soul forces and the God forces that live within you. This kind of "moderated" dual awareness can bring you excitement, enthusiasm, joy, and fulfillment as both a *human* being, and as an *eternal* being temporarily living in earth. (We will help you with this in later portions of this book.)

BECOMING AN INDEPENDENT PERSONALITY

To help you understand the way in which your present personality has come to exist, you could imagine that you are living in a time in the ancient past when there is no longer the dual awareness of personality and soul. And you are coming into a human existence to express a new kind of reality that is the experience of being totally immersed in human life—the experience of being simply one human being. As we have said, the reason the souls desired this experience of being one human being was to rejoice in the intensity of earth life, unhampered by confusions caused by memory of the eternal portions. This new kind of personality experience would be a "specialization" of the soul, created so that the soul could temporarily "lose" itself in the beauty of the earth life in order to experience an intensification of joy and love.

To bring about the experience of yourself as that early human personality intensely involved in earth life, it was necessary for your soul to create an *illusion* for you that would dim your awareness of the eternal portions of yourself. It was necessary for the souls to create energies that would cause the human personalities to temporarily feel: "I am simply a human being. First, I am born. I live. Then, I die." This illusion helps the personality believe in its own body, and in its own physical life. It helps the personality to feel that earth is important. It helps the personality to believe that it belongs to earth. Yet, this is the illusion. It is not true that your personality belongs in earth. Your personality is a force of your eternal soul. It is your *body* that belongs in earth.

Begin to feel now that you are temporarily your personality. You are not your body. You, as the soul, have created your body with the forces of God so that it could be a vehicle for your human earth experience. And, through all of your many human lifetimes, you as a soul have created the body that was perfect for each of those lifetimes. All of your human bodies were perfect for you as a soul to unfold your many desires and purposes through your human personalities.

You could see this as though you are a soul playing a game of cards. There are many cards in the hand to play, but, by the rules of the game, you can only play one card at a time. So, you choose the most perfect card to play in any moment, instead of throwing all of the cards on the table at the same time. You play the cards one after another, choosing with wisdom, understanding, and complete knowledge of the game. And so it is with the soul of yourself. Your soul can know, and see, and understand with perfect clarity what it wishes to experience throughout all of its personality projections, throughout all of earth time. It has many different personalities that it wishes to play, and, in order to align with the energies of physical time and space, your soul will play the personalities one after another.

Yet, your soul is faced with the added complexity that each of its personality projections will be quite free to do as it pleases during its earth life. So, we would need to extend our analogy here by imagining a player of cards who would play the card most perfect for the situation, but then, the card would rise up and change itself. And this would change the entire nature of the game. When the soul plays the next card, it must adjust in order to compensate for the different circumstances that were created by what the last card chose to become.

In the same way, your soul understands, in a very complex and intricate manner, what it desires to experience through all of its personalities. But each personality that it projects into earth life, each phase of *you*, has the freedom to rise up as a human being and use your personality forces (which are soul forces and God forces) in ways that perhaps the soul did not even imagine, or desire, or plan. You as a personality can create any situations that please you.

But, no matter what you create as a personality, whether it was the intention of your soul or not, your soul will continue to feed you with divine wisdom, knowledge, and love. As an independent personality, you are free to focus upon and accept these divine forces, or you can ignore them. *No matter what you choose to do, your soul chooses to love you.*

PERSONALITY AND REINCARNATION

Because of the freedom of human personalities to alter human life at will, there is needed an arena of vastness and broadness within which the souls can play out all of their cards of personality in the game of human life. The entirety of all human evolution within time and space is that arena. What you speak of as reincarnation is the process of playing one card after another—the step by step unfoldment of the process of life as lived through individual human personalities that the souls did set into motion in the beginning of earth life. The entire process of life and birth and death, again and again, is the souls' creation. It is the way in which souls desire to unfold the God forces in physical form. The process is built on love and goodness. Any negativity that you may see in the process is introduced by the subjective creation of the individual human personalities. The strange human belief that you ones enter into earth, then you make error, and then you are forced to return again to repay that error, is human confusion and misunderstanding, not truth.

If we would now attempt to use many words to more accurately describe the complex and presently unknown energy forces that make up this reincarnation system, it would create confusion for you. In a future teaching we can explore this more fully for you. For now, understanding reincarnation as the game that the souls have decided to play, and understanding your many personalities as the different cards played in that game, is a clear and simple way for you to grasp this reality. Yet, to understand our simple vision of reincarnation in the truest sense, you must imagine yourself as both the soul, the player of the game, as well as the cards, the personalities of each lifetime.

YOUR PERSONALITY AND YOUR PHYSICAL BODY

To clearly understand the relationship between your human personality and your physical body, you would need to see your body as *a product of earth*. Your body is ruled by earth forces. It is woven with the physical energies of earth, including the forces of birth, growth, and death. Your personality is *not* ruled by those forces. Your personality energies stream forth from the forces of your soul.

In all of your human lives, you as a personality living within a body have had an opportunity to rise up and project your eternal soul forces into earth as creativity, fulfillment, and love. You have always had the choice of identifying with your body and the earth limits that bind it, or living in ways that reflect the eternal magnificence of your being as a soul. In some of your many lifetimes, you ones of earth have brilliantly shown forth the beauty of the eternal soul forces within your personality. And, in some of those past lives, you have created much fear, and you have projected forth experiences of limit that reflected the temporal physical forces of earth that rule the body.

No matter which choices you have made in the past, all of your *experiences* of those choices have taken place within your personality. Your experience of the eternal forces of love, and your experience of your earth bodily sensations of pleasure and pain, both take place inside your personality. Thus, the personality is a "crossroads" where the earth forces of the body intermingle with the eternal forces of the soul. Within your personality where these forces intermingle, *there is the power to transform earth.* This power lies within your *human choice.* In your personality, you can choose to identify with the earth physical forces that rule your body, coming to believe that you *are* your body. Making this choice, you create a certain heaviness throughout your life, which makes it difficult to lift up your personality experience. What you create in this way reinforces the limited nature of earth reality. On the other hand, you are free to choose to identify with the eternal forces that animate your personality. *By choosing to identify with eternal forces, you lift up your personality experience and thereby project into the earth reality the eternal energies of your soul, and of the God force. This brings into the earth a force of beauty and love that is so great that it has a transformational effect upon the energies of the physical earth reality.*

This identification with your eternal nature, with the God force, does not involve denial of the joys of living in a physical human body. You can rejoice in the beauty of your body and your physical life, loving it, fulfilling within it. At the same time, you can infuse yourself with a sense of the eternal magnificence in a way that brings you the deep fulfillment of the soul, while not distracting you from your earth life. You can consciously live the eternal forces within your personality in a way that will enable you to feel day after day: "I am not this body. I am the eternal force of my soul, of God itself." Living your life in this way will enable you to give into earth, strong forces of love that will bless those around you, even as they become a part of the magnificent transformation of earth that is taking place in this time.

CREATING YOUR PRESENT PERSONALITY

Now we will turn our attention to the way that your soul manifested your present personality in your present body. To understand this, we ask that you now imagine yourself as your soul, and feel yourself standing beyond earth, before your present lifetime. As a soul, you stand with a vast knowledge of all of the personalities that you have ever projected into human life since the beginning of earth time. You as a soul can see what all of those personalities have experienced through their human existence. You can see the love, and the beauty, and the creativity that is the primary experience of all of your past personalities. The energies of those past experiences are of the same structure as your energies as an eternal soul. Thus, those experiences of human love and joy that were created by your past personalities have been taken into you and have become a part of you as an eternal soul.

You as a soul can also see, here and there, experiences in which your past human personalities acted in fear. Those experiences created energies that were of the same vibration as the *limited* energy structure of the physical earth.

Those limited energies were brought forth during times in which your personalities created pain and suffering in their own subjective realities, or they intentionally took actions that caused pain to other human beings. Those fearful energies do not match the vibration of your energies as an eternal soul. Thus, the energy of those past fearful personality experiences cannot mingle with your soul energy. Those fearful human energies remain in earth. From your point of view as a soul looking into earth, those fearful energies look like small dark clouds on the face of earth.

Since the fearful energies of your past personalities are "earth forces," they are of the nature of animal life. When you as a human person have passed through death in any lifetime, there comes a brief after-death transition period during which you learn to identify the patterns in your personality that were woven with the earth energies of fear, and you disassociate yourself from them. You leave them behind as you return to an awareness of yourself as your soul. To simplify for you, we could say that those negative energies are left in earth as small dark "packets" of heavy energy. Those energies are not badness. They are not wrongness. They are simply unmatched to the vibration of the perfect love of you as a soul. They are matched to the heavy, limited energies of earth, so they are drawn to earth. They remain in earth as invisible energies. (This does not mean that the nature of earth forces is negative. The nature of earth forces is *heaviness* and *limitedness*. The sense of negativity arises from human judgment.)

This phenomenon of the personality leaving behind small packets of heavy energy is quite complex, so we will take a closer look at it. We remind you that the feeling of *negativity* in painful personality experiences is entirely human. Your soul understands that earth life is quite temporary, and can see clearly that pain and suffering do not damage your personality matrix that lives within your human body. Even though you as a personality can subjectively feel, "I am being damaged," in truth, you are *creating* that feeling. The feeling of damage inside you is a mental-emotional creation. Even if your physical body is damaged, you are not that body, and within the body you are not damaged. There are earth experiences that can be painful, discouraging, frightening, and depressing for your personality. However, these are realities only in your subjective earth experience.

The "natural" human response to painful personality experiences is to believe that they are bad. Thus, creating the illusion of badness can be said to be an ordinary human response to painful and challenging earth experiences. When confused and frightened, you ones create the illusion of badness.

For human beings, bodily pain is an experience of badness. Pleasure is an experience of goodness. You learn that it is wise to avoid physical pain if you can, and it is satisfying to seek pleasure. Such responses are necessary in order to instinctively guide yourselves away from dangerous situations that could, if not avoided, damage your body, and, could possibly end the physical life of your body by causing death. These instinctive responses are protective functions of the earth animal life that are woven into your human existence as a physical being.

However, these instinctive animal responses often bleed through into your emotions and your thoughts. You begin to feel that your own painful emotions and thoughts might damage you. Thus, having learned that it is wise to avoid physical pain, you instinctively try to avoid the emotional pain of your own negative feelings and thoughts. You can also begin to feel that since other people seem to be able to cause you emotional or mental pain, then they can inflict damage upon you. You can thus become frightened of others and begin to avoid them. If you become frightened enough, you may wish to strike out to damage them before they damage you.

Here you have the root cause of the violence and pain that human beings inflict upon one another. If human beings become so confused that they begin to do violence to one another, then you have a situation in which a person's *perception* of forces of God living within other human beings has become distorted by human fear. Their human personality has become so afraid that others persons will damage them in some way that they are willing to take violent action to protect themselves from the damage.

There is also great confusion caused in human beings by fearful *responses* to violence. For example, if there is a male-one who has become so distorted by his fear that he murders many people, the negativity of his actions appears very large to your human mind. Perhaps you may feel: "There is great badness in this person. There cannot be God in such a human being. There must be evil here." Then, in your own subjectivity, prompted by your own fear and hatred of the murderer, *you have created evil and badness for yourself by imagining that it exists within the murderer.* Instead of seeing the distortion of human fear inside the murderer that has caused him to bring so much pain to others, you have created the illusion of evil through your feelings and your thoughts about him.

Now, when this human being who has murdered others finally comes to his own death, there is a period of time during which he gradually disengages from all of the human patterns of fear that he created that led him to murder. He gradually shakes off the distortion of his fearful personality patterns, and, eventually, he returns to conscious awareness of himself as a divine soul. Thus, even though his *actions* have been extremely negative from the earth point of view, they have not diminished the goodness that lives within his eternal being.

The human fear patterns that this male-one has disengaged from will remain in earth as the heavy energy packets that we have spoken of. They are not necessarily more negative than other packets left by human beings who were not violent. The packets of heavy energy left by a murderer do not cause other human beings to murder. They simply have a slight effect of intensifying fear, *if* human beings persistently, over many years, create similar fears in themselves and unconsciously align with these packets of heavy energy. In other words, the heavy energies left behind in earth by the murderer cannot *impose* themselves on human beings. They can only be *attracted* when other human beings create the same matching energies over a long period of time. Even then, the impact of the heavy energies is very slight; and takes place at an unconscious level. Those energies cannot disturb the conscious life of other human beings.

Yet, the soul of the murderer does not desire to leave the packets of heavy energy behind. Thus, the murderer's soul will create future lives in which new personalities will return in human form to work diligently to transform the packets of heavy energy. The future personalities of this soul will also attempt to love the human beings who were caused such pain by the personality that was the murderer.

Understand that the soul who projected the personality forces that became the murderer certainly did not desire to create a personality that would be responsible for the death of other human beings. This soul desired for that personality to heal strong negative fear patterns from previous lifetimes in the past, hoping that the new personality would transform those past patterns through creativity, sensitivity, and love. But, that particular human being who became the murderer did, throughout his lifetime, respond to life with such lack of trust, criticism, judgment, and feelings of insecurity and fright about his own safety that his fear grew to such extremes that he became distorted enough to murder.

It is difficult for human beings to understand the truth about people who take such dramatic negative actions toward others. It could help you if you would take an attitude such as this: "I do not rejoice in violent actions taken by one person against another. And, as a human being, I will do all that I can to prevent human beings from engaging in such negative choices. But, as an eternal soul, and as one desiring truth, I must be willing to believe that the negativity created by human beings who act violently is not prompted by evil, or badness. It is caused by *fear*. If I am ever to know truth, I must be willing to at least *imagine* that in some time, and in some place, that fear *can* be healed, the negative personality patterns can be dissolved, and the goodness will prevail." This is a difficult area for you ones. It is highly charged with your own fears that negativity created by other human beings will harm you and those you love. But we say to you, there is so much love in human beings that if you ones could give it freely to all ones in earth, you would eventually heal all of the fears, and never again would human beings strike out in violence against one another. If each of you could love enough, then you would all live the magnificence and beauty of the forces of your souls that live within your personalities.

Now, you as a *soul*, standing before your present birth, can see quite clearly the small dark packets of heavy energy that your past personalities have left behind in earth. You also understand that when present human beings create fear within their personalities, they can be drawn to the packets of fear energy left by your personalities. These packets have a tendency to amplify, in slight ways, the fear and pain of the living human beings. You as a soul can see that your personalities' heavy energies are not doing service to those human beings who still walk in earth. Thus, you as a soul, in your great love for human beings, desire to *dissolve* those heavy energies left behind by your personalities. But, you understand quite clearly that these packets of heavy energy are a portion of the earth system of energies. Therefore, they must be changed by a *human being* from *within* the earth system. (We simplify the extremely complex types of energies in all of this. Understand that our words are symbols that are intended to capture the *feeling* of the truth.)

So, imagining that you are now your soul, see yourself standing before your birth into your present earth life. You have taken into your soul self the magnificent forces of creativity, beauty, and love that your past human personalities have made in their many lifetimes, and you now desire a new personality to extend and amplify those forces in a new human life. You are also seeing the small packets of heavy energies that remain in earth that you desire to transform. With a desire to express greater beauty, and a desire to transform the past heaviness that your personalities have left in earth, you begin to create the new forces that will eventually become your present personality.

These new forces are first imbued with all of the capacities of human love, creativity, genius, kindness, courage, strength, forcefulness, patience, sensitivity, and all of the other qualities that you would understand as human goodness. You as the soul also weave into this new personality matrix certain complex energies from the eternal realities that are the forces of God. Desiring that your new human being will be motivated to transform some of those past patterns of heavy energy, you also place into the personality forces very small streams of human tendencies toward fear. These tendencies to be more frightened in one situation than another accurately reflect the past patterns of fear that were created by you as different human personalities in the past. Perhaps there will be a tendency toward jealousy, if that is one of the patterns needing to be transformed, or healed. Perhaps you will implant a tendency toward insecurity, or a tendency to be frightened in situations where others stand in power over you. Many complexities of human personality patterns that are related to past experiences in other lifetimes will be balanced and harmonized with the magnificence of the new personality forces.

All of these kinds of tendencies toward fear that you as a soul implant into your new personality matrix will be slight; not so strong that they will dominate the new personality. They will simply tend to cause challenges for you as the new personality, prompting you to find a way to respond with all the love that has been woven into your personality. The perfect combination of energies that you create in this personality matrix will lead you as a new personality to creatively find a way to use your power in order to love, to heal, and to transform the past energies of heaviness.

Thus, the new personality matrix is created from the forces of God, the forces of your soul's wisdom and eternal knowledge, the creativity and love from your past personality expressions, and the various eternal forces and patterns needed to inspire transformation of the packets of heavy earth energy. All of this is woven in an extremely complex way into your new personality matrix, and, at this point, all of it exists as *non-physical* forces and energies.

CREATING YOUR PHYSICAL BODY

As your soul, you next begin to create the perfect place in earth to "plant" this new personality energy matrix. First, you look about earth with a vision that can see all human beings on the face of earth with a deep kind of knowing that is a *feeling* understanding of all past lifetimes of all present human beings. You can see humans who are projections of souls that are your "favorite" souls. (Here this description distorts a bit, but it gives you the feeling.) You are joined to all souls in a perfect love, but in a certain sense, there are souls that exist with you that are your favorite souls; and there are quite a number of these—from the earth point of view, thousands of them.

Looking into earth with your eternal feeling-vision, you as a soul locate thousands of human beings who are projections of your favorite souls. And these human beings have also walked with you as a human being many times in the past in earth. From amongst these thousands of human beings, you locate those who would be the perfect family for your new personality, in light of the many complex energies and purposes woven into your personality matrix.

You as a soul then, selecting from all of the possibilities of earth, have now chosen two human beings to be your physical father and your physical mother. All of this has been done in perfect alignment with the *souls* of the two human beings, and with the unconscious portions of their human personalities.

You as your soul, along with the souls of your new father and mother, and aligned with all souls, and with the forces of God, begin to affect the bodies of your father and mother. In most cases, the two human beings will usually have been drawn together in love, and they will desire to make a sexual expression that will produce impregnation of the female-one. Together then, all of the souls, in a great joyous celebration, orchestrate the energies and forces that begin to affect the very cells, glandular functionings, and physical systems of the physical bodies of the father and mother.

The souls also work in this magnificent way even in cases where the impregnation was not created in joy, from the earth point of view. In the cases of accidental impregnation, or perhaps impregnation through the act of rape, certainly there is not a joyful earth decision to create a child. But, in order to know truth, you must be willing to at least imagine that the souls of the humans involved have chosen that particular earth event as the most important way to eventually accomplish the joy and happiness that the soul desires. Eventually, that which is painful for the human beings involved will be transformed by their courage and wisdom into joy.

As in any area in which human beings have painful experiences, this is one that is difficult for you to understand. But we would say to you most gently and most lovingly, if you are unwilling to imagine that within negative situations such as these there are deeper purposes that are aligned with the forces of God, then you open yourself to believe that these situations *impose badness* upon you. You can come to feel that there are energies of chaos in earth that can force negativity upon your life. You can begin to feel that you are helpless against such forces. This can bring you a great deal of confusion and pain. Thus, it is worth a bit of experimentation with your beliefs and attitudes to attempt to penetrate the truth that lies beneath such painful earth situations.

The inner work that is done by the souls with the bodies of your mother and father would be what you consider in earth to be *heredity*. The souls exert an influence of complex forces upon the sperm of the father and the ovum of the mother. This causes certain responses in the process of conception that bring about the creation of the individualized forces that eventually become the physical, mental, and emotional characteristics of the child.

In this complex process of influencing your father and mother, in a sense, *you are creating yourself.* You as your soul have created your new personality forces, and now you are literally creating the body that those forces will inhabit.

If you as a soul decide that the growth and the fulfillment of this new personality will require the challenge of an impaired physical body, then, during the process of influencing the father and mother, you will bring about the forces that will result in what you would speak of as a "birth defect" in the child. You would integrate such necessities with all of the other forces that determine the mental, emotional, and physical capacities of the fetus that will become the child that will be you.

For many human beings, it is difficult to believe that they have created their own body, particularly if that body came forth at birth with an impediment of some kind. For those who have a challenge here, we suggest that you simply consider our explanation to be an interesting theory at this time. Experiment with the feelings of it, and apply it to your life in ways that you wish. See what changes will occur in your feelings when you say to yourself: "I am responsible for all that has taken place in my life. I have created my life. No longer can I blame my father, or my mother, or fate, or God. I have created everything that I am." If you are willing to do this, eventually you will come to a place of great power where you can say to yourself: "Since I have created my life, then I am the one who can *change* any parts of my life that do not please me."

After you as a soul have influenced your chosen father and mother so that the perfect fetus form for you has been conceived in the womb of your mother, you continue to influence the fetus form during the period of gestation. You as a soul, along with the soul of your father and mother, and in harmony with the various patterns in their personalities, continually manipulate the growing fetus in order to achieve the results you desire. In the early stages of gestation, all of the energy systems of the fetus are quite flexible and changeable. Eventually, the rigidity of the earth forces takes over within the fetus body. After the fetus reaches this stage, the influences of the soul on the physical body begin to withdraw. At this point, you are *physically* formed.

Even though your new fetus body is formed, your personality tendencies developing within your fetus body remain quite flexible and changeable. They continue to be adjusted by you as a soul. You exert non-physical pressures upon the glandular functionings of the stabilized fetus body in order to change certain hormonal functionings of the body that are related to personality traits. In this way, you as a soul can make changes in tangible personality structures up to the time of birth. Even after birth, you as a soul, with the unconscious permission of your new personality structure, can affect the glands of your newly-born child body in ways that will bring about a change in the moods and other subjective personality experiences of the child.

THE BIRTH OF YOUR PHYSICAL BODY

Next comes the physical birth process, in which your new fetus body is transformed into a living human child. As you are aware, much confusion exists among human beings concerning the birth process and the beginning of life.

Some believe that the life of the child begins before birth. Many believe that the child's life begins at the time of the birth of the fetus. Eventually, you will learn to see that the life of the child actually begins *when the personality matrix of eternal soul energies springs forth into self-awareness within the child body*. The real birth occurs when self-awareness springs to life in the new physical body.

The differing beliefs of human beings about the birth process become particularly challenging as they relate to the intentional ending of the gestation period before birth. For clarity here, you would need to understand that, for many reasons, the soul will hold back the self-awareness of the personality until the newly-born child form is quite stable and established in physical strength. Thus, the self-awareness of the child could begin *after* the birth of the physical body. There are many complexities involved here. To know the truth for yourself, you must work for *flexibility* in your understanding of the birth process. You are free to choose what you believe about this, according to the present truths that you live by. But know that the soul, expressing the perfection of God itself, will determine the perfect moment in which the self-awareness forces come alive within the child's physical body. When that takes place, then the human life has truly begun.

In a situation in which the human parents of the fetus choose to make abortion, the soul of this fetus would be aware of this as a *possibility*. The soul may desire that the parents continue with the process of gestation and give birth to a child. But, the soul understands that the human beings are free to make any choice, and the soul would bless them with love, no matter what their decision might be. If they did choose abortion, then the soul could possibly work toward creation of another fetus form in a future time with the same parents, or, the soul could choose from among unlimited possibilities to create a child with other human parents. In all cases, you would know that there is no badness here. The souls are aware of *all* possibilities and will adjust to them. The souls would never condemn the human beings for choosing not to complete the birth of a fetus form.

For those human beings who now have a deep troubling in your heart about the area of abortion, you must understand that it is like all events in your life. The *badness* that you find in it lies within *you*, not within the event. If it troubles you, then you must express your feelings and your attitudes, but you need not believe it is bad. We can assure you that *life* is not destroyed at the death of a human body, whether it is a child body, an adult body, or an aged body. Death is simply the ending of a physical body. The life within that body is the eternal soul force that has animated the body, and that force continues to live without ceasing. You as human beings mastering your present earth life must *choose* how you will believe about this issue of abortion; how you will legislate it, or not legislate it. But for each of you in your own heart, in order to know truth, you will need to say to yourself: "How have I created my viewpoint about the issue of abortion? How much *fear* have I infused into this viewpoint? How much love? Do I truly create good by *forcing* my vision upon other human beings?" It would also be wise to ask the same questions about any viewpoint that you have about any portion of your earth life.

Now, still seeing yourself as your soul, we would ask you to imagine yourself completing the process of weaving all of the complex non-physical personality forces into perfect harmony with the physical energies of the newborn child body that you have created. This would be a gradual process, as you would imagine from observing children and the way they grow from the newborn stage. There are certain kinds of *physical* awarenesses that are present in the infant body from the moment of birth—the awareness of sight, sound, touch, smell, and taste. These are qualities that you could consider to be "animal" qualities, in the sense that the *eternal awareness forces* of the soul have not yet been infused into the infant body where these physical awarenesses have been created. You as a soul then, complete the complex process of implanting a portion of your eternal awareness into the personality matrix that you are weaving within the infant body. This is a gradual process that is usually completed within the first month after the birth of the child.

THE FREEDOM OF THE HUMAN BEING

After self-awareness arises within the infant, for all intents and purposes, you as a soul have completed your *direct* work with the new human being that will become you. Now the child gradually begins its process of becoming autonomous, preparing to choose its way through life. Yet, you as a soul will *inwardly* guide and love this human being during every moment of its physical lifetime. Also, woven into the inner personality matrix of this new person are the forces of guiding souls, and of God itself. These eternal forces continually speak to the heart of the new person throughout its lifetime.

However, this new human being is free to do as it pleases. It can focus totally on the physical earth circumstances that surround it as it grows. It can listen to, or ignore the inner guidance of the soul, of guiding-ones, and of God. But, no matter what the human being chooses to do throughout its life on earth, there is *never* a separation between you as the soul and you as this new human being.

Within your present personality matrix, your ability to be consciously aware of yourself as a human being is an ability that is *made* of the eternal energies of your soul. Your self-awareness is your soul. *Your self-awareness is a divine force.* It is *God* itself expressing through your soul, and now through your new human personality. This divine force is never absent from you. It cannot be diminished.

We have said that you as a personality are free to become consciously aware of the eternal forces if you choose. However, many find that when they begin to turn their desire in this direction, it is not a simple matter to feel and perceive the eternal realities. Within yourself as an individual human being, your key to feeling the truth of the God forces that live within you is your human *creativity*, and your *imagination* imbued with *feeling*. You must be willing to creatively imagine the beauty of eternal realities before you can clearly perceive them. Thus, we continue to stress your capacity to imagine, and the importance of feeling, love, and idealism.

Given the way your present personality is structured by your soul, under normal circumstances it is not possible for you to directly perceive the divine forces that make up your personality matrix, just as it is not possible to see your own face without there being a reflection of that face in another source, such as a mirror. You can also perceive what *reflects* the divine forces in your personality, and that is your *inner* life—your thoughts, your feelings, your imaginings, and all of your inner subjective experience. You can also *feel* divine energies by reflecting them through your inner and outer *creations*. And you can create with your imagination. You can create imaginings of the kinds of eternal realities that we have attempted to describe for you, even if you cannot yet directly perceive them. You can create inner images and visions of your soul and all eternal realities, even if you cannot yet perceive them.

These imaginings are only the first step. If they do not spark in you a *feeling* of love and truth, they will not take you very far. But, if you can imagine, with a sense of love and magnificence, that the very forces of God live in your heart, and if you can begin to feel those forces as love and beauty within you, then you will begin to open certain *new capacities* that are now being woven by souls and planted into human personalities. These new capacities will enable you to *directly perceive* the eternal realities and the eternal forces that live within you. These capacities eventually will enable you, through your own creativity, to make a very clear mirror in which you indeed can see your soul. In other words, first you must be willing to imagine the forces of your soul and of God within you, and eventually, if you persist in your opening in love and wisdom, your imagining will become transformed into direct perception.

This can seem to be a strange process when it is described in words. But when it is *practiced* by you day after day, in any way that seems appropriate to you (no matter how vague you may feel about it), it can help you develop the ability to directly experience and perceive the forces of God that are the truth of you, and to *know* through your experience that within your being, within all beings, there is only this force of life and goodness that is God. So, the key then, does lie in your creativity and imagination, and in your willingness to use these in love, idealism, and hope, and not by harnessing your imagination to the negativity, pessimism, and despair that often come in the experience of earth life. We will give further teaching on how to use your imagination to attune to the eternal realities throughout this book.

TRANSCENDING PERSONALITY LIMITS

In addition to your capacity to attune to the eternal forces of life, there are energies within your present personality matrix that will someday enable you to *transcend* the physical limits of earth life that affect your personality. There are several kinds of human situations in which this becomes possible.

First, it can take place *within your own subjective experience.* For example, imagine that you are in pain due to a cut upon your foot. If you believe that there is badness in having a cut foot, and you begin to feel frightened, and you create a heaviness in your emotions, then you are being ruled by the physical forces of your body. You are responding in a natural earth manner, in the animal way of pain and pleasure that is intended to keep your body safe from harm.

If, on the other hand, you would say inwardly: "There is great pain here, but this pain cannot harm me. It is temporary. It will pass. I am not my foot. I am not my body. I am an eternal force of love and beauty. I am also a human being, and I must care for my foot and doctor it. But I need not believe that this cut to my foot has brought badness into my life. It has brought only temporary pain that will heal, just as my foot will heal. I can believe that I have the wisdom, the strength, and the courage to continue to live a life of joy, even with a cut foot." This is a simple way in which the personality forces have the power to transcend earth realities and situations within the inner experience of life.

At the other extreme, there would be human beings who are imbued with a conviction that the earth forces are not imprisoning to the personality, and they have come to believe strongly that within their personality there is a force of mind, or a psychic, or mystical force that can manipulate matter. *When such human beliefs are aligned with purposes that the soul wishes to accomplish through that personality*, and when certain conditions are appropriate, then there can be instances of human beings manipulating physical matter beyond the ordinary laws of matter. There can be events and experiences that you ones would consider to be miraculous.

As you may have observed, such events are quite rare. They are not a part of the *ordinary* human experience. That is because such events are not so important to what each human personality is attempting to accomplish in earth, which is: to develop the capacity to live fully within the ordinary present human personality and to master that personality; to love and be loved by other human beings; to fulfill the personality desires in physical reality; and, to transform earth life from *within* the ordinary human reality that you ones created as souls, and that you now agree to live within as human beings.

What we have spoken of up to this point can serve as general guidelines that can help you understand, in a simplified way, the complexities of your own human beingness. Working daily with the thoughts, feelings, and imaginings that we have suggested can help you feel your *eternal* nature in a clearer way so that you may understand it, live it, and rejoice in it. These guidelines can help you put your physical earth reality into the proper perspective in relation to your soul, your guiding-ones, and God.

Even though we have emphasized the eternal portions of your being, we would not desire for you to diminish the importance of your physical body, your physical life, and the fulfillments of it. You have come into earth to experience the intensity of human life in physical form. So, you will need to celebrate those portions of your life. But, as you have learned, when you lose the feeling that you are eternal, and you begin to feel the heaviness and the limits of physical earth reality, then your joy and fulfillment in life are diminished. When you can go forth to fulfill yourself mentally, emotionally, and physically in the ways of earth, and, at the same time, can weave this with a clear awareness of the eternal realities, then the joy and fulfillment of your earth life are expanded.

Thus, in your desire to fulfill yourself, you can work with these teachings concerning your evolution as a human personality by reminding yourself:

"The personality forces within me are projections of myself as an eternal soul. As an eternal soul, I am projections of the force of God."

It is through these kinds of thoughts and feelings that you can always help your personality to understand, feel, and know that it is indeed an expression of God living in human form. If you would know this deeply, it would guide all of your choices, all of your viewpoints, and all of your actions as you go forth into earth to live a life of love and fulfillment.

CHAPTER FIVE

Your Life as a Personality

Since your entire human existence is experienced through your personality, understanding that personality is very important to a complete expression of your life. To help you move toward such an understanding, we will now speak of aspects of your personality that determine the quality of your subjective life on earth.

We will look at your human personality as *energies*, projected on the wings of soul forces, come to live temporarily within your physical human body. The various streams of energy originally implanted into your personality by your soul have become the different aspects of your present personality. By understanding these aspects, you can eventually master them and move toward the fulfillment that you seek in this lifetime.

EARLY DEVELOPMENT OF YOUR PERSONALITY

The non-physical personality matrix of energies from your soul begins to manifest within your physical body in the early periods of your growth as a child. Gradually, during the first year of your life, your personality structure gains a certain *authority* over your physical body, meaning that your personality forces can now cause actual physical change in your body. Other authority over your body comes forth from your soul forces that work beneath your conscious awareness to augment your personality throughout your lifetime as a human being.

As your child body develops, the influence of your personality will change, according to the *choices* that you make as a developing human being. If you consistently fall into habits of fear mover a number of years, then some of your personality forces are unintentionally aligned with the illusion of negativity, and your thoughts and emotions are used in ways that can create negative subjective experiences. If you consistently choose to focus upon creativity and love, even in the face of challenges, then your personality forces are allowed to fill your human being with experiences that reflect the true perfection of your soul that is woven into your personality matrix.

There is also the possibility that if there are severe negative influences from human beings around you as a growing child, and these influences could prematurely hamper your developing abilities as a child, then your soul *may* override those negative influences by sending forth extremely powerful forces of strength and love into your personality matrix while you are a child. This assures that your child development will not be too severely squeezed by emotional turmoil caused unintentionally by the adults around you.

The influences of your soul can also help the development of your physical body when those around you as a growing child cause conditions of great earth negativity. Ordinarily, the sadness caused to you by an extremely negative environment would influence your child body in negative ways, perhaps causing illness. If your soul feels that this illness would not serve your personality growth, then your soul may shoot forth extremely powerful forces of rejuvenation into your child body to help it maintain its strength during the challenging period.

If there would be two children in a family where the adults create much negativity, and one child grows strong while the other has illness, you would know that the child who becomes ill is aligned with very important soul purposes. It is important for that child's growth to pass through the period of illness. It will strengthen the child for later earth experiences. It is not that one child is being cheated of health, while the other child is given an easier life.

Now, in order to bring you closer to an understanding of that which makes up your personality, we will describe the various forces of your personality matrix that your soul has created. For clarity of communication, we will speak of these forces as separate threads of energy, but keep in mind that they are actually woven into a beautiful *whole* within your personality.

YOUR IMPORTANT INTUITING CAPACITY

The first stream of energy that we would address is what we would call a capacity for *sensing*, or *intuiting*. The intuiting capacity has a bit to do with emotion, since you can have a certain intuitive perception that can stir a feeling within you. But your intuiting goes deeper than emotion.

In the early years of your childhood, your intuitive sensing is ordinarily quite strong. Usually, your intuiting capacity diminishes as you grow toward a fully conscious adult. In later periods of adult human life, when the intuiting capacity occasionally rises up into conscious awareness, you ones have come to recognize it as intuitive knowing. Some even consider it to be *psychic* perception.

Your intuiting capacity is the deepest capacity in your conscious personality. This intuitive ability stands on the threshold between conscious awareness and *un*conscious forces. At all times in your life, your intuiting capacity is bringing you forces and energies from your soul that do not rise up into your conscious awareness.

Ordinarily, your intuiting capacity goes unrecognized because the conscious areas of thought, feeling, and desire are so intensely impactful that they receive most of your attention. This is quite a natural situation since your earth life is so demanding of your energies. Thus, for most human beings, the intuiting capacity will remain mostly unconscious throughout their adult lives.

When you decide to bring more of your intuiting capacity into your conscious awareness, you will need to work with the next two important streams of energy within your personality matrix, which are: your *emotions* and your *mind*.

YOUR HUMAN EMOTIONS

The energy stream that is your emotions is "closer" to your intuitive sensings than any other stream of energy within your personality matrix. Your emotions are closely connected to the deep eternal portions of your being, thus they work with your intuitive sensings to bring you guidance from your soul, and from guiding-ones. This is not to say that your emotions always bring you *truth*. Many times your emotions will be aligned with your human fear, not with truth.

When your soul feeds you wisdom and truth (which takes place unconsciously every moment of your human life) those eternal energies are brought into the unconscious portions of your personality by your intuiting capacity. The first *conscious* awareness you have of this feeding will come to you as a *feeling*. Ordinarily, it is through your feelings that you will be aware of the influence of your soul and your guiding-ones, as well as the forces of God. You will *feel* those influences, usually as a deep sense of well-being, as an emotion of joy or love, and perhaps as a magnificent feeling of transcendence.

Your emotions are intended to be a *receiver* of signals being sent to your personality from eternal sources. Thus, your *conscious* awareness of truth usually begins in your emotions. To reinforce this truth in your mind you could say to yourself: "My emotions are quite important as a bridge between what my soul unconsciously feeds me and what I consciously experience in life. If I build this bridge of emotions soundly, with wisdom, honesty, and love, then I can expect that the forces of guidance coming to me from my soul and my guiding-ones, fed through my intuitive sensings, can reach my conscious awareness without being distorted by my negative emotions."

The original intention of your soul in creating your human personality matrix was to establish the emotions within your personality as a receiver of all of the forces of perfection and love that were projected from all of the eternal sources. In the early beginnings of human life, when you lived physically in those pristine periods before human beings began to respond to earth life in ways that generated fear, these forces of the eternal energies were received within your human emotions quite clearly, without distortion. As the confusions of fear began to arise in human life, the emotions were turned more toward earth affairs, particularly to earth relationships between human beings.

You must understand that this was a very *beneficial* change for the human race. If you ones had not turned your emotions toward other human beings, it would have been difficult for you to love one another and to maintain societies built on a personal love and caring. If the emotions had not been brought into human affairs, there would have been a great aloofness from earth life, a great emotional distance between human beings. You ones would have relied on your *mind* alone to live your earth life. Rather than being deeply feeling human beings, you ones would most likely have developed into coldly calculating creatures involved in an unemotional manipulation of earth life. (It is not surprising that you can recognize exaggerations of these qualities in present human beings who have not developed their emotional capacities.)

Thus, in addition to creating the emotions to be the receiver of impulses from intuitive sensings, the souls also desired them to be a vehicle within the personality structure whereby human beings would be able to grow in love for one another. So, as early human beings began to turn their emotions toward one another, they were fulfilling the second purpose for which the souls created emotions within the human personality matrix.

The souls did not *intend* for early human beings to become frightened of losing their possessions or loved ones. They did not intend for human beings to become self-involved. But, since this is what human beings chose, the souls did not condemn it. They respected it as the unique unfolding of human choice, knowing that there was not badness in the fear that humans created, because they knew that eventually the love must prevail. In fact, the souls now attempt to teach this kind of acceptance and trust to human beings of the present time as a part of the *healing* of the fear that humanity has created. If you wish to completely fulfill yourself in this life, you will need to learn this loving acceptance, to understand the choices you make that temporarily bring pain and confusion, without condemning yourself, and without condemning your choices. If you condemn your choices, *you will begin to fear to choose*, fearing to make error, and fearing to suffer your own wrath for making error. If you condemn yourself, then you will begin to judge others in the same way. You will find fault with them, and eventually you will feel that there is badness all around you.

So, as you think about the evolution of human personality, and as you relate it to your own personality, you could say to yourself:

"My soul did not intend for my emotions to become confused and disoriented in ways that would bring me pain. Yet if I create such emotions, I must not see this as badness. It is a portion of my human life.

It is not a thing for me to condemn or to judge. My negative emotions are a portion of my personality that I can learn to understand and grow from. And, if I choose, I can learn to transform them."

In present human personalities, the emotions function in a way that helps you feel *all* of earth life. When you give your emotions freedom, they will respond to all that occurs in your life. They respond in a particularly strong way in areas of your life that are important to your subjective happiness, such as love, earth accomplishments, money, and health.

You could see your emotions as a small pond that ordinarily is quite clean and sweet to drink from. Occasionally, that pond becomes tainted by certain chemicals that taste bad, but they do not harm the body. In the same way, your pool of emotions will be clean and joyful when there is not fear. Occasionally, your emotions can become filled with patterns of fear that can cause temporary discomfort, or pain. But, *your emotions cannot harm you. Your emotions are still your eternal soul's vehicle for bringing you truth from your intuitive sensings*. At any moment, you are capable of letting your emotions fill you with joy and love, no matter what is taking place in your life.

You can expand your understanding of your emotions in this way. Say to yourself: "My emotions are a pond. A part of that pond is quite fresh. A part of it is a bit sour tasting. My pond is a bit polluted. I am free to choose where I drink in my pond. But even if I continue to drink from the fresh side, I still know the sour side is there. So, eventually I will desire to clean the whole pond. Yet, I will not know the pond is clean unless I am occasionally willing to drink from the sour side to test it. Perhaps I will even need to swim in the polluted side in order to infuse it with new kinds of cleansing forces." In other words, in your emotions now, you must be willing to *experience* the ones that seem to be negative. Much learning and growing can come from this.

You can also use your emotions to communicate more clearly with your soul. The souls have observed that over many generations, human beings have focused their emotions intensely into subjective earth affairs, and they have often ignored the portions of the emotions that are attuned to the intuiting capacity that brings forth eternal truths. Thus, in addition to communicating to you through your intuiting capacity, the souls have begun to use the emotions to communicate more directly. So you could say: "At times when I become a bit too frightened, or I have unintentionally numbed my intuiting capacity out of pain and fear, I can expect my emotions to be an indicator of what my eternal soul is attempting to communicate to me."

Even some of your negative emotions can be used in this way. For example, if you are mated to a deeply beloved one to you, and you have unconsciously ignored a pattern of jealousy within you because you fear that if you are jealous you will lose the love of this mating-one, then you have quite cleverly hidden from your conscious self the fact that you have a streak of jealousy. Perhaps you will notice that when your mating-one becomes passionately interested in a certain area of study, you begin to have an emotion of irritation. Your soul, in helping you to unfold your personality patterns, notices that you have unintentionally hidden a thread of jealousy that you truly desire to heal and that your soul desires you to heal. Thus, your soul will help you spark that sense of irritation with your mating-one's interest in the area of study. Your soul understands that you will allow a sense of irritation to come into your conscious awareness, but you will not let *jealousy* come because of your fear and your old habits. So, in a certain sense, your soul is attempting to communicate with you through the emotion of irritation, and to say to you most gently and lovingly: "There is a thing in your feelings that needs your attention." Eventually, you will understand that it is jealousy, but, for the moment, it feels like irritation. If you address that emotion of irritation, feeling it, exploring it, and communicating it lovingly to the mating-one, then gradually you will reveal the underlying jealousy. When you can feel that jealousy, then you can heal it.

We give you this example so that you may place a greater value upon your negative emotions, instead of condemning them, or condemning yourself for having such feelings. Instead, you may say: "*Perhaps* there is a lesson here." We say *perhaps*, for at times you may have certain negative emotions and no matter how diligently you look, you will not find a lesson. Do not be over-rigid here, but look for lessons in negative emotions when *you* feel there is benefit in doing so.

Thus, to summarize the emotional energies that live within your personality matrix, we could say that they are presently important as a way of experiencing human life and human relationships. They are important in helping you experience the love that joins you to others. Your emotions enable you to create joy and fulfillment in your subjective life. They are also important as a way of helping you learn and grow within the personality structure that you have built. In addition, they are still important as receptors of intuitive sensings by which your soul, your guiding-ones, and God feed you forces of eternal reality and truth. No matter what you are *consciously* aware of in your emotions each day, *unconsciously* you are being fed with love and eternal truth through your intuitive sensings. You always have the capacity to feel these in your emotions. This capacity will never cease; it will never diminish.

The two important streams of energy in your personality matrix—your intuiting capacity and your emotions—are closely related. Although your intuiting capacity lives within your personality, in a certain sense it remains the "property" of your soul. You can voluntarily increase or decrease your *conscious awareness* of this capacity, but you will not change the nature of the truth of your intuitive sensings, for that is controlled by the soul.

Your intuiting capacity stands at the threshold between the eternal nature of your soul and the earth life of your personality. When you move from the eternal intuiting capacity toward the personality, you come to the emotions. In your emotions, your conscious personality self is taking over control. You have more power to affect your emotions than you do to affect your intuiting capacity. Most of your choice in relation to your intuitive sensings is a matter of whether you will pay attention to them, or whether you will ignore them.

Your emotions and your intuiting capacity live in your personality matrix as a divine force of perfection to guide you; as a mirror to use whenever you need to see the truth of you apart from subjective earth confusions. Whenever you desire, you can look deeply into your heart, you can draw forth your intuitive sensings, and you can begin to *feel* the truth. You can feel that the truth of all life is love. The truth is goodness. The truth is the perfection of God. And always it is flowing into your personality matrix through your intuiting capacity linked to your emotions.

Now, even though we have said that you have a power over your emotional area, you may often feel that you are not in control of your emotions. When you feel out of control of your emotions, then either your emotions are responding to negative habit patterns that you have chosen, consciously or unconsciously, throughout this lifetime, or, your emotions are being affected by you responding negatively to what is taking place about you. At times you will feel a certain mastery and control over emotions, and at other times you will not. The emotional patterns within your personality matrix are very dynamic, intense, and volatile. Your emotions respond to many kinds of inward and outward pressures, and to many different cycles in your makeup. They are difficult to understand at times, but if your remind yourself that they cannot harm you, then your subjective fear of fully living your emotions will diminish.

Your emotions are like the sea. At times they are calm and quite beautiful. At other times they are stormy, turbulent, and frightening. But they are still the sea, and you can cross them if you please. If you have learned to navigate well, you will not have so much "wreckage" in your personality experience. If you have not paid clear attention to your earth truths, and if you have not developed your wisdom, trust, and love, then at times your emotions will *appear* to damage you. We can promise you, this is an illusion of your subjective experience. No matter how rough the seas of your emotions might become, they always rest on the solid bed of eternal love that lies beneath them. No matter what you feel, you are always the magnificence of God. You are never damaged in any way by your emotions.

YOUR HUMAN MIND

The next stream of energy within your personality matrix is your mind—your mental capacities. This is an area over which you have even more conscious control.

The human mind is quite similar in structure to a capacity within the soul that is best understood as *the creative force of God*. From your point of view, the most important aspect of your mind is its capacity to *create. This is more important than the mind's capacity to know truth*. We are not suggesting that the mind cannot know truth, but the capacity to know truth in the mind is open to many more storms than the emotions. And the storms of the mind are very subtle. You can create vast, complex, cosmic thought structures that seem to you to be quite real and true. Yet, even as you believe you are perceiving truth, those thoughts can be so filled with human misunderstanding that they are influencing you to actually walk away from the truth of your life.

Your mind is very important. It is important as a creative function of your human personality. It is indeed beneficial for you to use your mind and create with it. Yet, if you desire to know *truth*, then you must be quite cautious when working with your mind and your thoughts. Most of the time, what you hold in your thoughts as true is a very crude approximation of what your heart can *feel* as truth, if you are willing to love.

Now that we have spoken of some of the potential limits of the mind, we can speak of its creative power, especially its capacity to *create* truth. Even though the mind may not be ideal for *perceiving* truth, it is very effective in creating approximations of truth within a human personality.

It is important to remember that your mind is a function of your creativity. You do not *perceive* with your mind, except in the sense that you become consciously aware of your physical perceptions within your mind. *You* continually fill your mind with input that *you create* with your feelings, your subjective responses to your environment, your desires, your own particular set of beliefs and attitudes, and your intuitive sensings. You fill your mind with thought symbols and words, images of earth objects and people and places, complex sets of memories, and many imaginings and fantasizings.

It is important to understand that you are free to fill your mind with what pleases you. However, many times what you fill it with is not what pleases you. Your mind is often filled with a reflection of what you have unintentionally filled your emotions with, which is negative and painful subjective experience woven with fear.

The true purpose of your mind, as created by your soul, is to feed your personality with understandings of God, and to give you a God-like capacity to create worlds and universes. Right now, you can use your mind to create beautiful worlds and universes in your imagination. You can also use your mind to create thoughts that frighten you. You can create thoughts about being alone in a hostile universe. You can create thoughts about how life or other people will harm you. Ordinarily you do this in response to pain that you have felt in your emotions. Many times that pain is associated with human beings around you who, in their fear, have taken actions toward you that cause you emotional or physical pain.

Much of the confusion that fills the minds of human beings is a response to emotional turmoil within the personality. The emotions can become a cause of mental turmoil when the emotions are totally saturated with the affairs of earth; when you do not allow time in your day to day life to fill your emotions with your intuitive sensings, which are continually filling your unconscious patterns with love and joy. When you do not allow time for these unconscious soul energies to rise up into your emotions so that you may consciously feel them as harmony and unity with life, particularly if you are living a difficult, complex, strenuous earth life that involves much emotional turmoil and strain, then you can expect your mind to be quite chaotic. And you can expect that it will be quite difficult for you to know the truth of life through your thoughts.

We will make this more concrete by the use of an example. Imagine a male-one who has lived a life of emotional turmoil and pain as a child. And, in developing his personality patterns through his own choice, in response to all of the pain filling his emotional life, he has come to believe that human beings cannot be trusted to love him; that they will always cause him pain. Unconsciously, he has made deep adjustments in his emotional patterns to protect the sensitivity of his heart from this pain. Over many years, he has come to numb his feelings in order to avoid the emotions of pain. In so doing, he has also unintentionally numbed his feelings of warmth and love for other human beings. He has come to genuinely feel that human beings are not important. In fact, he feels that human beings are quite negative and they must be avoided. Thus, he has developed a personality that is quite withdrawn and reclusive.

Let us imagine that his intellectual capacities are quite great, even astounding. And, in his fear of human beings, he begins to escape into the intellectual pursuits of earth. He becomes a one of scientific pursuit—a chemist. He begins to develop research projects to heal certain human diseases through chemical means. From his work, there comes a benefit to human beings, and his life is quite productive and rather satisfying. But, within his heart, there is a belief that *truth lies in scientific pursuit,* and it has nothing to do with human beings, who are felt to be negative. Gradually, his mind builds thoughts that say that the truth of life is to be found in *physical matter.* Beyond matter there is no life. All of human life is contained in the physical body, and when the body is dead, there is no human life.

In spite of this man's brilliance of mental capacities, and in spite of the clear feeling he has that says, "I am perceiving truth with my mind," he has completely distorted the reality of life *because his mind has fed him thoughts that he created out of fearful emotions.* The fear coming from the pain in his emotional life that he would not acknowledge and experience led him to fear human beings, which led him to use his mind to create an understanding of the world that placed physical matter above human beings.

All of you in earth have distorted your thoughts to one degree or another. Using your great creative power of the mind, which is the creative capacity of God itself, you have at times made conclusions in your mind that have been colored by negativity that came from your personality. Under such conditions, you would not expect your mind to feed you truth.

Now, even though your mental capacities do not always bring you truth, they are still very important to your personality. So, you could say to yourself: "Just as I must not condemn my emotions, I must not condemn my mind. For it is a thing of great value. I must learn to use it and rejoice in it freely, without fear that it will mislead me." We suggest that you take a playful, bold, experimental attitude toward your mind. Let it be free to think what it pleases. But, if what it thinks does not please *you*, then change those thoughts. If what it thinks brings confusion to you, or feelings of negativity about you and other human beings, then we suggest that you question what your mind is feeding you, and that you consider changing your thoughts. Your mind is an instrument of God itself, and if you can learn to adjust it in certain loving ways, then your mind can align quite clearly and accurately with the perfection of God, the perfection of your soul, and the perfection of your guiding-ones. Your mind can be aligned with your emotions and your intuitive sensings in a way that can eventually bring you truth.

Always, during your lifetime as a human being in

earth, your perceptions of truth will be woven with your subjective creativity. It will be *your* vision of truth. One of the purposes of human life is to give you the opportunity as a human being to create your own truth. But you desire deeply, as your soul does desire, to create that truth as a mirror that is in perfect alignment with the truth of the universe.

So, to establish a sound attitude toward the stream of energy that is your mind, you could say to yourself each day:

"My present personality is infused with mental capacities that I wish to consciously and willfully use to create beauty for myself and others. I will use my mind as an instrument for infusing into physical earth life, the forces of love that surge through me as creativity in my thoughts."

YOUR HUMAN WILL

Turning now to another important stream of energy within your personality matrix, we will look at what you would understand as *will*. Your will is closely woven with your *desire*.

In the simplest sense, you could consider that your will is the key to *how* you create this life for yourself. As with all of the other streams that intertwine in your personality, when your will is aligned with love, understanding, and the truth of your soul, of your guiding-ones, and of the forces of God, then the use of your will can bring joy to yourself and to all ones. And, as you could imagine, when your will is aligned with factors that stream from fear and self-created negativity within your emotions and your thoughts, then you could expect that there would arise challenges from the actions that you take through such a use of your will.

Just as you are always free to think and feel what pleases you, most certainly you are free to *will* what you desire. Yet, you may find that it is not so simple to clearly understand your will. For example, you may desire great wealth, or a perfect love relationship. But, at times there are patterns of belief in your thoughts and emotions that immediately say: "You may will this, but you can never succeed in manifesting it." Ordinarily, you do this unconsciously, because you feel you are unworthy to have what you desire. Or, you may feel that there are so many earth obstacles to your fulfillment that it is impossible to manifest what you desire. This comes from an inner belief that you are weak or helpless. There are many inner confusions that can cloud your use of your will.

There are two different areas of the will to look at. First, your inner life of your thoughts, feelings, desires, and so forth, in which you are free to will what pleases you. Then, the outer life of action in the physical world, in which you are *potentially* free to do what pleases you, but so many times you *believe* there are constraints and limits in the physical realities of this outer life.

For the moment, let us keep our attention focused on the inner life of your personality. Your will stands on the threshold between your inner life of *experiencing*, and your outer life of *acting* and *accomplishing*. When you think and feel, you are transforming the eternal forces of your soul into earth energies of thought and emotion. Through *your* creation, divine forces have become a part of earth, but they still live only within you. They are inner creations. This inner creation comes to the threshold of outer physical reality first through your desire. Next, it becomes your will to fulfill that desire. If your desire is strong enough, you can will yourself to act to fulfill the desire. In your *action*, your inner creations cross over the threshold to become outer reality—you make some kind of impact on the outer physical world of people, places, and things.

Your will is your outward *force* into earth. It is similar to the force of your soul that created your personality. Your soul has taken the God forces, assimilated them within itself, and then has shot them forth as streams of energy to form your personality. You as a human being, through your intuitive sensings, have taken the divine forces of your soul, assimilated them into your personality, and then, through the use of your will, have shot them forth into earth reality as your creative *actions*.

The key here is to understand that the power is wielded first through your *will*, and then it becomes action. *You have the power to will actions that are aligned with love, thereby creating earth realities that reflect eternal truth. You also have the power to will actions aligned with your fear, thereby creating pain as your contribution to the earth reality.*

EXPERIENCING YOUR PERSONALITY STREAMS

You can learn to *feel* the way in which all of these various energy streams of your personality interact. This involves a steady process of growth that unfolds throughout your life. First, you would work to become aware of your intuiting capacity. Then you would learn to more deeply experience your emotions. Next you would learn to more profoundly experience your thoughts, and you would use your mind to integrate this with an understanding of the other streams of your personality.

As you deepen your experience of your personality, you become more clearly aware that the complex streams of your personality energies are continually involved in an interaction that affects your sense of yourself. This interaction will determine whether you experience yourself as important or unimportant, loved or not loved. All that you feel yourself to be is a product of this complex interaction between your intuitive sensings, your emotions, your thoughts, and the other aspects of your personality. Eventually, you will learn to balance all of the streams of energy within your personality and to align them harmoniously with desires, and then to *will* some of the desires into action.

We explain this in detail so that you can understand that creating what you desire in your life is not simply a matter of adjusting your outer actions in the world. It also involves a process of creating love and understanding within the complexities of the personality streams in your inner life. The process of fulfilling yourself begins in the inner life of your personality, for it is there that you begin to create your reality. It is there that you, as an expression of the God force, begin to create earth. Because your inner life is so important to your happiness, attempts to find fulfillment by frantically acting in the outer life only, to accumulate wealth, or sexual fulfillment, or power, or any of the earth pleasures, can only take you so far. Eventually, you come to a point of satiation and you begin to look for deeper fulfillment.

YOUR HUMAN MEMORY

What you understand as memory is that portion of your personality matrix that allows you to recall completed experience to present conscious awareness. As we now look at this capacity of memory, we will begin with this observation: your memory is closely aligned with the stream of energies in your personality matrix that are your self-awareness. The force of memory is a unique kind of energy that can be *directed* by your self-awareness, by your self-consciousness. Even though your past experiences are ended, your conscious awareness has a great flexibility in determining what kind of memories you have about those past experiences. It is as if you are standing upon a mountaintop—even though the mountain is formed and fixed, you still have many choices about how you relate to that mountain. You can choose to stay on top of the mountain, you can go down the mountainside, or you can go climb another mountain.

You have a great flexibility in the use of your memory. Your capacity to use your memory to recall *past* experience is quite similar to your capacity to use self-awareness to focus on your *present* experience. Using your conscious awareness of yourself, you can focus your attention on what you please. Your self-awareness of the present is a steady stream of energy that you can harness to your will, and you can say, for example: "I am taking notice, I am paying attention, and I now choose to become aware of my physical body. Next, I choose to become aware of my emotional sensations. Now I wish to think about money." The steady stream of your self-awareness can be directed where you wish to direct it.

You can also harness your awareness and will to your memory, and you can say to yourself: "I now choose to remember a wonderful time that I spent with a certain beloved one in a particular past period. I am now turning my attention toward recalling the experience of that past time." You can turn your memory in any direction that you please.

Your memory is an *energy* that exists in your personality matrix that you can touch into quite consciously. All of your past experiences have registered upon your personality in complex ways that create certain kinds of energy forms for each specific memory. All of those individual energies make up your whole memory, and they all combine with your ability to re-create past experience in the present moment.

As soon as your will is directed toward remembering a particular past experience, then certain "energy compartments" are opened within your personality matrix and the feelings, visions, tangible physical sensations, thoughts, and impressions involved in your past subjective experience are instantly *re-created* by you in the present moment. It is done consciously, or unconsciously. This is done by a complex interaction between your brain and your inner personality energies.

An important thing for you to understand in working with your memory is that your memory of a past experience is not the same thing as the past experience itself. You must guard against assuming that the feelings you recall in the present about the past are the same feelings that you had in the past. The feelings that you have in the present when you remember the past are totally new creations. You are not reliving the past feelings. *You are creating new feelings that seem the same as the feelings that you had in the past.* It is important to remember this, otherwise, each time you recall a negative, painful experience from the past, it will be tempting to believe that the negativity is imposing itself on you from the past. You will feel that the negativity is alive and visits you again each time you remember the past. You can eventually come to feel that you are a victim to the past. If you realize that you are using your memory capacity to re-create the negativity in the present, it will be easier to eventually stop re-creating that negativity.

Seen from this point of view, you can understand that, in truth, there is no such thing as memory, in the sense that you are actually bringing a thing from the past into the present moment. More accurately, you are creating "duplicates" in your present subjective reality that are similar to impressions that you had in a past moment.

To help clarify this, imagine that you are recalling a fulfilling past experience with a beloved one. In the present moment in which you remember the experience with the loved one, you are creating feelings of warmth, beauty, and love that are similar to what you felt in the past. You can even create, in the present, inner images of that loved person as they appeared physically in that past experience.

Now, you understand that you are not *seeing* that person. You are *creating* your impression of them in the present. The feelings you are having are not the same feelings that you had in the past, because those past feelings are ended. These are *new* feelings that have been created by you now, in the present moment.

When it comes to healing your negative experiences of the past, it is very important for you to be clear in your understanding that the past is ended and that you use memory to re-create that past. *Your past negative experiences do not exist in the present until you re-create them in the present through the use of your memory.* Often, you will cause pain in your personality by an unenlightened use of your memory, using it to convince yourself that there is negativity in the present because you remember negativity from the past. To heal this, you will need to be aware that a single memory is a combination of impressions of an experience that has taken place in the past, but your present awareness of that past experience is created by you in the present.

From what we have said, you can see that there are two important components of memory to consider. The first is the large reservoir of impressions that all of your past experiences have left in the energy of your personality matrix. These impressions are retained as *unconscious energy constructions* within your personality. The second component is the one we have just discussed—the ability to re-create past experiences by making duplicates of them in the present. When you are using your memory, you are reaching into your energy reservoir of past impressions and you are reminding your present self to become aware of whichever of those past impressions you desire to recall, then, you re-create those impressions within your awareness in the present moment.

Now, it is important to remind yourself that your use of memory is not a matter of re-creating a past experience *exactly* as it happened. You can understand that the reservoir of impressions made by your past experiences also contains impressions of your subjective responses to those experiences. Thus, at times, when you reach into your memory reservoir, what you draw out is not really an accurate memory of a past event, but rather your *interpretation* of that event. You have within you not only the past experience as it occurred, but your own subjective reactions to the experience are imprinted on your energy patterns. So, if you were frightened by your father shouting at you in a past time, then you have the memory of him shouting, along with a feeling of your own fear impressed into your personality energies. Your memory of this event can also be complicated by impressions from experiences that you may have had with your father in past lifetimes. These impressions are further intertwined with your responses to other people at the time that he shouted at you, and your responses to your environment. In other words, within your energy reservoir of memory, the impression of one single experience from the past is woven together with *all that you were subjectively* in the moment in which the past experience impressed you.

When you come into the present and you become involved in situations that are similar to this event with your father—perhaps your boss yells at you—this can trigger feelings of fear in the present moment that are *duplicates* of the negative feelings that were associated with the impressions made at the time of the experience with your father. It is possible that you will not be consciously aware that the memory of your father is being triggered, so, when you feel the duplicated fear in the present, you become frightened of your boss, when the fear is actually being caused by the unconscious re-creation of the memory of the experience with your father.

One of the most potentially confusing aspects of memory is that *your memory impressions of the past can be duplicated in the present even without your conscious participation.* They can be triggered by unconscious patterns that are built around strong emotional content. So, even though your memory is tied to your self-awareness, there are portions of your memory reservoir that are activated and brought to the present without your awareness.

The unconscious influence of memory is a complex area that can be illuminated further as you work with these teachings. At this point, for clarity, we would suggest that you retain the simple vision of the two aspects of memory that we have given: the reservoir of impressions of the past that you can consciously recall and become aware of; and, your capacity to create duplicates of those impressions in the present moment. In your daily affairs, you can remind yourself that at times you may also *unconsciously* create duplicates of past experiences that can influence your experience of the present moment.

Now, you could also remind yourself that unconscious memories from other lifetimes that you have lived in earth (and beyond earth) are also woven into the energies of your memory reservoir. It is not necessary to give a great deal of attention to this area, since it is usually so difficult to bring to conscious awareness. Yet, such memories of other lifetimes can unconsciously affect your present subjective experience in ways that are similar to your unconscious memories of this lifetime. However, the memories of past lifetimes are not *imposed* upon you in the present. They are *invited* by you, for they are triggered by your present personality patterns. Thus, if you are creating great patterns of fear in the present, you could expect to "attract" unconscious fearful memories from your past lifetimes. If you are consciously working to love and to heal fear, you could expect to attract past memories of love and healing.

However, with unconscious memories of past lifetimes there is a quality that is different from your memories of the present life. Since your memories of past times of earth are not under your conscious control, they are over watched and orchestrated by your soul. Under certain circumstances, your soul will choose to spark an impression within you from a past lifetime of earth that would be very valuable for your experience of the present. Your soul will attempt to intensify that past impression and bring it to your conscious awareness. Now, you as a personality are free to ignore the impression that your soul brings to you. You are also free to develop a sensitivity within your personality and become consciously aware of the memory of the past lifetime that is being sparked by your soul for the benefit of your personality.

If you desire, you can work within your personality and attempt to consciously remember your past lifetimes of earth. However, you would need to remind yourself that it is not a simple matter to gain such conscious memory, and this area can be colored by your present personality. Many times when ones of earth attempt to recall events of past times of earth they are *imagining* events that did not take place in the past. However, at other times they are actually bringing to their present conscious awareness impressions that *were* formed in their past lifetimes. For simplicity, you could view this complex area in this way, saying to yourself: "Indeed, my memory reservoir does include memories of all of my past times of earth. But, most likely in this lifetime it will not benefit me to bring many of these memories to conscious awareness. It will be of more benefit to me to keep my conscious awareness focused on my present personality and my present lifetime."

These aspects of your personality that we have spoken about are some of the important factors that you will need to understand in order to move toward fulfillment in your life. All of these are vital to develop and master in order to bring about the complete manifestation of your soul capacities through your human personality.

By looking at your own personality as a creation of your soul, and an expression of God, you are taking the first step toward deeper fulfillment in your life. We remind you again that no matter what you may think or feel in this moment, we can assure you that within your personality there is a goodness, a perfection, and a love, all of which are brilliant reflections of the God force that has created life. All of this can be temporarily hidden from your conscious awareness, but these eternal realities never cease to flow into your human personality through your intuiting capacity.

To remind yourself of the truth of this, you could say to yourself each day:

"In this moment, if I am aware of myself in a way that is not fulfilling to me, then I am not experiencing the truth of myself. In this moment, if I have inner patterns of condemning myself, of feeling inadequate, of feeling that there is no purpose or meaning for me in this lifetime, then I am not perceiving truth. I am perceiving the negative products of my own creation. I am perceiving thoughts and emotions that I have unintentionally filled with fear and self-created negativity.

"If I desire fulfillment and joy in this lifetime, there are many things that I can do to work with my inner personality life—with my thoughts, my emotions, my will, my desires, and my memory. But all of these things that I can do will be colored by my attitude about myself. So, in this moment, I need to understand that, until I am willing to adopt the attitude that there is the perfection of God living within my personality, it will be difficult to create the magnificent inner life that I desire."

You can understand now that *the most important factor in your unfoldment of joy and fulfillment in this lifetime is how you feel about yourself as a human being.* If you are not presently feeling that there is goodness and perfection within you, then, in order to completely fulfill yourself as a human being, you will eventually need to come to an attitude that is infused with this truth about you.

However, for this moment, simply *create* a feeling in your heart that you are the perfection of God. Even if your mind would say, "I am not perfection and love," in this moment, perhaps you would be willing to take a moment of silence with yourself and say to yourself:

"Whether my mind will agree or not, in this moment, I choose to fill myself with the feeling that my personality is infused with the perfection of God. I now imagine this, I feel it, and I attempt to live it in this moment."

If you are willing to do this in every day, we can promise you that eventually you will come to know that this magnificence of you is indeed *truth*, and you will live this truth throughout your lifetime.

CHAPTER SIX

The Stages of Your Earth Life

A ll of the aspects of your human personality that we have spoken of so far are brought forth in your present life in different ways, depending upon the stages of your earth existence. There are different stages of your human life that begin with your physical birth and that end with the death of your physical body. In order to live a fulfilling life, you will need to harmoniously integrate the various aspects of your personality into the complexities of the various life stages. To help you gain the understanding necessary to accomplish this, we will now speak of ways in which your personality unfolds throughout your life, from birth to death.

If you will study the knowledge given concerning the various stages of personality expression during human life, you will be able to recognize areas of your life, past and present, that need your attention, either because there is pain there that needs to healed, or there is joy there that has not been fully appreciated by you and it needs to be focused on and expanded. By looking, with love and honesty, at the various stages that you have already passed through in this lifetime, you can gain the insight and understanding to live the stages that lie before you with an intense joy and fulfillment that will enable you to complete the important purposes for which you entered into your present human personality.

YOUR PERSONALITY AND YOUR BODY

We would begin by looking at how your personality matrix, which is a *non*-physical sphere of energy, is related to your physical human body. First, we would need to speak about the *blood* of the body. This may seem a bit strange to some, but the blood is the first part of your physical body to receive impressions from the non-physical energies of your personality matrix. In a very complex way, the blood is activated by these non-physical impressions even before the brain receives them.

To give a simple description of a complex process, we would say that in the building of your human fetus form within your mother's womb, your soul begins to weave in qualities of the personality matrix it has created for your developing fetus body. The souls of yourself, your mother, and your father implant the non-physical energies of your new personality qualities into the blood of your mother and your fetus body. This process eventually results in what you would speak of as the *genetic* influences being activated within the fetus form. The genetic influences that you attribute to "heredity" are actually brought about by the forces of your souls implanted into the blood of the growing fetus.

During the gestation process, the living cells within the blood of your fetus form are constantly receiving impressions from your soul. Later, after your physical birth, your blood will continue to receive influences from your soul, but these will tend to be overshadowed by the stronger impressions from your own emotions, thoughts, and other subjective responses within your personality. These subjective influences can have quite a dramatic impact upon your body. For example, it is possible for you to continually focus on fearful thoughts and emotions over a number of years, and those kinds of self-created negative energies can accumulate to actually cause a physical change in the chemical structure of the blood in your body. Under certain conditions, this could subsequently develop into a disease process in your body.

In your developing fetus form, before your physical birth, the blood of your growing body receives all of the potent non-physical energies of your new personality matrix as they are brought forth from your soul. At this point, your body is still at the level of animal awareness. There is no self-awareness as you now know it.

THE MIRACLE OF YOUR SELF-AWARENESS

During the gestation period of your fetus body, your self-awareness is still a potential, or *pattern* being infused into the blood of your fetus form. The blood will interact with all of the cells of your fetus body, feeding each cell with all of the non-physical energies of the personality matrix, including the energy that is the pattern for self-awareness. Eventually, this creates a kind of "cellular awareness" throughout your entire fetus body. If you could enter into one single cell of your fetus body and activate your human sensory apparatus in order to feel what it is to be that cell, you would say: "I am aware of myself now as one discreet cell in the body of this new fetus." This is a bit distorting to describe it in this way, but it captures the feeling quite nicely.

As your fetus body grows, every cell within it is impregnated with this relatively weak form of self-awareness—the cells simply realize that they belong to this body. Eventually, around the time of the birth of the body, the cells begin to feel that they also belong to the new *personality*. The overall awareness of the fetus follows the same general pattern. First, it is aware of itself as a physical body, in a simple "animal" sense. Later, after the birth of the body, there will eventually come the awareness of being a human personality.

The personality awareness that comes after the birth of your body evolves slowly. First, it begins as a weak awareness in each cell, but from the point of view of yourself as the new child it is an unconscious awareness. The mind of your new child body is not yet aware of what the cells of your body can perceive.

Usually, within one month after a child is born (although it could be perhaps six months or longer, depending upon certain children and their circumstances) all of the cells within the child body are fully aware of their participation in a new human personality. This awareness energy is extremely strong in the cells that make up the *brain matter* of the child. The cells of the brain are quite unique and extraordinary because they are more intensely imbued with certain powerful non-physical forces of the soul. In the aggregate or conglomeration of these brains cells, there is an *intensification* of the kind of self-awareness that exists in each cell of the body. The cell awareness is a weak and feeble energy. The intensified and magnified awareness produced in the brain is a much stronger form of that awareness energy. If this energy were to be equated with sound, we would say that the energy of a cell's awareness would be inaudible sound. The accumulated awareness energy of the brain cells would intensify that sound so that suddenly it is loud enough to be heard.

Thus, in the brain, the awareness energy in each brain cell crosses over a *threshold* that is similar to making weak sounds audible. Except, in the brain, it is not only a process of bringing a quite feeble self-awareness into a greater intensity, but it also involves creating a *new kind of awareness*. Using the example of sound, the weak sounds have not only been made audible, but suddenly they have been transformed from random sounds into a beautifully orchestrated symphony. *The intensified, magnified awareness that the soul is able to stimulate in the physical cells of the brain is so strong that the energy of that self-awareness in the brain of your child body becomes a great brilliant "light" of consciousness that suddenly explodes within all of the energies of the personality matrix.*

This quite miraculous explosion of consciousness makes possible human *self-awareness* within the physical child body. Amplified by the brain cells, *this awareness energy becomes so strong that it springs into life as an independent, self-aware personality entity that is you.* Due to this extraordinary manipulation of energy by your soul, your "animal" child body has been transformed into a self-aware vehicle for the expression of divine forces into physical reality. You have become a new *human being*, living in a physical child body that is woven with all of the energies of your personality matrix which were given to you by your soul, but these energies have now been "brought to life" in the real earth sense by that final explosion of self-awareness caused by transformed energies in your brain.

Now, if you wished to physically locate this magnificent explosion of self-awareness, we would say that it "takes place" within the brain of your new child body, even though it involves all of the cells of your body. Yet, the brain reaction is most intense and unusual because of a certain quite extraordinary functioning of the physical brain cells. This extraordinary functioning was implanted in the brain cells of your fetus body by the forces of your soul during the period of gestation. It gives the brain an ability to duplicate the non-physical energy of self-awareness that existed around the child body, with the brain bringing the duplicate alive within the physical reality of the brain cells. As a result of this unique functioning of brain cells, the *etheric, non-physical* self-awareness that hovered around the child body can suddenly leap into being as a *physical* earth reality.

Understand that your self-awareness did exist before this explosion within your child body. But, you were aware of yourself as your soul, hovering *outside* of the new child body, having the exquisite experience of feeling yourself as an eternal soul about to become a human being again. After the explosion of self-awareness within your child brain, you were then aware of yourself as a human being living *inside* the physical body of the child. Your new body and your personality energies merged with a portion of your soul's awareness to become the beginning of what you now experience as your normal human conscious awareness. The "other portions" of your soul continued outside of your body in the eternal soul awareness, even as your soul rejoiced in also experiencing your new human awareness with you. Now, from your point of view, your present human awareness is conscious, while the rest of your eternal soul's vast awareness remains unconscious during your physical lifetime.

To truly understand the mystery of human life, you would need to develop a deep appreciation for the miraculous nature of this explosion of self-awareness that brought you alive as a human being. As your etheric self-awareness was hovering about the human child body, before it was taken into the body and the eternal awareness of the soul was cut off, there came a brilliant, delicate point at which many complexities of God, and soul, and man took place in a magnificent symphony of the creative forces of God itself. It was this miraculous interaction of the creative forces of God that enabled your soul to bring about the extraordinary capacity of the brain cells that led to the explosion of human self-awareness within your new child body.

This explosion of self-awareness in the child is the *true* birth of a human being, not the moment at which the fetus body emerges from the womb. The moment of attainment of self-awareness in the child is the time to celebrate your soul's completion of the very complex and intricate process of *bringing alive, within a physical human animal form, a divine awareness of self that is the culmination of the desires of the God force as they interact with matter within the earth system.* For human beings this is an *invisible* birth, since ordinarily, it is not possible for you ones to see when this true birth takes place.

Once the explosion of self-awareness has taken place within the child body, then all of your present human scientific understandings of brain functions, and the relationship between the brain and the personality, would be relatively accurate in describing the development of the child. But, what you would need to understand beyond your scientific observations and psychological introspections is that the power and the energy and the force that *maintains* the experience of self-awareness within the physical body is a *divine* force. It is not simply the physical energies of the brain. It is the force of your eternal soul. It is the force of God. Without the continual infusion of these divine forces, you would not be able to maintain your human self-awareness inside your body. Your physical body would exist only as a living animal form and you would spring forth from earth reality and regain conscious awareness of your eternal existence.

YOUR GROWTH AS A CHILD

To begin an understanding of your growth as a child, imagine that it is three weeks after your physical birth, and the explosion of self-conscious awareness has just taken place within your personality matrix. For three weeks you have been an unaware animal responding instinctively to light, sound, physical touch, heat, and the other physical stimuli around you. But now, suddenly, you are fully human, in the sense that you are aware, in very simple ways that are difficult to put in words, that you are a baby human child.

At this point, most likely, you have many conscious memories of past lifetimes of earth swirling about in your new personality awareness, along with your human animal sensations of hunger, pleasure, pain, and the physical experiences that have been present since your birth. But now, unconsciously, you begin to give *meaning* to your many new experiences. In essence, the inner learning process begins, and it will continue for you as a human being throughout this lifetime.

At first, this learning process is closely guided by forces of your soul that are bringing into your personality matrix the wisdom and the many talents and abilities that you have developed in your past human lifetimes. Your soul implants these as energy patterns within your personality matrix. They will live within your unconscious patterns until you begin to unfold your desires and they become intuitive capacities, artistic abilities, and all of the more tangible inner impulses of your growing personality.

As you grow as a child, everything that you do is woven with your process of inner learning. When you move your own finger and see it with your eyes, you are learning. Rapidly, in the most brilliant way imaginable, you grow and learn within the new child body.

Your *outer* learning is also set into motion as other human beings interact with you. Human communication begins. In certain ways, even before your birth, your fetus cells have been communicated with by the environment of your mother, and, to some extent, by her responses to her environment. But, your true outer learning begins with human beings speaking to you. All of the actions and communications of the human beings around you are registered in your child personality matrix, and they become impressions for your future use.

As you would imagine, your brain is quite active as this inner and outer learning unfolds. During this early period of development, your human brain is assimilating all of the necessary information from your past lifetimes, which most likely will never register upon your conscious awareness, and your brain integrates this with the many impressions that you are absorbing from your present environment. The primary focus of your brain activity will be your *present* life, for you will live in the present, not in the past. Thus, all of your mighty soul energies that make up your personality, consciously and unconsciously, are directed toward the present where they interact with your growing brain and body.

During your early stages of inner and outer learning as an infant, your entire personality matrix is involved in carrying out all of the minute inner adjustments of *perception* that are associated with your brain functioning, interwoven with energies from your blood forces, and all of it harmonized with the responses taking place in your new body. This involves such things as human language acquisition and the restructuring of your capacity for seeing and envisioning according to the *present* period of history. All of this work is necessary in order to release from your present personality, the energies that are woven with dominating patterns from past lifetimes that were beneficial in the past, but could possibly hamper you if they were to override your present interpretation of physical reality.

Also, during your early learning period as an infant, your *imagination* is being sparked by the patterns that your soul is continually infusing into your new personality. This will later result in the development of your artistic creativity and intuitiveness.

Another important development that is taking place within your personality matrix is the unfoldment of your *emotional* capacity. Emotional energies from your past times of earth are being stirred by the complex unfoldment of your brain, while your present emotional capacities are quickly being associated with sights, sounds, and thoughts that relate to your present environment.

As you grow as a child, you are beginning to be more strongly influenced by your family and those human beings about you. Your learning begins to occur in a rather crude trial and error way, as adults respond to your actions. If your actions please those around you, then you are encouraged to continue to experiment with those actions. If you make an action that seems to displease adults and brings a response of harshness from them, you are discouraged from continuing that action. So, gradually, in your learning, you come to be temporarily "at the mercy" of the human beings around you.

Many people have noticed that the influence of the adults around them during their childhood growth period was quite negative and painful. Thus, they believe that they have reason to blame their family for the pain that they now suffer. To encourage such feelings of blame in yourself will not serve you. You must remind yourself: "My soul, in its eternal wisdom, knew full well that there was a likelihood that this family would not be able to love me enough to restrain some of their own behaviors saturated with fear. My soul knew that perhaps my childhood would be a period of pain; it would be the beginning of my challenges as a human being." Thus, your soul, in its vast wisdom, knowing that the family challenge would be a part of your childhood learning period, planted within your personality matrix extremely intense qualities of *strength, courage, patience,* and *love*—more than it would have given you had there not been the possibility of this challenge.

We could say then, that your soul has simply chosen a path of courage and strength, as opposed to one of early ease, comfort, and smoothness. You must assume an intelligence and wisdom in your soul's choice, knowing that the choice will eventually lead to joy and fulfillment for you in this lifetime. It is only when you feel that you have been *damaged* by your painful childhood experiences that you would believe that there was badness in your soul's choice of a challenging childhood for you.

Now, from your birth, until you are two or three years old, even though in a certain sense you are at the mercy of those around you, you must understand the innate cleverness, creativeness, and inventiveness that you have in adjusting to your environment. You perform ingenious kinds of adjustments to adapt to harshness, or to encourage love. Intuitively, you respond in ways that are not only guided by the wisdom of your soul, but are aided by an earth cleverness of adjustment that you have brought forth from your many past lifetimes as a human being. Even if there is fear in some of your responses, you would understand that those responses are most appropriate and most brilliant, given the situation in which you find yourself.

Around the age of three years, your personal *will* begins to show itself in obvious ways. You become more independent, or more frightened, or more loving, or more discouraged, depending upon the many unique complexities of your personality matrix, your soul's desires, the individuals about you, your environment, the health of your body, and the many other factors impinging upon your child personality.

Also, at approximately three years of age, you become a true *physical* human being, highly responsive to all of the earth factors around you. Your intuitive memories of eternal realities and past earth lifetimes have gradually dropped away. Your present human personality patterns begin to grow so strongly that by the time you are five years of age, you will have essentially established what will be the personality patterns of a lifetime. We are not suggesting here that your personality patterns are inflexible and cannot be changed, but the general foundation for most of your patterns throughout this lifetime will be formed by the time you are five years old.

If you now feel that your own patterns that were established up to five years of age were negative, again, you must understand the perfection of the adjustments that you were able to intuitively make as a child, even if you cannot now remember them. You must understand the capacity of a child to create love, even in challenging situations. No matter how negative your memories of your own childhood may be, we can assure you that there was love around you, and love and creativity were involved in the personality patterns that you consciously and unconsciously created from birth until five years of age.

From five to seven years of age, there is a gradual loss of the last threads of knowledge of eternal realities from your *conscious* awareness. The eternal truths continue to flow into you without ceasing throughout this lifetime, but, by the time you are seven years old, these eternal influences coming into your intuiting capacity have been relegated to their unconscious functioning. The deep intuitive sensings of early childhood will most likely have vanished. This does not mean that throughout your lifetime there will never again be intuitive sensings brought to conscious awareness. But, at this point, you are setting about the business of focusing upon and specializing in your present human personality, and you desire to do this without distraction from the complexity of the eternal realities. The important task at hand is becoming a fully functioning human being, autonomous in your behavior, exercising your freedom to unfold your personality as you desire.

At approximately seven years of age (this can vary with different children), assuming that you have a family environment that is not overly frightening or traumatic for you, and that you are a relatively stable child, even though perhaps you have challenges here and there, you are beginning to freely *choose* your way through life. You will still learn and grow to a certain extent from those around you, but you as that seven-year-old child have essentially been cut free from most *restraining* influences. You are no longer mastered or restrained by your soul's desires and influences because they have become unconscious. In a *feeling* sense, you have developed your own ego to such an extent that you are no longer restrained by the wishes and desires of your family, even though in the way you live *physically* you will most likely obey and grow within their wishes and desires. Yet, *emotionally* you begin to realize: "I am free *not* to obey if I choose. I am free to rebel against anything, if I choose to do so."

This then is the beginning of the process of gaining *individual freedom*. This is a process that can be quite confusing and difficult as it continues throughout your growing years as a child. For some, it is possible that the struggle for individual freedom can carry over into adulthood, perhaps even lasting an entire lifetime. In other words, there are some adults who never seem to be able to take their freedom into their own hands. They become overly dependent upon so many things in their lives-family, teaching-ones, business, artistic areas, political areas, religious beliefs— striving to find fulfillment *outside* of their own personality. There are others who mature quite quickly, and even before they are physically mature they can feel within themselves: "I am free to live this life as it pleases me. I am free to unfold the magnificent abilities within me in any way that I choose." This does not mean they are alone, or separate from other human beings. In their maturity, they recognize that they are woven to other human beings by bonds of love and cooperation.

Children who are able to unfold their individual freedom will marshal the clarity, honesty, strength, sensitivity, and love to grow within what you would consider "normal" bounds. The range of normal growth patterns is quite wide, and it would encompass many different kinds of personalities.

YOUR YOUNG ADULT YEARS

Even with strong healthy growth during childhood, ordinarily, when you reach your young adult years-from fifteen to nineteen years—there is usually a great force of *rebelliousness* that develops. This grows out of a quite natural need to stamp your individual freedom upon your environment. It is a desire to project your unique personality quite forcefully upon your society. Thus, as you may have observed, in this age group there is often a marked unruliness, a boisterousness and vitality, as these ones struggle with their inner rebelliousness.

At this fifteen to nineteen year stage, you are an emerging adult, becoming free and independent as a human being. Your soul has made its creation by projecting your personality matrix into living human form. You are now preparing to make *your* creation by the kind of life you choose to live as an adult in your physical world. The God forces that began with the creation of your own soul have now evolved into full personality expression, and they are about to be expressed through your human choices as thoughts, feelings, words, and deeds that will pour forth those God forces into earth reality.

Now, to help you more clearly understand how you have grown from a child to your present stage of life, we would look more closely at the period that you speak of as the "high school" years. During these years, human relationships can become extremely important to you, particularly relationships that involve passionate *attraction*, and at times *repulsion*, with other human beings. Thus, in addition to polishing your ability to more brilliantly use mental, emotional, and physical patterns as a maturing adult, you can also have great passionate feelings of romantic love, and many times intense feelings of struggle and strife against others that repulse you. This flaming up of passion and desire is one of the most important aspects of this period of growth. If you do not understand that it is a natural cycle of expression of the developing personality matrix within you, then you can become confused and critical of your own development.

Combined with this unleashing of passion and vitality, there is also an emerging stream of strong *desire* that makes the earth concerns of more importance to your blossoming personality, whether these concerns are love, money, sports, politics, or whatever. Now, if you would look back at your high school years and find that your desires seem to have been smothered during that time, you may find in those years the beginning of fear patterns that continue to plague you in the present moment, dampening your passion for your present life.

For example, if you came forth toward another person during that period with a great feeling of romantic attraction, and, for some reason, the person did not respond kindly and you felt the pain of rejection, that may have been the beginning of a fear that *desire* eventually leads to *pain*. Perhaps the pain occurred in other arenas. Perhaps in creativity, where you would make a painting and others would condemn it. Or, perhaps you would write a poem and others would ridicule it. You would attempt to make success in sports and you would fail. In any area where your desires naturally were very strong and important to you, and you had painful experiences attempting to fulfill those desires, there you could find the beginning of a fear of pain that would lead you to smother your desires. There you may find the beginning of an emotional tightening and squeezing inside of you that perhaps has continued to this day. Perhaps it is in those high school experiences that you began to set the stage for emotional pain, turmoil, and sadness that would plague your adult life.

Of course, some of your fears and challenges have their roots in earlier childhood. But, in this particular high school period in which the natural unfoldment of your personality matrix requires a free, honest, and loving fulfillment of your intense passions and desires, strong painful blockages in the seeking of fulfillment can begin a process of diminishing your personal confidence, and, unintentionally restricting the magnificence of your own being within self-created walls of human negativity.

In working with your own growth in the present time, you can examine your high school years to see if they hold the beginning of the process of smothering your desires, closing your heart, and thereby hampering and diminishing your joy, enthusiasm, creativity, strength, and love. Perhaps it was there that you began the process of hiding your magnificence from yourself *because you became more concerned with protecting yourself from pain* than you were with expressing your passionate desires, fulfilling them, and following the energetic and potent impulses for growth that were welling up within you during that period. Even though all periods of your life have a potential for painful experience which can cause you to draw inward, for most human beings, this particular high school period can be quite impactful upon the patterns of withdrawal that will unfold later in life.

Now, during the high school period, if you were able to successfully let your desires arise, and at least partially act upon them and fulfill them, then you have gained a certain "head start" on creating joy in your adult life. We are not speaking of selfish, unrestrained desire fulfillment or actions that impinge upon others, or that bring about situations that are not loving and beneficial for you and others. We are speaking here of desires fulfilled within the harmonious realm of human relationships and creativity, within the societal norms and the structure that you consider to be idealism and morality. If you were able to fulfill your strong desires freely within such a structure, then you have successfully associated your intense desires with experiences of encouragement to continue to grow, to explore yourself, to respect yourself, and to love yourself.

Those who were able to bring together all of these factors during the high school period usually will rush into adult life excitedly, and most generally successfully. For those who were *not* able to accomplish this, there is certainly not badness in their lives, nor are there any barriers that they cannot overcome. There is simply a different situation. As an adult they may have feelings of struggle that are more intense. Perhaps they may experience less intense feelings of joy and beauty. But, there is no badness in this. They are simply propelled into the young adult years of the twenties with subjective experiences that perhaps have less happiness, perhaps less sense of balance and confidence, but certainly *not with less good* within their personality matrix. There is simply more time spent working with painful situations, feelings, thoughts, and relationships. This may be a different subjective reality from those who fulfilled more in the high school periods, but still, this is a life of beauty because all of the soul's forces and all of the forces of God are flowing as strongly into this person as they are into the one who was able to fulfill more.

To make any kind of comparison and say that one path of growth is better that another is not only unnecessary, but it can be deeply confusing. It can cause resentment within you, and it can cause you to blame your environment, or friends, or family, or life in general. Instead of making such comparisons, you ones of earth could say to yourselves: "If I came forth from my growing years with a great explosiveness of fulfillment and satisfaction, I rejoice in gratitude. If I came with less than that, then I rejoice in gratitude that I have had experiences that strengthen me even more than fulfillment of desire would have strengthened me. These experiences have challenged me to draw more upon my deep strengths and capacities. I still desire fulfillment, and I shall create it for myself. But, I will not condemn my present path because the past did not contain enough desire fulfillment for me."

We would remind you that in using your memory, you are free to focus upon impressions of the past that you consider negative, and you can re-create them in the present and convince yourself that you can never be happy in the present because you have been hurt by pain in the past. And this can last for an entire lifetime. You are also free, when you recall painful impressions of the past, to remind yourself that they are *ended. If you do not re-create them in the present, then they no longer exist.* You could say to yourself: "Certainly I do not wish to re-create past painful experiences in this present moment. *I now freely choose to create the passion, and the enthusiasm, and the fulfillment of desire that I was frightened to create during those past periods*."

You can turn this kind of understanding toward your entire childhood and all of your growth periods. If you are one who now feels, "I was cheated by life, I was not joyful and passionate and fulfilled during my growth periods," then *now* is the time to create the fulfillment you believe you have missed. You have even more need now to be passionate and excited about your life. You have even more need now to push through your fears and do what you desire, fulfilling all of your desires for successfulness, accomplishment, love, and joy. You can *now* create the meaning and purpose in life that you may feel you lacked in the past.

YOUR SEXUAL EXPRESSION

As a transition between the high school stage and the adult stage of life, we will focus for a moment on the area of human sexual expression. This is an area that can become quite important during the high school period, and from then on it comes to be a major concern throughout the adult life.

When you observe human beings experiencing their personality, you notice that sexual desire and its fulfillment play an important role in the inner life of most human beings. You would also notice that sexual desire and sexual expression permeate your literature, your visual communications, and your interactions with one another. The intensity of this interest, in the *first* sense, is due to the animal nature of the physical body and the forces implanted by the souls when they created the early animal-human forms. These soul forces emphasized tendencies that were most beneficial to the continued evolution of the physical bodily forms. Thus, the desire for sexual union was given into bodies with a great intensity to spark the reproduction of human forms. You are given a strong sexual drive as a portion of your bodily functionings, just as you are given smell, taste, appetite, and many other attributes.

Next, there comes the influence of your subjective personality, which will determine your own unique adjustment to the sexual drive given to you by your body. The mental and emotional patterns that you build, along with all of the complex energies of your personality matrix will weave with the innate sexual drive, and the result will be your own particular way of responding to sexual desire and its fulfillment. Thus, there will be great differences among human beings in their interest in the sexual area.

For example, imagine a female who has come into her present body with many patterns that have to do with healing old fears from past lifetimes of earth, fears that grew out of experiences that were painful in the area of sexual union. To make the healing more joyful in this lifetime, her soul would implant into her present personality matrix a great passion, along with lustful appetites. These would reflect patterns from her different past lifetimes in which she *rejoiced* in the sexual union, and was able to live in great love, woven with passionate fulfillment. For this female then, the force of the natural physical urge toward sexual expression is intensified by these other patterns. Thus, in this lifetime, she would be a one of quite passionate nature in whom the sexual aspects of life are extremely important.

On the other hand, imagine another female who perhaps in past times of earth became so preoccupied with the pleasure of sexual union that she ignored the sensitivity of love and gentleness, the depth of deep communication between herself and others, simply to indulge in the physical aspects of sexual pleasure. In this lifetime, among the many other things that she will accomplish, she is coming to heal the tendency to ignore important portions of her life because of a desire for over-indulgence in sexual pleasure. The soul of this one would implant into her personality structure, certain of lack of interest in the sexual arena. She would have a small appetite for sexual pleasure. The soul perhaps would also weave certain sexual fears from other lifetimes into the personality so that the lack of interest in sexual expression would give her a more objective viewpoint from which to heal the old fears. Thus, this one comes to be a female to whom the sexual area is not so important. She can easily bring her attention to other areas of her life, such as intimacy, warmth in love and mating, creativity, searching for God, and other areas that perhaps were overshadowed in the past by passion. For her, the natural sexual impulse is *diminished* by the needs of the personality

We give these as simple examples to help you feel how the importance of sexual expression will vary within each human being as a result of the many unique and complex patterns within their particular personality matrix.

To help you more clearly understand the intense widespread interest in sexual expression in your present society, we would point out that in this present period of earth life there are many human beings alive who have brought into their personalities an extraordinarily intense desire for intimacy, love, and fulfillment with other human beings. Therefore, romantic relationships are extremely important to many ones in this time. Yet, due to different widespread societal influences, many individuals have forgotten how to feel deeply for themselves and for others. Out of fear of pain and rejection, they have covered over their great capacity for sensitivity and love. Of course, the degree to which this has been done varies with each individual, but, as a broad generalization, it would be accurate to say that in your society *there has come to be a general decrease in the capacity to experience intimacy in human relationships.* This has greatly diminished the ability to create intense fulfillment in romantic relationships.

As a result of these factors, there are now many human beings walking in this earth who have a feeling of lack of intensity in romantic love areas. As an unconscious compensation for this emptiness, they are drawn toward the more easily attainable intensity of sexual experience. The sexual expression becomes one of the few areas in which they can experience the intensity of feeling that they desire. This brings about a temporary over-exaggeration of, and preoccupation with sexual expression. This results in a widespread intensifying of the natural interest in sex that you ones have as a result of your biological heritage.

Understand that this period of preoccupation with sexual expression will eventually bring much wisdom to you ones, after many learn through their own experience that to overemphasize sexual union without intimacy and love does not bring the intensity of fulfillment that you are seeking. Many ones will begin to make adjustments in their desires and passions, and they will bring their sexual appetites into alignment with their great sensitive hearts. They will be motivated to learn how to create fulfilling relationships of intimacy, sensitivity, honesty, and deep love, woven with a vigorous sexual expression. The deep inner wisdom that lives within the personality matrix of each of you ones will eventually lead you to adjust your sexual expression with intelligence and love, just as you adjust for all of the other complex areas of life in which your personality is involved as a human being.

YOUR ADULT LIFE

We will focus now upon the stages of adult life in a brief general way that will help you understand the major themes of each period. First, we will look at the young adult period, the years of the early twenties.

During the young adult period, most human beings will be propelled by a strong need to stabilize their personality within the social matrix in which they find themselves. This can manifest as a concern for solidifying a position in many social areas involving work, school, art, politics, religion, or family. This would be essentially your desire to carve out a place for yourself that is *your* creation, and that is sound, safe, and stable for you to live your life within. It is your attempt to create an arena in which you can fulfill your human desires and unfold your human personality throughout this lifetime. We are describing this from your personal subjective human point of view.

Looking from your *soul's* point of view, you would see the early twenties as a time in which you are building a solid foundation from which you can fully participate in the creation of earth. As a mature human being, you are now preparing to take all of the divine forces that your soul has implanted into your personality matrix and spew them forth into earth in tangible ways as your physical life. You will shower your creations out upon earth reality through the choices that you make in relationships, and the way in which you conduct those relationships; in the way you think, and feel, and communicate your thoughts and feelings; in the kind of work you do; and in all of the other actions that you take toward the outer world. Essentially, this is a period of outward *doing, acting,* and *accomplishing.* (This is quite generalized, and there are many other purposes and functions during this stage of life, but this would be the dominant pattern for most ones.)

During the period from the late twenties into the early thirties, for most human beings, there is much vitality, strength, confidence, and enthusiasm. This is not to say that you would be free from challenge or difficulty in your earth situations. Perhaps you would even have experiences that you would label as *failure.* But, essentially, this is a period of continuing *creation* in great intensity and confidence. There is an extension of previous accomplishment in career, family, or other fulfillments that are important to you.

Continuing now in this same way of generalizing, passing over the various complexities that exist in each individual human being, we would move then into the area of the fully mature adult—the thirties, the forties. This can be seen as a period of *solidifying accomplishment*. This is the period of *mastering* what you have worked toward. This is the period of advanced accomplishment, in relationships, in career, in pursuits of truth, in artistic activity, in all that you are attempting to fulfill in your life. During this period, some will rise to levels of superiority in various areas, bringing their earlier accomplishments to fruition in tangible ways.

Now, even if your earth accomplishments are great during this adult period, if you have gone a lifetime ignoring the *eternal* portions of yourself, not allowing an opportunity to bring into conscious awareness some of your intuitive sensings that are filled with the eternal forces from your soul, from your guiding-ones, and from God, then the period around forty years of age may possibly become a time of struggle, of disillusionment, and pain. For many, there will be the breakup of families, careers thrown aside, rebellion against old patterns, and frustration with many aspects of the personal life. This is usually brought about by a pervasive sense of discontent with life, a feeling that earth fulfillments are becoming hollow, and that life is not satisfying enough (there will be other factors that differ with each individual). This is accompanied by an intuitive prodding from your soul that can influence you toward *change* as your soul attempts to show you that you are overlooking a major purpose in your life—the integration of deeper portions of your being into earth life fulfillments.

During such a period of turmoil, your soul will attempt even more to begin a new birth of the *truth* within you, to inspire you to seek a fulfillment that is not simply rooted in your physical being and your concerns of earth. This is not to suggest that there is a badness in the earth accomplishments. Without such earth fulfillment you would find it difficult to enjoy human life. But, if it is *only* the earth affairs that have received your attention throughout your life, then at the mature adult period you may encounter upheaval in your life.

If you do come to experience such a period of upheaval, and you are able to view it as an opportunity to begin a new life, if you are able to trust that there is not badness in this upheaval, and if you are honest and loving with yourself, then this period will be a rebirth for you. All of the brilliant, magnificent eternal forces that live within you, and that have been ignored by you in the past, can be sparked and brought to life. It will depend on your willingness to examine the personality patterns that you have developed, to draw deeply on your own wisdom to find ways to change the patterns based in fear, and to bring forth your capacity to attune to the forces of love that live within the depths of your being.

During the late forties and through the fifties, there will be two general patterns of human expression that will be quite common. These, of course, do not apply to all human beings, and even those who express these patterns will do so in their own unique ways. By the time human beings reach the age of fifty, most of them have developed such unique personal ways of expressing themselves that they will not often fit generalizable patterns.

The first general stream of expression will be made up of those who continue to solidify and master the same paths of earth fulfillment that have been important to them in the past. Those who have achieved outstanding superiority in certain areas will assume leadership positions in those areas. Others will master more simple arenas of life, but will find that their confidence and command of those arenas will be quite great.

The second pattern of human expression will be one of *change*. Those in this group will usually abandon the old paths, whether they have mastered them or not, and they will set out in new directions, seeking new unfoldments. This will not necessarily be prompted by discontent or pain, but rather it will grow out of a sense of eagerness to explore different aspects of personality fulfillment in different human situations. Here you will find pioneers and innovators who are more interested in the *variety* of human expression than they are in mastery of one area.

As the mature years blend toward older age, from sixty to seventy, and this will vary with each individual, there usually comes a great *reassessment* period. Many will begin to notice a sense of *saturation* with the earth pleasures. Perhaps there will be a feeling of not yet having fulfilled the important purposes of life. Often, ones will have the feeling that they have not given enough to others in their lives. There can still be great rejoicing in earth affairs, a great satisfaction and fulfillment with the sensual pleasures of earth, but the desire for completing important purposes becomes very strong.

In most ones who allow themselves to open their hearts during this reassessment period, there comes an increased sensitivity to the eternal truths of life. Unconsciously, they begin to turn their attention toward deeper and broader issues of life. For many, there will be a conscious reaching out for the more eternal values through an involvement with religion, philosophy, artistic creativity, teaching, or other areas of human unfoldment that bring a deep feeling of purpose. They will often engage in activities that are of service to other human beings. In many ways, they will seek fulfillment that goes deeper than the earlier experiences in their lives.

There will also be those who have, throughout all of the earlier stages of their lives, felt an attunement to the deep eternal forces of life. They will have lived with a sense of purpose and meaning as they unfolded their personality, even though at times there were doubts, confusion, challenge, and pain. For ones such as this, the reassessment period will be more of a *reaffirming* period, a time in which they feel that the beauty of their life will continue to be rooted in eternal truth, just as it was in the past.

During the period of human life that spans the years between seventy and eighty (varying with different individuals), there begins a gradual, and natural process of *disentanglement* from earth life. At this point in life, assuming that there is not a disease process or health challenge to darken the development of the personality, there are many changes that come about to loosen the personality's hold on earth life. There is usually a natural decrease in the passion for earth pleasures, less conviction that earth is the only reality, greater patience, and many new insights about life that are a preparation for releasing the earth. (This is not to suggest that continued passion during this stage is unnatural. Each individual will live this period in their own unique way.) Much that takes place during this stage of life helps the earth personality matrix disentangle itself from the dense complexity of bodily cares and concerns, usually bringing about a closer attunement to eternal realities that lie beyond earth.

At this stage of life, there will be many ones who struggle with illness and disease. As a broad generalization (and some will have different patterns) we could say that many who have disease in the later years are making unconscious choices to continue to learn and master earth affairs right up to the end of life. They wish to stay totally engaged in the earth battle.

To convey the feeling of this, we will use here a metaphor of armies at war. Imagine that some have fought long and hard, but they begin to see that this battle will be neither won nor lost. *It will simply draw to a close.* Those who realize this are the ones who are willing to gracefully and joyfully disentangle themselves from the battle. They simply cease to fight the war.

In human life, these would be the ones who begin to have less desire to succeed and accomplish in earth terms, realizing that soon the brief period of earth life will draw to a close and the truth will be experienced again without the illusions of earth. These ones simply wander away from the earth battlefield and enjoy their time sitting in the shade, feeling the magnificence of their remaining time in life. Perhaps such ones would take up poetry, deepen their interest in philosophy or religion, or rejoice more in human relationships, or in nature.

Imagine others engaged in the same war who feel: "We shall win this battle if only we can fight harder." Ones with this attitude, as they come into the later years of life, will fight harder for success and fulfillment in earth. Many times they will intensify their desire to master what they feel have been the rigid forces of earth that have prevented them from fulfilling themselves. Often, within such persons, the pressure of many years of fear and doubt will have accumulated as negative forces upon the body, having caused disease or infirmity of some kind.

Those who battle life in this way can often be helped by ones of love around them. Loved ones can encourage them to attune to the inspiration from their soul, and from the forces of God. If they are able to do this, then gradually they will cease to struggle against life as if it were an enemy, and they will create joy and harmony in their lives. Some will continue to fight until the end, and they will not rejoice. They will move into death with confusion, frustration, fear, doubt, and pain. But, you understand that this is not badness, it is simply *painful*. After they have passed through death, the pain will gradually dissolve. (We will look closer at this in a later portion of these teachings.)

As you consider the elderly periods of human life, the most generalizable truth would be this: *in your elderly years, you will experience what you have built throughout your lifetime.* If you have built mostly fear, you will have fear and pain. If you have built love and trust, you will have love and trust. So, in any moment in your life, no matter what stage you are in, you can say to yourself:

"This is the moment in which I am building the remainder of my life. Let me build it in love and joy, and I can be certain that that will please me throughout this lifetime."

As a general guideline for assessing *all* of the various stages of your human personality growth throughout your lifetime, you could look at any stage in which you were unfulfilled and say: "I am not happy about the lack of fulfillment that I find here, so now I will rise up to make the next stage of my life the one in which I fulfill myself." If you look at a stage of your life and see that it was quite fulfilling and satisfying, then say to yourself: "That period has served me well, and I will assume that my strong growthful personality patterns will continue in the next period of my life. I will build upon those fulfilling experiences and expand them even further in the next stage that I am now entering."

YOUR PRESENT MOMENT

No matter what stage of your life you are now living, whether you are a youth, or whether you are an elderly one moving toward death, *your present moment is the most important time for you. Now* is the moment to let your desires and passions grow in you, whether they are for earth fulfillment, or for oneness with God. Now is the moment to fulfill your desires in love, honesty, idealism, and joy. *The present stage of your life is the one in which you can be fulfilled, no matter what you have experienced in the past stages.* It is never too late to fulfill yourself. All of the accumulated goodness and love of every past stage of your lifetime is carried into this moment. All of the goodness and love that you have ever experienced in all of your past lifetimes is brought forth as unconscious energies into your present moment.

Even though we have spoken of the various stages of your life in order to bring you clarity, you can understand that *in your inner experience of life, there is only the present moment.* Your life is one present moment of experience fading into the next present moment. Stages of growth are a human intellectual creation based upon *observation* of your life, made from a detached viewpoint. You can observe that indeed you were once a small child. Now you are a large adult. That is your intellectual observation. However, your *inner experience* has always been the same. It is the feeling:

"I am living now in this moment. I may have memories of the past, and I may have imaginings of the future, but my inner experience of living is taking place now, in this moment, and I can feel that I have always had this experience of living in the present moment."

If you will work with yourself each day to rejoice in every moment with as much love for yourself and others as you can bring forth, you will find that indeed the beauty of all of your human lifetimes lives within you in the present moment. The more you become consciously aware of this, the closer you will come to experiencing the magnificence of the divine forces of all of life that are woven into the perfection of the present moment that you are now living.

CHAPTER SEVEN

Death of the Human Body

We will now turn to the portion of your personality expression that you ones in earth would speak of as *death*. We will begin the understanding here by reminding you that the negative emotional intensity that most ones bring to the issue of death is primarily a result of human confusion and a lack of understanding. In other words, the fear of death is not a *natural* quality of your personality matrix. In fact, the souls of you ones have woven into the complexity of your non-physical personality matrix an inner knowing and certainty that *there is no death. Your soul has placed into your personality an intuitive knowledge that you are eternal.*

If you were to bring these soul influences into your conscious awareness, it would be quite clear to you that you are not your physical body. However, most ones living in human form tend to become so entwined in their subjective bodily expression that gradually they come to feel: "This body is me." Therefore, when they begin to think about losing that body through death, they quite naturally fear that they will lose *themselves*. Thus, for many human beings, the thought of moving toward death is a negative thought that sparks frightening emotions within their personalities.

When these negative thoughts and fearful emotions about death are dwelled upon, such as in the case of ones who would have intense fears of death and would spend much time preoccupied with those fears, there can come about a limiting of their ability to subjectively know the truth of life. There can come a distortion of the beautiful energies within the personality matrix. This distortion would begin to create a subjective feeling of darkness, heaviness, and oppression, rather than the feelings of joy that are natural to the personality. For ones who unfold their personality in this fearful way, they are literally creating a hell for themselves, in which they must exist until they are willing to change their own subjective creation. They will live in this painful experience until they are willing to see and believe: "I have created this feeling of darkness out of my own fear of death. Until I can live those feelings of fear, work with them patiently, and then heal them, I can expect to walk in emotional pain."

Even though it is not natural for your *personality* to fear death, there is a natural innate tendency to avoid danger to your body. Just as the sexual desire is given to you by your physical nature, there is also an intuitive *caution* that is an aspect of your animal physical nature that will lead you to fear situations that could cause physical damage or death to your body. In other words, as you would notice from your own human observations, there is a certain thread of self-preservation woven into your body. Due to this, it will be quite natural for you to have a certain amount of apprehension about death, particularly your own death. This kind of apprehension about death is not an indication that you have abnormal fears. You could say to yourself: "I will notice my own attitudes and feelings about death, and if I feel they are overly negative, I will look for the fear and gradually heal it. If I feel there is only slight apprehension, then I understand that this is to be expected, and, for this time, I need not be concerned with death. I need to be more concerned with *life*, as I am presently living it."

THE PROCESS OF DEATH

To bring you general knowledge about human death that can deepen your understanding, we will focus more closely on the *process* of death for the physical body.

First of all, we can assure you that the time, and place, and manner of your death is always chosen by a wise portion of you that is unconscious. This portion of you is aligned with your soul, and with the choices your soul has made in projecting your personality into earth, in this lifetime, and in all of the past human lifetimes in which you have passed through human birth and death.

So, even in human death situations that to your earth eyes might appear to be accidental and tragic, you can rest assured that the soul has given permission for that person to meet death. Thus, you can be certain that when you go forth to meet your own death, there will be no badness in it, and there will not be an inappropriateness to the time and circumstances of your death. Your death will be a part of your soul's choices.

Looking closer now at the choosing of the time, place, and manner of death, you would need to understand that in some human beings, the soul has a very clear intention, even before it creates the personality and the body of that human being, to bring about the death of that person's body at a particular time and place, and in a particular manner. Thus, for some human beings, these choices are made prior to birth.

For others, the soul desires a greater flexibility, and will wait until the circumstances of the human personality life are unfolded before the choice of death is made. For these human beings (the words distort the realities a bit here) the soul implants several "possible" death times, and places, and ways of dying. These different possibilities are chosen clearly by the soul for very important reasons that have benefit for the personality-reasons of growth, knowledge, and wisdom.

Then for other human beings, the soul does not implant any plan for death. These souls, who are of the most adventurous and spontaneous nature, leave that decision entirely dependent upon the life of the human personality. Ordinarily, such souls will manifest human personalities that are quite spontaneous, independent, and free in all areas of their lives. As the life of these human beings unfolds, the soul could determine, at any point in the life, that this is the perfect moment for death. The death could occur at any time throughout the life.

If you would desire to speculate about which kind of death your soul has chosen, we would suggest that again you use your imagination, and say to yourself, in a moment of deep silence: "I will now imagine I am my soul. Given my kind of personality, as I presently understand it, if I am my soul and I would match the death to my personality, what would I choose? Am I the kind of person who loves certainty? Then, most likely, I have chosen a death at quite an advanced age, and it will be quite simple and straightforward. Am I a personality, on the other hand, who likes flexibility, total freedom, spontaneity, and impulsiveness? Then, I will imagine that I am a soul who has chosen not to define at all the death time, place, and manner." If you feel, "I am a little bit of each," then you would say: "I will imagine I am a soul who has chosen the second alternative—several possible times and places and means of death." This is a way to make a very *general* assessment. However, if you are loving yourself and rejoicing in your life, then these areas of speculation about death are not of great concern to you, for you are quite busy living your life.

We can assure you that at the time of death, even in the case of physically painful deaths, the soul does come forth during the period of pain and infuses into the subjective personality awareness of the dying person a certain kind of eternal force that will help the person detach from the experience of pain and fear. Thus, during the process of death, even if from the outside it appears that the person is suffering, there is a certain *release* that the soul helps the person make so that the death process becomes not so painful, not so frightening.

Your soul does not abandon you during the process of death. Quite the contrary; your soul comes more closely into your conscious awareness, and, whether your death is slow or abrupt, your soul quite quickly begins to intensify the portions of your human personality that we have described as your intuiting capacity. Your soul activates, within your personality matrix, your capacity to be consciously aware of eternal realities of the soul and of God itself. *Your soul immediately helps you peel back the temporary illusion of being one human personality.* Thus, within the human personality matrix that you have experienced as yourself throughout your lifetime, at death, there is a rapid infusion of an awareness that you are an eternal being existing in a vast, magnificent reality beyond earth.

YOUR ATTITUDE TOWARD DEATH

In understanding human death, you can see it as the end of a play at the theater, a drama in which you have played a role. The curtain has now been drawn. It is no longer necessary for you to stay in character as the one that you played upon the stage. *You no longer need to limit your expression to the narrow range that was your one character.* The play is over. You have been enriched by the character that you have played. You can play it whenever it pleases you. However, you are now free to go far beyond the confines of that single limited role. You can play any role that you desire.

So it is with death. It is a releasing from a role that was necessarily limiting, due to its *human* nature. But, even though that role was limited, *it was not bad or wrong in any way.* You must understand this clearly: death is not to be seen as a way to gain freedom from your earth pains and negativity. If you would view death this way, then there would be no purpose for earth life. With this distorted attitude, your primary goal in life would be *to escape* life.

You would simply strive to die as quickly as possible.

Those who commit suicide in their lives have fallen into such fear and confusion that they come to believe that death is an escape from negativity and pain. They do not understand that, at the point of death, if you are filled with such fear and frustration, or such despair with earth life that you believe that death is an improvement, then *those strong patterns of negativity and fear will be carried through the door of death.* Your after-death period, for a while, could be quite confusing, painful, and frightening because the force of your negative human illusions would be so strong that they would endure, even after your body and brain were ended. For a while, you would create within your enduring personality matrix the same patterns of fear and darkness and pain that you created as a human being.

As you now look at death, you as a living human being could understand it as a returning to conscious awareness of the truth. If, in this lifetime, you have done all that you can to seek that conscious awareness of truth while you are living in human form, then you would most certainly have created experiences of love, and trust, and goodness in your life. Most likely you would have come to the conscious understanding that there is good in all of earth, even when you cannot feel it. Thus, you would take into your death a willingness to release the negative illusions of earth and to quite quickly regain your conscious awareness of your soul, of the God forces, of all eternal realities.

As you live your life day by day in an attempt to love yourself and those about you, in an attempt to understand your fears and to heal them, in an attempt to give to others and bless them by your actions and earth choices, then you are *perfectly* preparing for your death. So, as a *living* human being, you need not be concerned with death. You need not be concerned with preparing for death, because everything that is important for living a magnificent life automatically prepares you for the perfect death.

Only when the issue of death arises naturally in the course of your earth life does it need your attention. If you notice, for example, that you are passing through a period of discouragement, perhaps depression, and death begins to rise up in your awareness, then you would say: "This is a period of time in which I need to bring about an understanding of death. I need to understand what it is, and why it is drawing my attention." If you find that you are consciously avoiding the issue of death out of fear, that is another case in which death needs your attention. You would need to address the fear and heal it. If beloved ones to you are dying, or if they die and you enter into sadness and feelings of loss, then you would say: "Now is the time when the arena of death needs my attention. There are areas of my life that are important to understand because they relate to my feelings about death." But, when these areas are not present in your earth experience, you could say to yourself: "I am concerned with *life*, and I will trust that my death will take care of itself. I do not need to prepare for death. I do not need to be concerned about it. For now I am *living*, and that is where I will turn my attention."

YOUR AFTER-DEATH TRANSITION

Now we would turn our attention to that which occurs *after* the death of your physical body. The process that begins the after-death stage would be essentially the same for all human beings, whether they meet death naturally by failure of the body, or by disease, by violence, or in a manner that to your earth eyes appears to be accidental. However, the *subjective experience* of each personality in the after-death transition period can be quite different.

After the death of your physical body, your personality matrix of energies is released from your body. As a result of this, your conscious awareness of yourself will stand *outside* of physical reality. Yet, at that point, even though your soul is standing with you and has intensified your intuiting capacity so that you can be consciously aware of eternal realities, for a while, any unusually strong personality patterns that you created during your earth life can continue to color your subjective perception of the after-death reality, just as they colored your perception of physical reality.

For example, if your personality beliefs and attitudes during your life were strongly loving and positive, then, after death, this will be an inspiring and uplifting influence that will color your immediate after-death period in a very joyful way. And, since human love and experiences of subjective goodness are made of the same energy fabric as eternal realities, then these positive beliefs and attitudes that you bring from your human life will help you quickly open your awareness of eternal truth after death. Yet, there will be a small period in which your subjective experience immediately after death will be colored by the nature of your positive earth beliefs. Then, quickly, those beliefs will be adjusted to reflect *all* of truth.

We will use an example to clarify this for you. Let us

imagine that we have a male one before us who has a deep, sincere belief in the present Christian religion, particularly in the teaching that would describe the being of Jesus Christ as a most important focal point for human beings who desire to know God. Let us imagine that in most of the life of this male one there was a wonderful, intimate sense of communion with the Jesus being. There was a sense of the Jesus being watching over himself, protecting him, guiding him, and loving him. Then, after death, this male one would experience the presence of the Jesus being near him. That experience would be colored for a while by how the male one subjectively understood the Jesus being. This would be quite a magnificent experience for the personality of the male one. However, gradually, this experience of magnificence would *expand* beyond the awareness of the Jesus being to include *all other beings*. The expanded experience would be even more joyful and more magnificent. And, gradually, the subjective experience of the personality that had been the male one in earth would expand even further to rejoice in *all of God, in all of its manifestations.*

You must understand that in the period after death, *all* of the truths and realities of all universes are flowing about you, and your soul is consciously aware of them. However, you as a surviving personality matrix, having built strong thought and emotional patterns for a lifetime, will naturally bring those strong patterns with you into the immediate after-death period. So, as the eternal truths and realities swirl about you, even though they are recognized and experienced by your soul, they come into you as forces that you are not used to perceiving. They come into the intuiting capacity of your surviving personality matrix that has now been suddenly expanded by your soul. As these "different" forces come to you, at first you will tend to interpret them in the same way that you have become accustomed to interpreting your earth reality. Thus, if these forces cause you to feel a great sense of deep, all-consuming love, then you may interpret that from your earth habit as *romantic love*. And you may immediately *create* the experience of being with a beloved mating-one that you have known in your past lifetime. On the other hand, if a stream of the God forces is felt and noticed by you, and it has a certain quality that to you suggests the *nurturing of family*, you may interpret that immediately, according to your old earth habits, as the presence of your family.

Now, in truth, the love of your family and your beloved ones is actually there with you. Their love energies are a portion of the God forces. *All* energies are a portion of the God forces, and they are also with you. In other words, all realities that could possibly be, or have ever been, are swirling about you as you reestablish increased conscious awareness of all truth. But, during the early periods of this process, you will tend to *interpret* those truths *according to your past human understandings*. Thus, you may see family-ones, you may see mating-ones, you may experience religious teachers, you may find yourself in places of beauty that were extremely important to you in earth life. The underlying *realities* of these experiences are true—the *feelings* and the *energies*. However, the *images* and the *visions* that you see, for a while, will be colored by the recent earth understandings of your personality matrix, and they will tend to be smaller than the truth. In later periods, your images and visions of beloved ones will expand. They will eventually include vast magnificent portions of your beloved ones that you were unable to perceive for a while.

The quality of your immediate after-death experience can also be affected by intense degrees of human negativity that you have created during your earth lifetime. However, your negative patterns do not have the strength that they had while you were physically alive. When you are alive in earth in a physical body, your negative personality patterns have a certain "life" of their own. In other words, they have a certain *momentum*, and ordinarily it takes *time* to heal those patterns. Once you have left the body behind, your personality matrix functions in a way that is very free, because there is no time and space to restrict you. Thus, if you have entered the after-death period with extreme patterns of fear, those patterns do not have the momentum they had in earth, and, *it does not take time to heal them.* They can be healed *instantly*, as long as you can believe that this is possible.

Thus, if you are one of great fear, and you have made death, and you find yourself in a great darkness, as soon as you realize that *you are creating the darkness by your fear*, then you will be able to love enough and understand that in that instant you are free to release the fear and dissolve the darkness. This is what your soul is continually trying to influence you to choose to do.

For those human beings who have caused their own death by suicide, that action usually reinforces the fear patterns so much that after death it is very difficult for the personalities to believe that they can simply *release* the fear patterns that tortured them so much when they were alive.

While they were living, they believed so strongly that pain and darkness were being *inflicted* upon them by life, that they came to believe that the only way out was to escape life. This distracted them from the truth that it was their personality that was causing the darkness. So, since they died believing they did not *cause* the negativity, after death, they believe that they cannot *end* it. Thus, even after death, they will feel helpless for a while, feeling that they are now a victim of their new surroundings.

In truth, they are surrounded by the love of their soul, their own guiding-ones, other souls, and God. But they cannot perceive this love because they continue to unintentionally wrap themselves in the darkness of their own subjective negativity. Thus, during the after-death period, those who commit suicide will temporarily have a deeper struggle and greater confusion. Yet, eventually, this will pass, as soon as they realize that they can heal their own fear in any instant in which they are willing to love enough.

There could also be ones in human life who filled their personality with strong beliefs that there was not life after death, ones who were rigid in their insistence upon identifying with only their physical body. For such ones, after death, these belief patterns would have such intensity that they could remain in place for a while. So, it is possible that these ones would stand beyond earth, free from the body, yet with such intense rigid beliefs that they *are* the body that *this belief would instantly re-create the illusion of being in a physical body.* These ones would re-create an etheric *facsimile* of the physical body they had left behind. From the point of view of the subjective awareness of their personality, they could believe that they were still alive in earth.

For such ones, the soul would be pouring forth the eternal forces of truth, trying to attract the attention of the confused personalities who have unintentionally created an etheric replica of earth life. In that confused experience, the powerful soul forces being poured into the intuitive sensings of the personalities would eventually become so strong that it would be impossible for the personalities to ignore them.

From the personalities' point of view, after a while, they would begin to notice that their reality that seemed so physical was beginning to fade at the edges. They would begin to notice that it seemed not so solid, and not so real. Gradually, the eternal forces of the soul would prevail, helping the personalities dissolve their illusions by sparking feelings of trust and love within each personality matrix. When the earth illusion was finally dissolved, the person- alities' conscious awareness of the magnificent eternal realities would return, and gradually, the personalities would proceed toward conscious merging with their souls.

YOUR ETERNAL AWARENESS

As we have mentioned, at the time of death, your soul begins to intensify, within your personality matrix, the intuiting capacity that brings eternal realities to your con- scious awareness. The eternal forces of your soul, your guiding-ones, and of God that have been continually flow- ing into you throughout your physical lifetime now begin to become conscious to you. The forces themselves were never diminished throughout your human lifetime. So, all that is actually increased at the time of death *is your capacity to be consciously aware of those forces*. Throughout your human lifetime, your soul, your guiding-ones, and the forces of God have been walking with you. You simply have not noticed them. At death, your soul, your guiding-ones, and God are walking with you, and your conscious awareness of them is returned.

Now, as we have said, if you meet death with great fear and misunderstanding, or particularly if you intentionally cause your own death out of fear, you can *temporarily* continue the blockages caused by your human fear patterns, making it difficult for you at first to regain your eternal awareness and to perceive your soul, your guiding-ones, and your God. However, they are standing beside you even more clearly than ever, and they are loving you. They are attempting to communicate to you in your fog of self-created negativity. And, during such an after-death period of confusion, if you are willing to trust and to release your belief in the negativity, you will hear the call, and you will guide yourself out of that self-created sphere of darkness, and you will become consciously aware of the eternal truths that have been living within you throughout your physical lifetime, and by which you are surrounded during that after-death period of confusion.

In light of what we have pointed out here, you can understand the importance of learning to trust and love while you are physically alive. Not only will it bring you greater joy and fulfillment while you are living, but it will bring you a quicker conscious awareness of the eternal truths after you pass through death. Thus, you could say to yourself: "If in this lifetime I attempt to love as deeply as I

know how, and if I work to recognize my fears and heal
them to the best of my ability, then I can assume that after I
have passed through death, there will not be a period of
lack of awareness of the eternal truths. I will have immediate awareness of the majesty of God living within me, and
surrounding me. I will have immediate awareness of my
beloved guiding-ones. And I will have immediate awareness of myself as a soul."

Now, after your death, there will be a brief period in
which you will continue to have an awareness of yourself
as that human being that you were in your lifetime that has
just ended. The intensity of this awareness will depend
upon how completely you were identified with your body
during your earth lifetime. A normal, passionate involvement with earth life would not cause any undue confusion
during this period. If you have over-identified with the
physical body, or if you have a fearful desire to cling to the
body because of a belief that you are *only* your body, this
could slow the after-death clearing process.

However, regardless of your degree of identification
with your physical body, gradually, you become more
aware of yourself as your soul. Your human personality
matrix is gradually merged into the eternal forces of your
soul, and, eventually you regain total conscious awareness
of all eternal realities.

As your eternal awareness returns, you understand that
your soul is deeply enriched by the energies of your human
personality matrix that has just passed through the earth
life. This will be true whether you believe your life was
positive or negative. You as a soul will take that personality
into yourself, and you will rejoice in it. In a certain sense,

you are still that personality, but now you are not limited by it. Now, you are *all* of the human personalities that you have ever been. You are aware of them, and you rejoice in them. However, you are also aware of all of the magnificent *eternal* realities that are love, and beauty, and fulfillment.

What we have discussed is the immediate after-death transition period. This occurs before you become *fully* conscious of yourself as an eternal soul. To conclude this look at the after-death transition period, we would ask that you now bring forth your imagination again and we will give you a simple vision that perhaps can communicate more deeply than words.

Imagine yourself coming forth into a beautiful meadow that is warm and green. There are flowers all about. In this meadow you are rejoicing with beloved ones, and it is so magnificent. You are happy and fulfilled. Then, you notice that near this meadow there is a large lake. You say to your beloved ones, "Let us go swim in this lake." They would say to you that they do not desire to swim at this time. In great appreciation of their enjoyment of the meadow, you bless them and you say: "I desire swimming. I shall go now and swim." And you go forth and you plunge into the cold water. At first, there is a bit of a shock, but then you rejoice in your swimming. Now, during that swimming, you do not bemoan the fact that your beloved ones are in the meadow. For you understand quite clearly that you are free to cease swimming anytime it pleases you and again rejoice with them in the meadow.

We are bringing this vision forth to help you understand the *feelings* that are involved in moving from life to death, and then returning to a physical life again. The feeling that we have described in this vision is the kind of feeling that grows in you during the after-death transition period. During that period, all of the temporary veils that seem to separate life and death begin to dissolve. Perhaps during life you felt that there was badness in death because it separates you from your loved ones. As the veils dissolve, you see that life and death are right next to one another, and there is truly no separation. So, if you would imagine the meadow as your earth life, and you would imagine the lake as the immediate after-death period, you would vaguely understand what your feeling will be in the after-death period. You can see your beloved ones in the meadow next to the lake, and you know that you are still joined with them. You understand clearly that death does not separate you from them. Even though they still walk in physical bodies, there is no time and space, and you walk with them. You live in their hearts. From the eternal viewpoint, you are larger than them. So it is that you can be in your magnificent after-death period throwing off the limits of the personality matrix, while at the same time you can look over and participate in their hearts, and love them, and rejoice in them as they remain in earth. This will be the feeling of wonder and magnificence that is involved in the after-death period as truth is returned to your conscious awareness.

Gradually, as you near the end of the after-death transition period, you will have an experience that you could imagine as choosing not to play in the meadow, and not to swim. You have decided to climb a mountain. You know that you are still with your friends of earth in the meadow; you are also with friends who are now swimming in the lake of the after-death stage. But, as you climb the mountain, you suddenly realize that you are in a vast kingdom that includes *eternal* beloved ones that you had forgotten. And yet, your new kingdom includes the meadow and the lake. In other words, from the mountaintop where you are rejoicing with *all* beloved ones, you can see *everything*. And you recognize that everything is all the same wonderful land, with no limits, no restrictions, and no separations. Gradually, the feeling of total magnificence that has always lived in you as a human being throughout your physical life, comes back to your *conscious* awareness. Gradually, *you become your eternal soul.*

Thus, the after-death transition period is an experience of magnificence, wonder, and beauty. Just as the earth life did not separate you from God, the period of the after-death experience cannot separate you. Nothing can separate you from the majesty of life and love that is God.

It will be important for you to carry this feeling with you throughout this lifetime. Even though in these teachings we have created words and concepts that would describe earth life and the after-death stage as being different, they are *only perceived* as different when viewed from within the personality matrix. They are not different in reality. They are both an expression of the magnificent, unlimited force of God. *They are all you.*

Always, in time and space, and beyond time and space, there is no separation. There is no distance between you and all of life. There is only love, beauty, joy, and the fulfillment that is God itself. Feel this each day of your life and you will rejoice in this lifetime—both in the life of it, and in the death of it.

CHAPTER EIGHT

Creating a New Personality

After you have met death as a human being, and after your personality matrix has passed through the after-death transition period in which the layers of earth confusion are peeled away and dissolved, there comes a point at which your personality matrix returns to a full awareness of itself as your soul. You become your soul again. Then, if you desire, you will begin the process of creating a new personality matrix that will eventually return into earth as your new human being. We shall put this process of creating a new human personality into words in order to lead you to a clearer understanding of how you as a soul participate in the unfoldment of earth life.

BECOMING YOUR SOUL AGAIN

First, during the after-death transition process, your personality becomes so deeply attuned to the eternal forces within your intuiting capacity that this becomes larger than all of the other "earth" capacities that are woven into your personality matrix. Your former capacities that sustained your human awareness, such as thought, emotion, ideation, conceptualization, and all of the other abilities that helped you live in earth while you were a human being, are over-shadowed by the magnificence of your reawakening *eternal* awareness, which is so much larger than your human capacities.

Then, as you come to the end of the after-death transition period, with your intuiting capacity now filled with the qualities of your eternal soul, rather than with the capacities of your human personality matrix, you begin to experience a reality that is *completely* filled with the divine forces of perfection, beauty, creativity, and love. All of your old limited and rigid human personality patterns dissolve. Everything that you have learned as an earth human being that is of value to your soul and the eternal universes begins to be infused with these growing forces of eternal truth within your inner sensings.

This is a magnificent, miraculous process in which *you are transforming yourself from a limited human personality back into the eternal soul that created that personality.* During this process, your conscious awareness of the incoming forces of your soul becomes stronger and stronger, until eventually, the process is complete when you realize: *"I am the soul!"* Then, rather than experiencing yourself as a human personality infused by a soul, *you once again experience the truth of yourself as an eternal soul that has created the human personality into which it pro-jected a portion of its consciousness.* That portion of soul consciousness that you previously experienced as your human self is expanded and merged with your full awareness of your eternal nature.

At this point, you are standing in the midst of the real truth that was obscured while you were a human being. You are totally aware of the magnificence and perfection of all of the vast universes in which you have your being as an eternal soul. You become aware of your intensely fulfilling and unending love relationship with the forces of God as they continually create you and sustain you in a constantly expanding experience of happiness and joy. You become aware of the vast continuous communication between all souls, and you consciously participate again in the subjective experience of each soul as a portion of their beings.

EVALUATING YOUR PAST LIFETIME

In this experience of awakening that we have described, you as a soul also have a complete knowledge of earth, including its origins, purposes, and destiny. You understand how it is that souls can rejoice in all portions of human life, even those that are so challenging for human beings, because you can directly experience that there is only good and love in all moments of reality.

Standing as your soul, you are aware of how you, along with other souls, drawing upon your perfect vision of all realities, have over watched the earth drama from its beginning, hoping that the human beings that the souls have created would use their free will to trust and love and understand one another, and thereby create in earth the perfection that you souls clearly perceive as all of reality.

With this vast, perfect understanding of earth life, you as a soul begin to look closely at the overall experience of your last human personality in order to assess its impact upon earth reality, and to integrate it perfectly into eternal reality. You are totally aware of each individual strand of the extremely complex consequences of every instant of the human life that your personality has just lived. You can see the many ways that your personality affected all of the human beings around it moment by moment throughout its earth lifetime. You can see clearly through all of the illusions that you created as a human being. You can see through the judgments, criticisms, doubts, and all of the fear that arose within your human personality. You can also see all of the creativity and love that your personality experienced, including the magnificent forces that existed in your personality that your personality was not aware of.

Next, you as a soul enter a period of intense study of your contribution to earth life. This study will expand your knowledge of creation. You look back at your most recent human life and relate it to all of your other human lifetimes in order to fill in the missing pieces, and to understand the many complexities that were hidden from your personality while you walked in earth. You work to broaden your soul understanding of the mysteries of earth life, to answer all of the questions that you generated as a human being, and to solve all of the riddles and puzzles for yourself, now that you have returned to your eternal awareness.

You also bring from your past personality matrix into your eternal soul a certain *newness* and *freshness* of energies. These are different energies that come from the subjective experiences of your past human personality matrix. They are energies that were created by that personality in its quite original and unpredictable use of human free will. These energies make a unique contribution to you as a soul. The realities of these energies could not have been created in any other way except by the individual way that you as a personality chose to live your human life on earth. The experiences created by "you-as-a-personality" are new and unique experiences that never existed prior to your living as that human being. Thus, you-as-a-personality have brought magnificent gifts to you-as-an-eternal-soul. Even though as a soul you experience yourself in eternal perfection, this perfection is not *closed*. It is not finalized. It is flexible, and changeable, and expandable. Thus, you as a soul, in accepting the gifts of your personality experience, have the great joy of experiencing yourself as an eternal soul who is being added to and expanded by the new and unique personality experiences that you created in your human lifetime. In this sense, your human lives are very important to you as a soul. They bring you a unique kind of expansiveness and fulfillment that you could not receive in any other way. In light of this, you can understand that your present human experience that you are living right now is not to be underestimated or taken lightly.

As you stand in your awareness of yourself as an eternal soul, it is quite obvious to you that nothing that your personality did in its just-completed lifetime as a human being was *bad*. As a soul, you have perfect understanding of all of the complicated factors that affected your human personality in each moment, all of the inner forces that were a portion of your personality's decisions and choices. You understand the fear that caused the personality, at times, to take actions that caused pain to others. You understand the reasons for all of the feelings, actions, and experiences that as a human being you would have judged to be negative. Thus, as you stand as your eternal soul, you can see your personality self in total goodness, with complete understanding. Therefore, as you assess the earth life of your personality, there is no judgment, criticism, or any other experience of negativity.

In this process of assessing your earth life, all of the other souls stand about you and work with you. They also view your earth creations in love, without making any judgments against your human personality. In the same way, God itself rejoices in your personality creation in total love, without judgment.

Judgment, criticism, and negativity are entirely human. They do not exist beyond the earth life. They exist only in the dimensions of reality in which the personality matrix is the largest subjective experience. Negativity is a creation of the human personality matrix living in physical forms. It can be carried forth for a while into the immediate period after death, because during that period the personality matrix is in charge. As we have pointed out, if the personality has strong habits of creating negativity, then those habits have a certain momentum, and they will take a while to fade away. But, they do not exist anywhere except within the *subjective experience* of the human personality matrix. And, they will eventually be dissolved in the love that is the truth of all reality.

CELEBRATING YOUR PAST PERSONALITY

To help you feel what it is like to have completed the after-death transition period and to stand as your true self, your eternal soul, merging with all of the experiences of your last personality matrix, we would ask that you would imagine a vision of a beautiful mountain. You have lived on this mountain for a long time, and it has been quite joyful for you. But, you desired to explore the other mountains and valleys around you, so you sent your beloved child forth to explore those areas for you. This beloved one is such an intimate part of you that what that one experiences will be your experience. Thus, your child has gone forth for many years to explore the other mountains and valleys. Now that child has returned, and you call together all of your friends and your beloved ones who live with you on this mountain peak and you make a grand feast to celebrate the matured child who has returned to you. All of you gather about in great joy and love to embrace this returned traveler. There is feasting, laughing, singing, and dancing as all of the souls celebrate the return.

These are the human equivalents of the kinds of feelings that you would have as a soul when you take your personality matrix back into your being. While this personality has been living in earth, you have been aware of yourself as an eternal soul. Now, as you celebrate the return of your personality, you are giving to your personality the great experiences of joy that you have had as the eternal soul, and your personality is giving to you its experiences of the earth realities that it has explored in its human life.

To extend our image further, you could see the returned traveler telling the assembled souls great tales of the earth adventures, sharing experiences with them in a much more intense way than earth words share when you tell stories. You as a soul create energies that allow your personality matrix to share in a way that literally *re-creates* all of the earth experiences that the personality had in earth. Thus, in this period of celebration, all of the assembled souls can re-live all of the earth experiences with your personality and with you as a soul. The souls literally participate in the adventures of the returned personality matrix through merging with you as a soul.

Through the same kinds of energies, you as a soul also participate in the earth experiences of the returned personalities of all other souls who are concerned with earth. So, there is a vast, continuous, complex process of celebrating and rejoicing and absorbing all of the earth experiences of all souls. However, you as a soul feel more uniquely aligned with and aware of the earth experiences of your own particular personality matrix that you have projected into earth, and that has now returned to you through death.

Now, there is an even more complex process taking place within you as a soul that is quite difficult to capture in words. As you absorb your returning personality matrix, you are also experiencing and celebrating all of your past personality projections that have lived in earth through all of the eons of earth time. Also, in very deep ways, you are participating in all of the vast personality projections of all of the many souls who are concerned with earth. Even though in human words this seems vastly complex, to you as a soul it is simply your ordinary reality. And, it is a magnificent, beautiful, stimulating, and fulfilling reality.

So that we would not stray too far from the important issues of your present life, we would not wish to go further into the larger experiences of the soul. For the time, let us leave it at this. Say to yourself in this moment:

"If I wish to imagine what it feels like to be standing as my soul, having merged with the energies that are my present human personality matrix, then I can use this vision and this feeling to come near to the truth. I can imagine myself in the beautiful, magnificent feasting hall, celebrating in total love, joy, and creativity, all that this personality has lived and experienced throughout its lifetime. As a soul with total understanding and love, I am joyfully absorbing even the experiences that seemed negative to my personality. I feel myself embracing my personality in love, and I am being loved in return by it. I feel the eternal majesty of all love, all being. Here is the truth of my existence, and here is the truth of that loving force of God that animates all life. In this I am complete. I am whole. So it always has been. So it always shall be."

If you would work with these truths each day, you would find that your understanding of yourself as an eternal soul would grow, and this would illuminate your present experience as a human being.

YOUR REMAINING EARTH PATTERNS

After this period of celebrating and rejoicing at the return of your personality matrix, there comes a point at which you as an eternal soul, clearly aware of what you and all souls are attempting to create in the earth reality, begin to determine which of the forces left behind in earth by your last personality tend to amplify and exaggerate the negative forces that living human beings are creating out of their fear. To do this, you will look back into earth from your soul point of view, seeing the entire life of your personality in different ways. First, you see it, and understand it, and feel it as all of the *subjective experiences* that your personality had while it lived. At the same time, you will experience other layers that your personality was not aware of, including all of the patterns of all of your past personalities. You will have a perfect understanding of how the most recent lifetime as a human being will either heal some of the old negative patterns from previous personalities, or how it will tend to exaggerate those patterns. Even though all of these patterns are vastly complex, they will be perfectly clear to you, and you will immediately begin to make plans for new adjustments of those patterns that do not clearly reflect the eternal perfection of God. You will be adjusting the patterns of pain, misunderstanding, depression, judgment, guilt, and so forth—all of the areas that arise from human fear—that were created by your past personality.

To help you clarify this, we will return to the idea discussed earlier: that the individual subjective patterns that your personality brings to the door of death are "packets" of energy. The packets of energy that your personality created in love, understanding, and honesty are of the same frequency or vibration rate as the eternal forces of your existence as a soul. Thus, those energies pass through death along with the personality matrix and are soon merged with you as the soul. However, the human experiences of your personality that grew out of human fear, and that were dark and painful, are of a heavy, dense frequency that has a reality only in physical matter. In the eternal sense, these "negative" energies are not real, thus there is no way for them to exist beyond physical death, unless they are temporarily kept alive in the subjective experience of the personality matrix for a short while after death. But, eventually, the negative energies are thrown off and are no longer a part of your personality matrix or of you as a soul. They then become the packets of heavy energy that can exist only within the temporary energy vibrations of the physical earth.

Thus, the energy of the negative experiences of your personality are left behind in earth. That is the only place where energies of such a dense vibration can exist. Since they have been created by you as a human personality infused with divine force, then they are creations imbued with a certain power, or *continuing* force. They are rather weak energies, but they do temporarily have a continuing life, even though they are not embodied in physical form. In a certain sense, they are forces of God that have been entrusted into the personality matrix, and, through the unintentional distortion of those energies by the fear of the human personality, they have been made so heavy and dense that they cannot continue to evolve through earth unless they are transformed.

For example, if you have lived as a human being with a great hatred for your neighbor, while you were alive that hatred existed only within your subjective experience within your body. When you have completed the after-death transition period, the hatred cannot go with the eternal forces of your personality matrix because the hatred is of a different energy. Yet, since it was created by you as a human being infused with divine force, the hatred will not simply evaporate or dissolve. It has a certain feeble kind of energy existence of its own. After the death of your body, this negative energy packet becomes a small dark cloud in the energy of the earth.

Now, from the earth point of view, the problem here is that *you* are the only one who can dissolve that cloud. Ordinarily, the dark, heavy energy packets created by your personality cannot be altered by any other human being, or any other soul. The agreement of souls in their creation of earth is that each soul will take responsibility for its own creations, and the projection of the soul as a human person-ality matrix in a physical body will be the vehicle by which the earth forces will be manipulated.

All of the souls see this situation in perfect love and understanding, for there is no fear or negativity of any kind in the souls. The souls understand that the heavy energy packets left behind in earth are not bad. They are only distortions that cannot be immediately assimilated into the eternal fabric of life. They are unintentional "mutations" of the God forces that the souls do not desire to continue.

So, as you stand as a soul reviewing the kinds of nega-tive energy packets that your last personality has left in earth, you begin to ascertain what kind of *new* personality matrix would be necessary to send into a human body in order to re-create some of the fear patterns that were involved in the original creation of the heavy energy packets. By re-creating the same fear patterns and combining them with strength, wisdom, understanding, and love in a new human personality, the new personality can face again the challenging experiences that caused the fear, and, *the personality can transform the fear patterns through love.*

What we have described in a very simple way is the experience of a soul who chooses to create *another* personality matrix and project it into another human form. However, if you as an eternal soul choose to *end* your direct participation in the earth reality, you can choose *not* to send forth another personality projection to dissolve those remaining heavy energy packets left behind. You can freely choose to "transfer" the responsibility for this task to another soul. Now, we must remind you that choices of this kind are always made in love and joy, with a recognition that there is no badness in those heavy earth packets of energy. There is no negative feeling at all in the soul that is asked to take on the responsibility for the transformation of those packets in your place. It is an intense joy for another soul to combine the transformation of your heavy energy packets with the transformation of its own.

This kind of reality is an area that simply cannot be conveyed accurately in words. So, we ask that you take our very simple explanation lightly and playfully, knowing that it has many more deep implications that cannot be verbalized. Our purpose here is to help you understand that you are truly *free* as a soul. You as a soul are not forced to project a personality into human form. It is an extraordinary *opportunity* for which you as a soul are extremely grateful. You are always free as a soul to choose to turn your attention *away* from earth reality whenever it pleases you. You are not trapped in earth expression simply because your personality matrix was unable to heal its patterns of fear in a human lifetime.

CREATING YOUR NEW PERSONALITY

To help you feel the unlimited freedom of choice that you have as a soul when you begin to create another personality matrix to project into earth form, we would ask you to imagine that you are now looking at a large *catalog*. This is such a vast catalog that it would take millions of volumes to contain it. And, you would imagine yourself as a soul able to *instantly* read all of the volumes of this catalog at the same time, and to know, in one instant, everything contained in the millions of volumes. The volumes contain *all* of the possible qualities of a human being. You as a soul are now sensing and perceiving *every conceivable potential that a human being could ever manifest. From this vast potential, without any restrictions, you are free to choose what you will put into your next personality matrix.*

It is very important that you as a presently living human being understand and feel that when your soul created your *present* personality, your soul had this total command of all possibilities. From all of those possibilities, your soul, aligned with the infinite wisdom of God itself, created what it considered to be the perfect personality for you in this lifetime. If you can understand this, then you can begin to feel the magnificence that lies within your present human personality.

Now, to return to the vision of you as a soul preparing

the next personality matrix that you will project into earth, first you would see yourself absorbing all of your understandings about your assessment of your past personality and its life. Then, using the eternal forces of God, you begin to create the energy patterns for the new personality matrix. Drawing from the infinite catalog of human capacities, you infuse into the new personality matrix all of the beautiful abilities that you wish to have fulfilled in the life of the new personality. This can include continuation of past lifetime experiences that were cut short or that were incompletely fulfilled in earth. You would also place into the new personality matrix all of the strengths and creative abilities that the personality will need in order to heal any packets of heavy earth energy that you are responsible for transforming.

Even though our words have made the transformation of the heavy packets of energy appear to be important, we must point out that in truth, this is a very minor consideration to you as a soul. If all of the beautiful purposes of your new personality were represented by millions of grains of sand on the shore, then the issue of transforming the heavy energy packets would be represented by only a few grains of that sand. You as a soul are primarily concerned with all of the qualities of magnificence that you wish to experience throughout the human lifetime of the new personality that you have created. Your primary focus as a soul is to weave into the energies of this personality matrix much beauty and love, and many capacities for that new personality to have human experiences of fulfillment that will directly reflect the perfection of yourself as a soul, and thereby the perfection of God.

As you create your new personality, you work with all of the souls who occupy themselves with earth. Their love and their creativity are forces that are woven into the energies of your new personality matrix. Also, in a very complex way, the God forces that create you as a soul, and that animate you and maintain your being, become a portion of this energy matrix that will be the new personality.

Due to the complexity, it would not be of benefit to you for us to describe in further detail the process of creating a new personality. Therefore, we will turn now to the kind of momentum that you would begin to create as a soul in order to make it possible for this energy matrix that will be your new personality to be re-directed into the forces that make up the physical earth reality.

PROJECTING YOUR PERSONALITY INTO EARTH

In order to project your new personality matrix into a new human body, you as a soul set into motion a process of reintegrating the non-physical energies of the new personality matrix into the physical energies of the earth reality. This will enable the personality to become a physical human being, born to human parents.

Imagine this new personality matrix as a vast sphere of energy. And here we will echo our original way of visualizing the coming into earth, as expressed in an earlier portion of these teachings. Imagine this vast, complex sphere of energy of the new personality matrix permeated with your awareness of yourself as a soul. At first, this new personality clearly feels itself to be a portion of you, the soul. Your subjective experience as a soul is that this new personality lives *inside* of you.

Gradually, as a soul, you begin to adjust the largest portion of this new sphere of personality energy, which is what we have called the intuiting capacity. Because of the focus upon the intuiting capacity, this sphere of personality energy is permeated primarily with the forces of intuitive perception of God, which is your nature as an eternal soul.

In this beginning period of manifestation, the new personality matrix and you as a soul are essentially the same. But, gradually, all of the other forces that are latent human qualities that exist in this sphere of personality begin to expand and grow larger. This expansion is guided by you as a soul, and by other souls, particularly the souls of those two human beings who will be the human father and mother to your new personality as it enters fetus form. There is a slow, gradual process of change of energies in which the latent *human* qualities become stronger in the personality matrix, and the intuiting capacity that brings awareness of *eternal* realities becomes weaker. This is the important movement and momentum that you as a soul will generate as you project the new personality matrix from yourself toward the physical earth reality.

Next, you would see the sphere of energy of the new personality coming "toward" the physical earth (speaking in terms of earth direction). As the personality sphere comes toward earth, the latent human qualities continue to expand, and the intuiting capacity continues to contract. As a result of this process, the *feeling* quality of this sphere of personality energy changes. Recalling that this sphere of personality energy is *aware of itself,* and, in its beginning period it was aware of itself as the soul that created it, as this process of change occurs, the personality begins to experience itself as being *different* than the soul. It begins to feel like a *personality*, with only a thread of eternal soul force in it.

BECOMING HUMAN AGAIN

You as the new personality begin to feel: "I am a personality, and I perceive clearly that I have been created by a soul that is eternal." This is the point at which you first begin to become *human* again. Instead of being aware of yourself as an eternal soul that has created a portion of yourself as a personality matrix, you now become aware of yourself as a new personality who has been created by a soul.

You as a personality also begin to feel that the soul is *larger* than you. This is an aspect of the necessary *diminishing* process that must take place in order for the divine forces of your personality matrix to be "squeezed" small enough to enter a physical body. The kind of awareness that can enter a physical body is much, much narrower than your true awareness that remains with your eternal soul. To say this in another way, the vibration rate of your eternal soul forces must be slowed down in order to enter the dense and heavy energy of the physical earth reality.

As you imagine these realities that we are describing, it will help you understand that in your present life, any feelings of human smallness are an *illusion*. Such feelings are simply a necessary aspect, at this point in human evolution, of coming into physical form. In future times of earth, when you ones as human beings have learned to love enough, and to expand your human personality enough, you will literally transform the nature of physical reality from inside of it. Eventually, you will make physical reality large enough so that the *entire* awareness of your eternal soul can exist within a human form.

After conception is achieved in the body of your new human mother, and after it has been determined that the birth of the child will be physically accomplished, you as a personality energy matrix will move closer to physical reality. As this takes place, there is a further diminishing of your awareness of the eternal realities. Eventually, you as a personality begin to experience yourself as *one unique being*. During this stage, you still have an awareness of the fact that you have been created by your soul, that you are joined to all other souls, and that you are a part of other new personalities who are in transition toward earth as you are. You are also aware that you are joined to all other beings who are expressing in earth in human forms, and you are clearly aware that you are joined to all beings who are coming through death and making their transition back to their souls. At this point, you have total awareness of all of reality, but your subjective feelings are that you are experiencing all of it *inside* of your unique personality matrix.

In coming closer to your physical birth as a new human being, as we have described earlier, you consciously participate with your soul and other souls in the manipulation of forces that will create the physical fetus form that your soul desires for you. You as a personality are aware of your relationship to all of the patterns that your soul wishes you to manifest in your forthcoming lifetime. However, gradually, you begin the process of identifying with the new fetus form; thus, your vision of the broader purposes will dim. At this point, your subjective experience would be very difficult to describe for you, but it would be similar to having the experience of hovering about your human mother and father, and beginning to perceive, in a faint cloudy way, what they experience in their physical reality. You would not be able to perceive the tangible earth reality in any clarity. That would not come until after you have access to your *physical* perceptive capacities that live in your growing fetus form.

As your fetus form is growing within the womb of your mother, in great love, you are hovering about the personality matrices of your new physical parents. You are also perceiving your soul and all of its purposes for projecting you into your present personality. So, at this point, you are clearly aware that there is only good. You see that there is only perfection in the earth life that you are about to enter. You are aware of any physical, mental, or emotional defects that your soul might purposely create in your new fetus form, as well as any challenging situations that may arise in your new family, and you have a complete understanding of how these will enrich the human life that you will live. You clearly understand the purpose of every single thread of energy that makes up the complex patterns of your new personality.

This is a period in which you as a personality are still experiencing total truth. You can clearly understand that shortly there will be your physical birth, and you will voluntarily relinquish your conscious awareness of the eternal realities, including your direct perception of your soul and the reality of God. You know that in order to live this new human life that you are about to undertake, in order to successfully fulfill and rejoice in this new earth adventure, it is necessary for you to begin to squeeze yourself into the limited perceptions of one ordinary human being who is aware of itself only as a *body*, a *mind*, and *emotions*. You know that you are about to enter what, from the earth point of view, appears to be a very narrow and limited mode of existence. But you as a new personality matrix, with your eternal wisdom still intact, are rejoicing because you understand that, indeed, your coming into a human life is a miraculous instant in creation in which you will experience *the intensified focus of God forces directed toward the unique experience of being one subjective human being.*

The intensity of the human subjective personality experience is indeed a miracle. The capacity of the soul to concentrate a portion of its eternal awareness into such a reduced band of the energy spectrum is an extraordinary achievement by the soul and the God forces. All of the intensity of thought and feeling that you have as a human being is a result of this achievement. In time, you ones of earth will understand the miracle of this. You will feel it, appreciate it, and rejoice in it. At the present time, for many human beings, if they compare their ordinary inner experience with the vastness of the universes and the broader affairs of the soul, they will judge their earth life to be not so important. This is a human response that will change in the near future.

However, you as that new personality matrix preparing for your physical birth can directly experience the miraculous nature of the human existence that you are about to begin. Thus, with great gratitude, you are celebrating your opportunity to enter into the brilliantly intense human experience once more. You are rejoicing in the love relationships that you will renew with those in earth who are joined to you from your past lifetimes. You are eagerly anticipating taking up again the passionate and exciting pursuits of earth life fulfillment. The adventure truly does beckon to you.

The next change that comes about in your movement toward your physical birth is a clouding over of your subjective experience that brings about a gradual diminishing of your conscious awareness of the eternal realities. This experience is similar to passing through a thick layer of fog. Before you enter the fog, you can clearly see your soul and all of the other eternal realities about you. As you go into the fog, these realities begin to fade. As you emerge from the fog, you find that your fetus body has been born as a living child and you are gradually beginning to receive your awareness of yourself as one human being living within a physical body.

Next comes the growth of your child body, and, eventually, the explosion of *self-awareness* in your body that we have described earlier. You become consciously aware of yourself as a human being, with only a very faint awareness of the eternal realities stirring in your intuitive sensings. As we have described earlier, your awareness of yourself gradually becomes associated with your physical body and your inner subjective *human* realities, while the awareness of eternal realities settles into unconscious patterns within your intuiting capacity. When all of this has been accomplished, you have truly been born as a new human being.

The truth of this human birth is indeed a cause for celebration, for it is an event of great magnitude. It is quite appropriate that you ones of earth celebrate birthdays in joy, laughter, singing, giving, and loving.

If you reflect upon this birth process that we have described for you, you can begin to understand how miraculous it is that your human birth enables you to live fully within the subjective intensity of one human being who can freely *create* life at will; who can create, moment after moment, for an entire lifetime, what you *desire* in your reality. And, due to the narrowed perceptions of your human personality, you have the luxury of creating your life as a human being without distraction by all of the complexities of the eternal realities.

Now, if at this point in your present life you have had experiences of sadness and pain that at times cause you to feel, "My birth does not seem to me to be such a fortunate event, for it has cast me into a world of sorrow, pain, and suffering," we can assure you, these are only your *emotions*. They are not the truth. You will learn to understand these emotions, to live them, and to heal them. And, eventually, if you are willing to love enough, in this lifetime you will know the truth of what we have said about human birth, and you will indeed celebrate your birth into this life. You will celebrate yourself as you build your life in joy, love, and deep fulfillment. You will come to bless yourself in this earth adventure, just as your soul, all other souls, and God itself continue to bless you moment by moment as you live your present human life.

CHOICES OTHER THAN HUMAN LIFE

As an eternal soul standing beyond earth, you are free to choose *not* to create a new personality matrix to infuse into human form. If that is your desire, then most likely you will choose to participate in a non-physical reality that is an *extension* of the earth reality. This would be an existence that is similar to human life, a world in which many souls who have chosen not to continue to project portions of themselves into human form create a new reality that is a further expression of their desire that led them to create physical reality in the first place.

To simplify this, we would say that these souls are expressing in what can be seen as, from your human point of view, the *next stage* of human evolution. They are expressing in a realm that is very similar to earth life, but in this extension of earth reality there are no energies of negativity. The love, joy, and beauty that you ones are now learning to create in earth is extended and magnified many fold to create an even more beautiful form of existence. This is made possible by the experience that the souls have gained by living in physical earth through their human personalities.

In this non-physical realm of existence, the souls can participate directly with the fullness of their beings. There is no need to project portions of themselves into personalities. Within the subjective experiences of the souls who exist in this realm, when there would arise feelings that in earth would have become fear, the soul in its enlightenment and wisdom can immediately understand such an impulse and can instantly transform it in love. Thus, in this new realm, there is no negativity, for there is such mastery that any such energy is dissolved by love before it can manifest tangibly.

The difficulty in communicating to you about this non-physical realm lies in the fact that in a very mysterious way, this new realm is woven together with your present earth experience. This realm is made up of some of the same divine energies as earth realities, and, in certain non-physical ways, the two worlds interpenetrate each other. So, if you stand as a soul beyond earth and choose not to return your energies and forces into earth as a new human personality, and if you choose to express in this new realm, which we would call for your purposes the "evolved earth," then you as a soul would contain within you a simultaneous conscious awareness of the evolved earth and the physical earth reality. You would "live" in the evolved earth, but, in very deep and intimate ways, you would be connected with physical human beings in earth.

As a soul living in the evolved earth, one of the choices that you could make would be to *guide* living human beings on earth, bringing forth your soul wisdom from your more evolved understanding. In such a capacity, you would be considered to be a spiritual guide, or guiding-one to a human being. Remind yourself that even as you functioned as such a guiding-one, you would still be aware of yourself as an eternal soul consciously experiencing all universes, all realities. Your own personal *subjective* experiences would be focused intensely and primarily in the evolved earth. You would also have an awareness of physical human beings walking in the present earth, and you would interact in non-physical ways with their subjective lives.

You as a guiding-one to a physical human being would literally live within the heart of that human being throughout their physical lifetime.

If you as a soul living in the evolved earth decided that you were satisfied with your experiences in that realm, then you could shift your existence into an even broader and more magnificent reality that would be a further extension of the evolved earth. You would have your existence in this even larger world, yet you would retain your awareness of both the evolved earth and the physical earth.

To express this in a simple way, we would say that in the stream of evolution that the souls have set into motion, an evolution that includes the physical earth, there are many unfolding non-physical realms of existence that grow out of one another, each new one larger and more beautiful than the one that has gone before. These evolving realities offer very intense experiences for you as an eternal soul. Over a period of what you in earth would speak of as *time* (and the period of which we are speaking would be extremely vast if expressed in a context of time), all of these evolving realities of the soul ultimately grow to the eternal completeness of the soul's *original* awareness of itself as an eternal portion of God.

The "first" stream of evolution was the God forces that brought about the existence of the souls and made possible their original awareness of themselves as a portion of God. The "second" stream of evolution consists of the evolving realities (including the earth reality) that have been set into motion by the souls themselves in their own creativity. This new second stream of evolution that you as a soul, working with all other souls, have been responsible for, has *intensi-*

fied the first eternal creation of God itself. Thus, you ones as souls, in concert with God, have augmented the majesty of creation in ways that are important to the souls and to God itself.

Therefore, we could say that beyond earth the choices of you as a soul are actually infinite. You have *chosen* to express within the earth reality, and you can choose to express beyond the earth reality in an infinite number of ways as an aspect of the "second" stream of evolution created by the souls.

For now, let us leave these vast realms of yourself as an eternal soul and return to your human personality as it presently exists in earth. To help you appreciate the beauty of your own personality as it lives in this magnificent earth adventure, we will now suggest a way of using your imagination to bring about greater feelings of love for yourself. If you would take a period of time to love yourself in each day, we can assure you that eventually your struggles, confusions, pains, and fears would be healed in the great energies of love that you would create within yourself.

We would ask that in this moment you would imagine that you are stepping outside of your present personality. Using the power of your imagination, see yourself as if you are your own beloved child. You have such love and appreciation for this beautiful child. You would never condemn or abuse this child. You would always understand this child, with gentleness and tenderness. In this moment, you can view yourself as this child that you are willing to love and appreciate. By allowing this love for yourself, you will be able to feel more clearly the magnificence of the eternal

forces that are now expressing through your personality—
the forces of your own soul, of your guiding-ones, and of
God itself.

By seeing the innocence of the child within you, you
soften your heart, you release any judgments that you have
toward yourself, and you allow a stronger flow of the
eternal love that lives within you. By taking a few moments
each day to step backward from the confusions of your
earth life and feel yourself as a beloved child, you will
establish a place in your heart where there is *always* love
for your personality. If you take this time each day to
experience feelings of love for yourself, then most certainly
you will come to rejoice in this human being that is you,
and you will live your life in confidence, joy, and great
fulfillment.

We believe that the teachings that we are communicating to you can help you in different ways. But we believe that the most important gift we can give you is to
stimulate your capacity to recognize the magnificence of
yourself as a human being; to encourage your willingness
to love the human being that you are in this moment. If you
can do this, then, even if you would accomplish nothing
else in this lifetime, you would rejoice throughout your life,
and you would celebrate and fulfill your desires until your
physical death.

So, in this moment, if you are willing to love yourself
as a human being, you are coming nearer to perceiving
yourself as an eternal soul. In this moment, if you are
willing to love yourself deeply enough, you are coming
closer to experiencing God. That God lives within you *now*,
within your human personality, and it lives within you

eternally, in your existence as a soul. Feel this now, to the best of your ability, and you will make a deep inroad to understanding all of life.

CHAPTER NINE

Living Your Soul In Earth

You can consciously adjust your personality as you live in the physical earth reality so that the eternal forces that come forth from your soul can be manifested in great perfection within your human life. There are many ways that this can be done. But, you as a personality must decide how much attention you wish to give to this pursuit in your day to day life.

You are free to choose to focus all of your attention on your earth life, which would include your physical desires, and your thoughts and feelings having to do with living a physical life. This can bring about an earth life of satisfaction and beauty that can deeply fulfill you as a human being under ordinary circumstances. However, in earth life, you may have noticed that there are experiences that arise at times that seem to cause you pain. When you live your life focused *only* on creating a pleasurable *physical* existence for yourself, you may discover that during periods of pain and deep crisis in your life, your "earth" focus is not stabilizing enough for you. You may come to feel that a life lived only at the physical level does not give you a deep enough feeling of goodness to bring you the comfort, trust, and healing that you need during periods of intense personal challenge.

In the ancient times of earth, when human beings first created the forces of fear that began to distort earth life, the confusion within the human race became so great that people came to believe that the physical earth reality was all that existed. Thus, the guiding influences projected from the souls to the human personalities of the time were directed in such a way as to influence the human beings to shake off their overbalanced preoccupation with physical earth reality. The souls attempted to inspire the human beings to become more deeply attuned to eternal aspects of reality—that which you would speak of as the *spiritual* forces of life.

However, since that early time, through many human civilizations, there have been different fluctuating cycles of experience for the human race in general. At certain times, the ability of human beings to attune to God and the spiritual forces of life became very great. This resulted in a period of time in which there was an over-balance toward the eternal realities, causing human beings to lose the intensity and excitement of the physical world. They became preoccupied with non-physical life beyond earth. During those periods, the guiding influence of the souls was directed toward bringing the human race back toward a love for the physical life.

In the *present* period of earth life in which you live, humanity is coming out of a cycle of preoccupation with *physical* reality. This is not to say that all human beings have been totally caught up in this, but simply that many ones have been over-focused upon their physical earth fulfillments, and have generally lost the sense of the eternal realities in their *conscious* subjective experience. Thus, there is now an influence from the souls to bring the attention of humanity back to the spiritual realities.

In the present time, even though there are many human beings preoccupied with physical fulfillment, there are also a growing number of people who have found that physical accomplishments do not always sustain them during periods of crisis. For example, many have discovered that at the time of the death of a loved one, as they struggle with their sorrow and pain, the size of their bank account is of little comfort to them. In the situation of a broken marriage and the loss of love, successfulness in a career is not always enough to help you feel fulfilled.

Thus, at this time, due to the past preoccupation with physical pleasures and accomplishments, many of you ones of earth are learning to turn toward the spiritual realities, often through challenging situations. The challenges create a need for you to believe that life goes deeper than the *physical* realities of earth, which can be very painful at times. When you are feeling lost, frightened, and in pain, there is a need to know that you are tied to a reality that is not painful; a reality that is beautiful, and good, and filled with love; a reality that can never be diminished by your present temporary pain.

There are other human beings who are now beginning to turn toward an understanding of the eternal realities out of a desire to expand the joy and love in human life. They are following the deep soul influences that are flowing into their intuiting capacities. This brings about the sense of happiness and fulfillment that is the *intended* experience for human beings walking the face of the earth.

We are not suggesting that this re-awakening of interest in the eternal realities of life will mean that you must turn away from your physical earth fulfillments. Those fulfillments are very important to you as an individual, and it is important to human life that individuals be fulfilled in their earth affairs. But, as many people are now learning, if you can weave your fulfillment in earth affairs with a deep capacity to live the *eternal* portions of your being, then you will find the greatest happiness, fulfillment, and joy throughout your lifetime.

As we now turn our attention toward the kind of human experiences that can help you gain perception of the eternal spiritual realities that infuse your personality, we will be speaking of forces that ordinarily remain unconscious in your life. We will examine certain areas that are quite different from your ordinary conscious experience. These are areas of experience that are on the "borderline" between the physical reality of earth and the non-physical reality of eternal realms. The most common of these borderline experiences is the state of *sleep*.

YOUR EXPERIENCE OF SLEEP

There are many things that take place in your personality as you sleep. Some of those things are related to your physical earth life, and some have to do with your soul and its eternal realities. Human sleep is a very broad and complex area, and each human being will have their own unique purposes to accomplish during sleep periods. Therefore, we will simplify by generalizing about the kinds of patterns that are unfolded by most human beings.

First of all, to help you understand what occurs in your sleep state, we will use a simple vision. Imagine that your physical body is represented by a small cabin by a lake. You have come to this cabin for a vacation from your ordinary life. You desire to fulfill yourself and to have an adventure. In a way similar to this, we could say that your soul projects a portion of itself into your present physical body in order to have an adventurous outing, a temporary adventure that is set apart from the ordinary experience of the soul.

When you go to your cabin for a vacation, if you spend the entire period of your adventure time staying in the cabin, your experience will be rather restricted. It is the same for that part of your soul that has come into your body as your personality. If your personality spends all of its time in the cabin of your bodily life—your daily waking experience—then your earth adventure will be restricted.

The fullness of the adventure comes when you can at times leave the cabin and go to the lake to swim and to fish. You are happiest when you can do things that are an *extension* of staying in the cabin, and are not limited by that narrower range of experience. It is similar with your soul. If you as a human being did not need to sleep for physical rejuvenation, and you remained awake and active in your earth body, mind, and emotions for an entire lifetime without ever sleeping, you would have an extremely limited experience of the earth adventure. This is because the period of sleep, in addition to being necessary for the physical rejuvenation of human bodies, was also created by the souls as a way of temporarily *extracting* the portion of themselves that is the human personality from the confines of the physical body in order to diversify and complexify the human experience. The sleep period allows the human personality matrix to temporarily step back from the limits of earth in order to expand itself into the larger eternal realities in which the soul exists. So, one of the most important purposes of human sleep is: *to temporarily free the personality matrix from the confines of the physical body, and to free the human self-awareness from the limits of subjective personality creations, including thoughts, emotions, ideas, and desires.*

However, most of this beneficial sleep activity takes place in a state of total unconsciousness, from your human point of view. The magnificent sleep work that is done with your personality by your soul will take place during a period of "blankness," during which you experience no dreams and no conscious awareness. Ordinarily, this will occur each evening, if you have not over-agitated your body prior to sleep through traumatic fearful experiences, or by the ingestion of too much of the chemicals of earth, such as caffeine, alcohol, or drugs of different kinds.

During this blank period of sleep, your *true* personality self—the portion of your soul consciousness that lives in your body—will experience a lifting up out of the heaviness and solidness of the earth reality. *This true self then becomes aware of the nature of all of the eternal realities.* This happens night after night throughout your entire human lifetime. Thus, you can understand that human life does not separate your personality from your soul reality.

Your human personality matrix is involved in this expanded experience in a rather complex way. Your ordinary *conscious* mind that is associated with your brain is blank, and it remains unaware of what is taking place. But, your human personality self, drawing upon a different portion of the personality matrix that is not tied to the physical body, is completely aware of being drawn away from the body and going forth to "study" with your own soul. This deeper aspect of your personality merges with your soul and with your own guiding-ones, to re-spark and rejuvenate the divine energies within your personality matrix.

Each day, in your *waking* conscious life, you are constantly being infused with the forces of your soul and of God, even though you are usually unaware of this. In your sleeping life, this infusion is intensified, and the deeper portion of your personality becomes aware of what is taking place.

In this union between your personality and your soul that occurs during sleep, you are studying the eternal realities in order to bring them back into your earth patterns. The hope of your soul is that this will spark your *conscious* mind, which is in control while you are awake, to become more sensitive to these unconscious truths that have been learned during sleep. Your soul is attempting to inspire your conscious mind to *choose* to draw the eternal forces up into conscious reality so that you will desire to understand the spiritual aspects of your nature. You are being fed with eternal forces that can later come into your conscious awareness as inspiration and motivation for your personality to seek truth, to seek knowledge of God.

For clarity, we will speak of the portion of your personality matrix that is aware of what is taking place during these blank periods of sleep as the *inner wisdom* portion of you. This inner wisdom portion stands in the middle between your ordinary waking consciousness and your soul. During your sleep, the inner wisdom portion of your personality, of which you are ordinarily unaware, attempts to *translate* the experiences of deep sleep learning with your soul into a knowledge that can be absorbed by your ordinary conscious mind. Thus, the inner wisdom portion of you will transform the experiences of spiritual learning that take place during the blank sleep period into input that your conscious mind can accept and understand. It does this by creating *dream* experiences. Although your conscious mind is not aware of your merging with your soul during the blank period of sleep, your mind *can* be aware of the dream experiences that your inner wisdom portion creates from the spiritual knowledge. Thus, these dream experiences can eventually become communications from your soul to your conscious personality.

The difficulty here is that the spiritual energies and forces that make up the experiences that you have when you study with your soul during sleep are of such a different quality of reality that they cannot be fed *directly* to your conscious mind. Your conscious mind simply could not perceive them or understand them. They are experiences of a totally different nature that are difficult to describe in words. They would be similar to intense feelings of love and majesty; yet, these spiritual realities go far beyond such human feelings.

Thus, your inner wisdom portion attempts to transform these spiritual energies into dream experiences that are roughly equivalent to the kinds of teachings that you receive as you study with your soul in those deep sleep periods each evening. However, at this point in human evolution, dreams are a very *crude* translation of the spiritual realities. Yet, they are all that the conscious minds of you ones will accept. Since human minds insist upon translating all realities into the images, feelings, and thoughts of your ordinary physical earth reality, for your dreams to be accepted by you, they need to be constructed so that they have the same look and feel as your physical life. This tends to distort them from the original spiritual reality from which they emerge.

The clarity of your human dreams is further confused when your mind and emotions are strained by experiences of fear, or by physical disturbances to your body. In other words, when your body, and your mental and emotional patterns are not balanced in your day to day waking life, then, during the dreaming period in which your inner wisdom portion is attempting to communicate the teachings of your soul to your conscious mind, your mental and emotional patterns that are rooted in earth confusion tend to *distort* the dream experiences created by your inner wisdom portion. Thus, your dream experiences can become confusing disturbances, rather than lessons of truth.

We will give an example to help you feel this area. Imagine that you are a male one who has lived in earth in many times in the past in which there was war and strife. At the present time, you tend to be quite frightened about the state of the earth, because of the many small wars that are taking place.

During your deep sleep period, when your conscious

mind is blank and you have left your body, your inner wisdom portion goes forth and learns from your soul that it is *human fear* that is causing the wars in earth. This portion of you learns that fear can be healed and that wars can cease. You learn the truth that there is no badness, and eventually the earth struggles will heal as human beings are willing to love. There is no reason to fear the present earth violence.

The inner wisdom portion of you attempts to bring this teaching of truth back to your ordinary conscious awareness as a dream in which you see different groups of human beings who are presently making war against one another, coming forth to resolve their differences and to create an earth civilization of great majesty and beauty. But, your fearful earth personality patterns are so strong and so deeply rooted in skepticism that you feel that peace is not possible. Then, those kind of negative patterns are unconsciously woven with the dream experience. This causes you to experience the dream as a cruel joke. In the dream you see a person believing that human beings will love one another and create peace, and you see that person as being ridiculous, a figure to laugh at, one of ignorance and unwillingness to face what you consider to be the earth *facts*. Then, instead of the dream teaching you the truth, it simply reinforces your own patterns of negativity.

We give this as an example so that you may understand the complexity that the inner wisdom portion of you faces in attempting to communicate truth to your conscious mind through dreams. Since your dreams can be so easily distorted, it is not beneficial to become too preoccupied with an understanding of your dreams. You can remind yourself that your primary purpose is to live the *waking* portions of your life.

If you wish to begin to investigate some of the mysteries of your own personality and your larger being, then your dreams can be a possible area of study. However, we remind you that it requires honesty and clarity on your part to recognize the unintentional distortions that your fearful personality patterns can bring to your dreams. Thus, in working with your dreams, you will need to say to yourself: "If my interpretations of my dreams lead me to believe that there is badness in myself, in others, or in life, then I can rest assured that this dream that I am studying, or my understanding of it, has been distorted by my own fear. If my interpretation of the dream is leading me to greater love, and to feelings of truth and strength, then I can consider the *possibility* that I am accurately understanding the truth that was taught in the blank portion of my sleep experience."

The study of dreams is a complex area, and it is not a simple task to find truth in dreams. You would need to work with your dreams patiently and slowly. For many, it will be much simpler to learn the truth of life from a loving and honest study of *waking* experiences.

WORKING WITH YOUR DREAMS

For those who do wish to work with their dreams and deepen their understanding of the truth that is taught during the deep sleep periods, we will suggest a simple method that can be quite effective.

First of all, you would need to remind yourself that the

results of the study of your dreams will be directly tied to your willingness to work with yourself in the waking state. Success will depend upon your willingness to love yourself and to work to heal your fears. If you give a great deal of attention to a study of dreams, but you do not love and heal fear in your waking state, then you can expect your study of dreams to be quite confusing and perhaps distorted. But, if you are, to the best of your ability, working each day to love yourself and to heal fear, you can assume that what you are doing in the waking state will support the study of your dreams.

In beginning a study of your dreams, always start with the thought that your dreams are temporary realities that may possibly contain threads of truth, yet they are woven with your own subjective *creations*. Your first task then is to begin to understand which portions of your dream experiences are the teachings of your soul and your guiding-ones, and which portions are caused by your subjective personality creations. In order to determine this, you will need first of all to retain the *memory* of your dream experiences.

We suggest that to heighten your memory of your dream experiences you work in this way. First, you will need to feel a sense of commitment to the work. You will need to make the period of dream study as important as other areas of your waking life. Create this commitment by determining the period of time each day that will be dedicated to the study of your dreams. Then, decide exactly how long you wish to do this work—whether for a week, or a month, or more—and *write on paper* a small agreement with yourself: "I will give full attention to my dreams for this much time each day, for this period of time."

Next, prepare a way to *capture* your dreams upon awakening each day. The simplest way is to write them in a notebook. Or, you may wish to speak them into tape recording machines. Whatever you decide, as you prepare for sleep each evening, prepare your equipment and have it beside your bed. You will use it before you go to sleep.

As you prepare to enter sleep, take time to write, or speak to your machine, in a way that will focus your conscious mind on what has occurred during your day. You can say to yourself: "Today, I have had a day in which these areas of my experience stand out the most to me." Very briefly you would outline for yourself what were the most influential forces in your day. For example, you may write: "Primarily, in this day I was excited about a large sum of money that I inherited from a relative. I was also disappointed by a friend who seemed to insult me. Other than this it was an ordinary day." Perhaps on another day you would say: "All that stands out at this point is the sense of appreciation I had for being alive." In other words, you will make a brief note to yourself so that upon awakening the following morning you will have before you the most likely *subjective forces* that your personality created that might have entered into your dreams in that evening.

Then, put aside your writing or tape machine and prepare for sleep. Gently release your earth thoughts and emotions as best you can. After calming yourself, say to your mind:

"I am now entering into a period of sleep during which I shall learn many truths. I open my con-

**scious mind to accept love and truth. During this
period of sleep, my body shall be rejuvenated. I
shall awaken in the morning with an alertness that
will allow me to have greater conscious memory of
my experiences of truth gained during sleep."**

Upon awakening in the morning, or if you should
awaken in the middle of the night and desire to capture
your dreams, *immediately* fasten your attention upon your
memory of your dreams. Then, begin to write or speak all
that you can remember. You can give attention to the
details of the dream situations, but the primary focus should
be on the *feelings* that you remember having about those
details. Write your feelings about *yourself* in the dream,
about *other human beings*, and about the *situations* and
events that unfolded.

After you have written all that you can recall, if you
have a sense of the *meaning* of the dream, record that; if
not, record what seemed most important about the dream,
along with your observations about the important aspects of
it.

All of your recording of your dreams can be done
quickly each morning, without analyzing what you record.
Simply develop the daily habit of recording the dreams.

Then, each day, when you come to the period of time
set aside for your dream study, gather up your recorded
material and pick one dream to work with. First, attempt to
re-create the *feeling* of the dream as best you can. Use your
imagination to spark your feelings. As you begin to bring
the dream alive again, notice carefully the various elements
of the dream as you wrote about them, and as you presently

feel about them. Then question yourself about the major elements and write down your answers. What are the major themes lived out in the dream, and how do you feel about them? Who are the major characters, and how do you feel about them? Ask yourself as many questions as you can. Notice what seemed to be positive and inspiring about the dream and attempt to feel deeply about that, then write about this under the heading: *Inspirations*. Then note anything that was frightening and disturbing, and list this under: *Fears*.

Next, re-examine what you recorded about your day before you went to sleep in the previous evening. See if there is a correlation between your day's experiences and your dream. This is an area of investigation that can be quite broad, and you can explore it as deeply as you desire. Make all of the connections that you can between your daily experience and your dream, noting how dream experiences of love, harmony, and beauty might be related to your previous day's subjective waking experience. Then, do the same for any fears or challenges.

As you work with your dreams, remind yourself that you are discovering *possible* truths. You will need to work intelligently and attempt to go beneath the surface of all that you learn. For example, imagine that you have had a dream in which you saw yourself standing before thousands of people, teaching them great truths by lecturing. As you study this dream, you experience a great sense of excitement, goodness, and fulfillment. You have a strong feeling: "This is my true destiny. I am destined to be a great orator." You would need to remind yourself that this is a possible truth. Perhaps it is simply that a portion of you that feels inadequate is being adjusted by the teaching of your soul translated into a dream of you standing before thousands. Perhaps your soul is really attempting to spark your confidence and appreciation of yourself, and it is not telling you that you will be a great orator. Or, your soul may simply be reminding you that you have great capacities for communication. Therefore, when you work with your dreams, rather than prematurely leaping to the conclusion that you have discovered truth, it would serve you well to look at the knowledge as *possible* truth.

What we have described is a simple process that can serve as a beginning for the study of your dreams. You can expand this process as far as you wish to take it. It is primarily a matter of how much time, attention, and energy you wish to give to your dreams. As long as you continue to work lovingly and honestly with your personality in your waking experience each day, then a deepened understanding of your dreams can help you come to greater wisdom and fulfillment in your life.

DISTORTIONS OF YOUR HUMAN AWARENESS

In order to help you understand some of the factors that can temporarily block your capacity to live your soul in earth life, we will look now at the way in which your conscious awareness of your human experience can be distorted as you pass through your life in earth. Such distortion may be caused by human fear, as well as by altering the subjective personality experience by introducing chemical substances, such as drugs and alcohol, into the body.

We will begin by reminding you that the *structure* of

your subjective experience, the way in which your subjective experience functions, *was created by the forces of God*, in perfect wisdom and understanding. This structure was implanted in your soul by the forces of God. Your soul transmitted this structure for subjective awareness to you as a human personality. Thus, your present human awareness is a reflection, even though a limited reflection, of the kind of awareness that is the eternal awareness of your soul, and the true awareness of God itself.

From this you can understand that the ordinary *healthy* human awareness is the *perfect* vehicle for what the soul is attempting to accomplish by projecting human personality into physical bodies. What we would speak of as a healthy human awareness is one in which the human subjective experience is not distorted by excessive pain, fear, or extraordinarily difficult earth challenges; a human being in which there is essentially happiness, joy, and balance, even though there may be difficult challenges in the life.

When your subjective experience of your life becomes saturated with fear and pain, then your healthy human consciousness is distorted. The perfect structure of consciousness that was created by your soul to bring joy to your personality, to bring fulfillment and celebration to your earth life, is distorted by the fear that you have unintentionally created. Then, instead of having an awareness of earth life as a magnificent experience filled with love, your human awareness begins to experience life as something dark and frightening. Instead of the healthy, *perfect* experience that your soul desired for your personality, your subjective human experience becomes a *distorted* experience in which there appears to be a great deal of negativity and unhappiness.

At times, such a distorted awareness can magnify the negative experience of life to such a degree that you can come to believe: "This negativity is reality. This is truth. The earth is frightening. It is a bad place." When you come to such beliefs, then there is naturally a desire to *escape* the negative subjective experiences. Since your own negative experiences are felt to be the reality of earth life, then, *you come to desire to escape your own experience.*

In the present period of earth, and this has been true in some past times also, the most frequently chosen way of escaping the personality experience is through *numbing* the feelings of negativity. At the present time, the way in which many human beings choose to numb their feelings of negativity is through the use of such things as alcohol, drugs, nicotine, or even excessive eating of food. Some are drawn to preoccupation with sexual pleasure. In other words, human beings seek immediate *pleasure* to help them numb the pain of the negative experience of earth that they are creating.

If, during the period of use of alcohol or drugs, you would have experiences that feel pleasurable and good, in which reality seems larger and more beautiful than your day to day life, it is *possible* that you are attuning to your capacity to experience the true goodness of life. It is also possible that you are using your imagination unconsciously to escape from your negative experience of earth. It would not be beneficial to make a general statement here for all human beings. It would depend entirely upon the subjective personality matrix of each individual. However, we can say quite strongly that if in your personality you tend to avoid

facing your fears and healing them, then you can assume
that any altered experiences that you create through drugs,
or alcohol, or any other earth means, will directly reflect
your fear patterns.

The point that you must focus upon in order to understand the effects of chemicals placed into your body is that
*chemicals will most certainly distort the natural process
whereby your soul attempts to communicate to your personality.* In other words, your soul did not *intend* for your
body, your mind, and your emotions to be influenced by
foreign chemical substances. The use of chemicals is a
human choice. Therefore, even if you would feel that there
is no harm or negative effect from using alcohol or chemicals, you will need to remind yourself that these were not
intended as a way of expanding your awareness of truth.

For most human beings, creating a belief that alcohol
and drugs can expand awareness of truth will generally
result in less confidence in your *natural* ability to expand
your awareness. Yet, we cannot say to you that there is
badness or wrongness in using foreign chemicals in your
body. We cannot say that you will harm yourself, for
nothing in earth can harm your *true* being. But, in all truth,
we must say to you that these chemicals are not areas of
expansiveness intended by your souls. They are not aligned
with deep soul purposes that you have, in terms of expanding your conscious awareness of life.

However, in certain times, if you feel in your own subjective reality that there is too much pain for you to bear,
and you can honestly say to yourself: "I desire in this day to
bring a bit of pleasure to my personality in order to numb
some of the pain caused by challenge, and I do this now

consciously through the use of chemicals," then, at least there will be clarity and honesty in what you do. With such honesty, perhaps you will come to a time in your life in which you will be willing to face the fears in you that have caused the negative distortion of your human awareness. Then, by healing those fears, you will draw forth the magnificence of your *natural* human awareness that is so perfect for leading you to fulfillment in your present lifetime.

When alcohol or drugs are used in a human body excessively, and in the case of some drugs, even when they are used a small number of times, there comes certain responses in the body that cause the subjective feeling of *dependence* upon the alcohol or the drug. What you become dependent upon is the sense of *pleasure* or *goodness* in your subjective experience that is associated with the chemical. The sense of pleasure becomes strongly contrasted with a great feeling of *helplessness*, because you have temporarily covered over your ability to create pleasure without the chemical.

In some cases, the *physiological* effect of the chemical can cause you to experience intense feelings of disturbance when you do not use the chemical. The pleasure of the chemical can become the *only* satisfaction in your subjective feelings. However, the chemical does not manipulate you or control you. You simply intensify your feelings of weakness and helplessness, and you increase your desire for the pleasure of the chemical to such an extent that you create the *belief* that you have no choice. You are still making choices, even though you believe you are helpless and at the mercy of your desire for the chemical. *Always,* the human choice is the greatest choice in the physical earth reality, even though those who believe that they are addicted would have difficulty feeling this and believing it.

UNDERSTANDING FEAR AND "BADNESS"

There are some human beings who fear that in making deep attunements to realities beyond the physical earth, they will open themselves to forces of negativity—forces of "badness" or "evil." If this is your attitude, then you will need to heal it before you begin to make such attunements. Until you can understand that there is only good in the universe, we suggest that you keep your attention focused upon your earth life and leave attunements for a future time.

We can assure you that in all universes, physical and nonphysical, there is only the goodness that is God. All beings, all realities, are created by, saturated with, and sustained by these God forces that are, from the earth point of view, *perfect, magnificent, totally loving.* In other words, in all realities, physical and non-physical, there exists only these forces of goodness and eternal creativity. There does *not* exist, as the earth mind would be tempted to create, *opposites* to these forces. There are simply the realities of good, conceived in what you would speak of as love, harmony, perfection and creativity.

Now, in the human reality of earth, there are *feelings* of badness. There are conclusions drawn by human beings that certain *actions* are bad, that certain *people* are bad. Some human beings conclude from such feelings that there must be an evil within human beings that causes them to create such badness. By drawing such conclusions, human beings can temporarily create the illusion of badness *in their thoughts and feelings*. Then, by drawing the conclusion that there is an *evil force* in people who cause badness, human beings can temporarily create the *illusion* of evil in their own thoughts and feelings. Such badness and evil exist *only* in the subjective experience of human beings.

The truth of all realities is: *There are no forces of badness. There are no forces of evil. These are imagined by human beings. There are no forces of negativity*, except those that you human ones experience *within your human subjectivity*. The only "negative" energies that exist-meaning energies that do not perfectly reflect the true nature of God—are the temporary forces of human fear that you ones can create and transmit to one another while you live in human personalities. There is nothing in your inner reality, or in the forces of life, that can harm or damage your eternal being. Only your physical body can be damaged, and you are not that body.

In all of the deep attunements that you make to eternal realities, *unless you bring your own fear into the attunement*, there will never be any negativity at all. There will only be the force of God. During your attunements, whether you are aware of the God forces or not, they will be filling you with love, expanding you, and uplifting you.

EXPANDED STATES OF AWARENESS

It is possible for human beings to have subjective experiences of expanded awareness that seem to arise quite spontaneously. For some individuals, they are experiences that have not been consciously sought after. For others, there is a *desire* for the expanded awareness, and perhaps they have even made attunements, or study, or meditation in that direction.

Experiences of expanded awareness are highly individual, and will have different purposes and results for each person. However, for all human beings, spontaneous experiences of expanded awareness that go beyond your ordinary human perceptions are in some way aligned with the wisdom of your own soul. Your inner wisdom portion has worked with your soul and has given permission for there to be an experience of expanded awareness in your conscious personality. The experience can be one of inspiration, or an experience that will stir up a dramatic change in your personality. Your inner wisdom will work with your soul to determine the kind of influence that is perfect for your personality.

Yet, it would not be accurate to say that experiences of expanded awareness are always *caused* by your soul. Many times they are caused by a deep *desire* in the human personality for a change in the subjective life, for a new understanding, for a new wisdom. Thus, experiences of expanded awareness are indirectly caused by the human personality and its choices.

For example, imagine a female one who has continually prayed that her life would have more meaning and more purpose. As a result of this personality desire, her inner wisdom portion and her soul make inner adjustments in her human awareness that bring about a temporary expanding of that female one's capacity to sense inner truth and to feel the forces of God as love and magnificence in her own personality. In such a case, the expansion of awareness within the personality of the female one began with her *desire*. Her desire consciously and unconsciously aligned her with her own soul forces, which expanded her conscious awareness.

The *quality* of the experience of expanded awareness for the human being will be woven with the ordinary personality patterns of that human being. Thus, for a fearful person, the response to an experience of expanded awareness could be fear. Such a person could feel a negative quality in the experience. A person of trust and love would most likely experience the expansion of awareness as quite magnificent and beautiful. Here we must keep this at a simple level, since there are so many individual complexities involved that could make each person's experience quite different.

Therefore, we would say that, for most human beings, the expanded areas of human experience that you would consider to be mystical, religious, inspirational, spiritual, or psychic, occur because of an "agreement" made, consciously or unconsciously, between your human personality and your soul. The *purpose* of such an experience, in general, is to cause a turning in your earth pathway as a human being; to inspire your human personality to consciously turn toward truth in a deeper, more intense way. However, as a human being, your subjective *response* to the expanded experience, as with all responses in your personality, will be intimately woven with the inner subjective patterns that you have created within yourself throughout this lifetime. Thus, although the expanded experience is *intended* by your soul to be quite beneficial to you as a personality, whether you experience it as negative or positive will depend upon what you have created in your day to day personality life.

DESIRE TO KNOW ETERNAL REALITIES

We would look now at the aspects of your reality that you would speak of as the eternal or spiritual realities. These are areas that are not a conscious part of your earth adventure. They are realities of existence that are woven into the *unseen* fabric of human physical life in earth. It is these unobservable spiritual realities that make your earth life possible.

Imagine that you wish to go swimming, and you go and find a pool of water. You leap in and swim about in great joy. Now, the water is not *making* you swim. *You* are doing the swimming. Yet, without the water, it would be impossible for you to do the swimming.

In the same way, the eternal forces that are the forces of God, of your soul, of guiding-ones to you, and of many other beings that need not be spoken of in these present teachings, have created the "water" of physical reality through which you can swim with your own human abilities. These eternal forces, working through the souls of you ones, have created the energy matrix within which this physical earth exists, and within which your human personality can express and fulfill itself in joy. *You* are doing the expressing as a physical human being, but, if there were no eternal forces, then there would be no physical reality for you to express within. This is a very crude way of communicating about complex energy forces that continually interact with one another to make your physical earth life possible.

The important point to understand here is that the eternal forces and realities *are not separate from you* as a human being. You are swimming in the midst of them. However, for reasons that we have previously discussed, you as a soul have decided that when you come into human form, your conscious awareness of these eternal forces will be left aside so that your personality can focus intensely upon the earth reality.

When you as a human being begin to have a desire to *consciously* know the eternal realities, then, in a sense, you are stirring up a desire to return to your true existence—your true home. However, this is not accomplished by *escaping* earth life. It is done by *completing* the earth adventure.

The earth experience is very important to you and your soul, because the earth reality is the one in which you can create the most *intense* personal experience into which a conscious understanding of eternal realities can be brought. In other words, you as a human being, when you can *totally* experience the forces of God within your personality (and this is what human evolution is moving toward), in a certain sense will be experiencing a certain kind of intensity of the forces of eternal life that was not experienced by your soul up to that point of your expanded human experience. The intensity of experiencing *one* focused stream of the force of God within your human ego and personality will be greater at that point than at any time in all of the universes that have gone before. We are speaking here only of *one* focused stream of God, and all of this is simplified for you. Keep in mind that as your earth life unfolds around the one focused stream of God that is your personality, your soul continues to intensely experience *all* streams of the eternal forces.

It would not be of benefit to go too deeply into those complexities at this time. What is important here is to know that once you as a human being, living in earth and fulfilling your earth desires, begin to desire *of your own free will* to turn your attention to the eternal realities within which you live, then you have begun to move toward a fulfillment that is one of the most magnificent possibilities in all of the universes. Thus, you can see that it is an important turning point when you begin to desire to attune to the eternal realities.

It would not be beneficial for you to *force* yourself in this direction out of a feeling of inadequacy or discontent with your earth life. Yet, you *can* use your ability to make a spiritual attunement to help bring joy into your life when you feel challenged. Here you will need to use your wisdom to find the right balance for yourself. At times it can be very beneficial for you to turn toward eternal realities, and toward experiences of God, of your soul, and of your guiding-ones, in order to ease your pain and to comfort yourself. This is a focus that can help you a great deal throughout your life, and you could do this as often as it pleases you. However, if you would feel, "I am an unworthy human being, and I must force myself onto a spiritual path in order to be better," then you will find much confusion as you attempt to attune to spiritual realities with the desire to eliminate badness in yourself. In this case, it would be of greater benefit to say to yourself:

"I am feeling pain. Earth seems quite empty and unsatisfying. I wish to attune now to God itself, to the eternal portions of reality, in order to re-inspire myself to bring joy into my human life, to bring an understanding of my true magnificence, to live more fully and more magnificently in this earth life."

To balance your spiritual pathway with your earth life, you will need to monitor your own *motives* for seeking knowledge of eternal realities. When you feel satisfied that your motives for attuning to the eternal portions of life are sound, according to *your* understanding of yourself, then we strongly encourage you to proceed on your path of discovery of the eternal realities by turning your thoughts and your attention toward your *guiding-ones*.

YOUR SPIRITUAL GUIDES

Some human beings in earth are just beginning to turn toward a pathway of attunement to eternal realities. Others have walked such a path for many years. Regardless of your stage of seeking, it is of great benefit to understand that you are not walking alone in your search for truth. Not only are you infused by the forces of your own soul, but you are also guided by the forces of other souls who align with you out of love for you as a soul, and as a human being. These other souls are your *spiritual guides*—your guiding-ones.

For human beings alive in earth now, these souls who guide you, that we speak of as guiding-ones, have in past times of earth walked in *their* human forms beside your human form. Your guiding-ones have lived as physical human beings with you in the past, but they have since left earth behind in order to express their souls in ways that are no longer physical.

We can assure you that in this present human life in which you find yourself, you are closely guided by these souls who are guiding-ones to you. These guiding-ones live *within* your own personality, in your heart. They are not separate from you. Throughout this lifetime, they will walk with you in your personality expression. They constantly infuse you with their wisdom, their knowledge, and their love.

Even though your spiritual guides work closely with you, your soul would not desire for them to interfere with the unfoldment of your *choice* as a human being. Thus, in their work with you, your guiding-ones will not dominate your subjective reality. They will not make your life choices for you. In a certain sense, you have the same relationship to your soul that you have to your guiding-ones: they will always be the force of love that uplifts you and inspires you, but they will never interfere with your free will as a human being. You as a human being *must* be free to do as you please in your earth life. You are free to ignore the deep subtle forces of your soul and your guiding-ones, or you are free to turn toward those forces, to integrate them into your own personality, and to align them with your will and your choice in order to make them a part of what you create in this lifetime.

In this present time of earth, many people desire to gain knowledge of their guiding-ones. We suggest that it is not *knowledge* of your guiding-ones that will be most beneficial to you. That which will uplift your personality is your capacity to feel the *love* and the *wisdom* with which these guiding-ones infuse you. And, your feeling of your guiding-ones will be interwoven with your own thoughts and your own feelings. Your guiding-ones would not override your thoughts and your feelings, or block them out and replace them with other forces. Thus, it is important that you continue to respect your own thoughts and feelings, to pay attention to them, and to work lovingly with them, for it is through your inner experience of your own personality that the forces of your guiding-ones will work.

There are some people in this period of time who desire to attune to their guiding-ones in order to push away what they consider to be their own "inferior" experience, and to have their guiding-ones come forth and replace those troubling thoughts and feelings with a greater truth from the eternal portions of life. Attuning to guiding-ones with such an attitude will cause confusion. Even though such an attitude can bring a certain feeling of *comfort* if you come to believe that your guiding-ones are living your life for you, and making your choices for you, working in this way can eventually cause you to feel insignificant and helpless as a human being. If you deeply need such comfort, we cannot discourage you from moving toward it. However, if you need this kind of comfort, we strongly recommend that you give yourself to *God*, not to your guiding-ones. Create feelings within you that it is God itself who is helping you and lifting you up.

Eventually, you will come to the place in your personality growth where you can feel: "I am the one who must

live this human life. I am the one who must make my
choices." To align your human choices with your spiritual
guides, you can say to yourself:

**"I desire to attune in love to my guiding-ones, to my
soul, and to God. This will help me bring eternal
wisdom and truth into my own human choices."**

With this attitude, you can uplift yourself, fulfill yourself, and fully express the forces of God through your
human personality.

If you would desire a simple method for attuning to
your own guiding-ones, we would suggest that you set
aside a time in each day in which you would release your
personality rigidities in order to become more receptive to
the love and the magnificence that your guiding-ones bring
to you moment by moment. To begin such an attunement,
you would first bring about a state of deep relaxation in
your physical body. Then, you would create a feeling of
lightness, and a feeling of being free of all of the tensions
and pressures of the earth life. Create this with your
thoughts and your feelings, using your imagination. You
may also wish to create in your imagination a vision of a
physical place that represents to you your joining with your
guiding-ones. For some, this could be a beautiful garden;
for others, a magnificent temple. As you create this place,
remind yourself:

**"My guiding-ones are never apart from me. What I
am doing now is creating a symbol to bring them
more fully into my conscious awareness. But,**

**throughout this lifetime, they live in my own inner
being."**

After you have created this mood and such a symbolic
meeting place, begin to feel as though the inner portion of
you, which you can imagine as being located in your heart,
is expanding. Begin to understand that in your daily life,
your ordinary awareness of your eternal realities is con-
tracted, it is squeezed, it is quite dense. In this period of
attunement to your guiding-ones, your awareness of eternal
realities, symbolized by feelings in your heart, begins to
expand. To help this expansion, create feelings of becoming less heavy, less dense. Let your feelings of yourself
grow larger and larger.

If you wish, you can imagine yourself at first as a solid
wooden ball. Then, gradually, that ball begins to expand.
Feel as though that ball becomes so large that you can now
feel the spaces between the molecules that make up that
sphere. Work gently and patiently to feel that what is
ordinarily you as a human being, which is generally quite
dense and tightly packed, has become so large and light,
and so filled with free-flowing forces of love and joy and
creativity, that there is now much space woven with the
forces that are you. Your personal energies, which are now
light and moving about quite beautifully, have spaces
woven between them.

Gradually, begin to feel and understand that these
spaces are filled with *forces* and streams of *energy* that are
similar to your energy. But these forces are the energies of
your own guiding-ones. They feel the same as you, but they
are different. They are the magnificence of other beings

who love you, who care for you, who rejoice in you. They are the forces of your guiding-ones, who would never criticize or find fault with your personality, no matter what you do. No matter what choices you make in any moment of this lifetime, the guiding-ones will continue to pour forth their streams of love, and they will continue to weave them with your streams of being.

This is a simple way to build a representation of the reality that takes place within your personality as your guiding-ones weave their love into you. You can use these images and feelings as they please you, expanding or contracting them, altering them in ways that feel more suited to your joy and your upliftment.

In your attunement period, after you have set these kinds of images and feelings into motion, then it is time to become quite passive. Say to yourself:

"I have now created the *atmosphere* in which I will become consciously aware of the love and wisdom of my guiding-ones. Now I release myself from earth life. I am a being of total magnificence and beauty. I am now infused with the unlimited love of my guiding-ones. I now give permission for my conscious personality self to be impregnated by the love and wisdom and inspiration of my guiding-ones."

Then, simply float in a silence of beauty and love, allowing yourself to drift, *not needing to create, or direct, or control*, but simply *rejoicing in what you feel*. You do not need to listen for words from your guiding-ones, or look for pictures. Simply feel. Let your guiding-ones communicate with you through *love*, through *feelings of magnificence*. Do this for as long as it pleases you. Then, gently begin to return yourself to your ordinary awareness, working slowly, patiently. As you return your attention to your ordinary awareness, create inspiring thoughts for yourself, such as this:

"I rejoice that I have been able to be more consciously aware of my guiding-ones. I rejoice that they will continue to infuse me with their love and wisdom as this attunement period ends. I now return to my earth life rejuvenated, inspired, and prepared to make my own choices now that I am filled with this deep wisdom that aligns with my own truths."

These kinds of thoughts will gently and easily guide you back to your ordinary awareness.

After you have worked with this kind of attunement over a period of time, and it may be a period of months or years, you will come to understand many truths through the *feelings* that you gain in your attunements with your guiding-ones. Gradually, you may notice that after your attunement period you are left with brilliant inspiring *thoughts* and *ideas*. Perhaps you would notice *images*, or you would hear words. You could say: "Perhaps this is guidance from my guiding-ones, from my soul, and from *me*." You will always need to evaluate such input with your human intelligence. Say to yourself. "Is this confusion from my personality, or is this truth from inner guidance."

The area of receiving inner guidance is quite complex for each human being, and it can be difficult at times to evaluate the truth of attunement experiences. Again, as with all of the other areas of your inner life that we have looked at, you will need to work patiently with your personality to love yourself, to honestly identify your fears, to experience them, and to heal them so that they do not color your attunement experience. If you ignore these portions of personality growth, and if you over-focus on your attunements to your guiding-ones, emphasizing that experience more than your life, then you can create confusion for your personality. You will find the greatest fulfillment when you harmoniously combine your desire to attune to your guiding-ones with your desire to unfold the beauty of all aspects of your human personality.

YOUR ATTUNEMENT TO ETERNAL REALITIES

In order to successfully and joyfully attune to eternal realities, you will need to have a rather stable philosophical and spiritual viewpoint that explains to your mind what you are doing when you attune, and why you are doing it. The challenge here is that your understanding of these areas can constantly change. Therefore, *you will need to hold an ideal that can withstand change.*

The most effective ideal by which you can guide yourself in your attunements to eternal realities, and the closest to truth that human words can come, could be expressed by saying this to yourself:

"No matter what my personality might think, or

feel, or believe, my subjective human experience cannot alter the truth. And the truth of me is a force of perfection, of love, of all that I can conceive of as goodness. That force of goodness can *never* be altered by any human experience that I might have."

A way for you to think about this truth, and to feel it, is to imagine an eternal stream of perfection energy that is constantly flowing within you as a human being. And, riding upon this eternal energy is the smaller stream of energy that is your temporary human experience of physical reality. The stream of eternal perfection energy is *always* you. That perfection is what you will be after the death of your present body. After your physical death, the smaller energy stream that represents your human experience will be refined and then assimilated into yourself as an eternal soul.

Another way to reinforce your ideal of truth is to remind yourself each day:

"No matter what takes place in my human life, it can never alter the fact that I am an eternal soul; a soul of perfection; a soul of love. Nothing can change that."

Being able to *know* this in any moment of your life is the essence of human trust. Even when your thoughts say, "There is badness, I am lost," and when your feelings say, "There is only pain, terror, and darkness," you will need to find a way to live those negative feelings and experience them without losing sight of the truth. This can be done by taking time each day, *before* you experience challenges, working in periods of calmness and relative stability, to make deep attunements to the truth—to feel it, to live it, and to bring it to your conscious awareness. This will help you remember that experiences that clearly are not aligned with the truth—experiences of fear, doubt, pain, and sadness—are *temporary*, and they do not diminish the goodness that is your true nature.

If you are unable to feel the eternal realities, it is possible that you could create confused feelings that would say to you: "My negative earth experience is the truth. My spiritual ideals are simply a fantasy that I have made up. All is lost. Earth is only darkness and pain. There is no good." By a steady, patient, persistent working with your ideals, and by persistently attuning to the eternal truths each day, without ignoring your human personality, you can heal such confused feelings, and you can come to know the truth of your eternal soul, and you can live the perfection of your soul in your human life.

THE PROCESS OF ATTUNING

In learning to make deep attunements to areas beyond the physical reality, the *process* of the attunement is the same whether you wish to attune to your guiding-ones, to your soul, or to God itself. The forces of your guiding-ones, your soul, and God are all woven together in the same eternal reality. You as a human being are woven into that reality.

Even though at times it may seem difficult for you to achieve the deep experiences that you desire from your attunements, it is not difficult to *do* the attunement. It is a very simple process. Whether you would speak of it as meditation, attunement to guiding-ones, or prayer to God, the *process* of the attunement can be carried out quite easily. Here are the simple steps of that process.

Step One. Begin by retreating into a physical place of pleasantness where you can enter into a beautiful silence with yourself to create an environment of love.

Step Two. Work with your physical body, creating relaxation and comfort for your body.

Step Three. Move to your mind, creating a stillness and calmness in your thoughts.

Step Four. Bring about a smoothness and tranquility in your emotions so that you can feel the deep underlying beauty of life.

Step Five. Set into motion a feeling of release from the earth reality. Create the feeling of slipping away from all that holds you to the heaviness of earth.

At different times, you will experience varying degrees of feelings of success with each of these steps. Your mind might say: "This is a bad attunement period. I am filled with earth complexities, not with truth." If you listen to your mind and believe that it is thinking truth, then you will create a blockage in your attunement. However, if you gently remind yourself, "These are my confused subjective responses; *I* am creating them; I now wish to *cease* creating them," then you can simply ignore the judgmental chatter of your mind and continue with the attunement.

At other times you may feel: "This is a magnificent attunement. I am feeling such expansiveness, such love. I am feeling so close to the eternal realities." Ordinarily, this will be followed by the feeling: "*I desire more*. I desire to deepen this experience." With such feelings, you will usually begin to try to *create* a deeper attunement. This will usually cause you to lose the thread of the feeling of depth and intensity. Thus, you will need to say to yourself: "The feeling of *pleasure* with this deep attunement is a subjective creation of my personality. I rejoice in it, but I now *release* it so that I may temporarily step back from my attempt to *control* this attunement. I now give myself fully, and in total trust, to the process of loving attunement that I am choosing to set into motion."

To attune deeply to eternal realities, you will need to remember that there are three separate phases of the attunement process. The first phase includes the steps that we have listed above, which involve working with your environment, your body, your mind, your emotions, and your ability to release earth. This is the *preparatory* phase. In this phase, you *do* take control with your will. You *will* yourself to go to your attunement place, to sit quietly, to make the relaxation of body, mind, and emotions. You *will* yourself to begin the feelings of release, and love, and whatever other preparations you desire to consciously make.

Then comes the second phase of the attunement in

which *you voluntarily give up your will.* You release yourself toward complete trust that you are giving yourself to
God, to your soul of eternal wisdom, and to guiding-ones
who have total love for you. Thus, the next step is:

**Step Six. Enter into the second phase of your attun-
ement in which you give up your will. You understand that all here is taken care of for you. All here
is guided by eternal perfection and love. You need
do nothing but rejoice in the magnificent experience
of perfection.**

During this step, you will simply *experience.* Let yourself drift in love, peace, and harmony. As much as possible,
refrain from attempting to *create* these feelings. Trust that
these feelings are *realities* that you are simply drifting into.
You are floating in beauty, joy, fulfillment, and love. It is
all given to you freely. You are closely guided and loved.
Drift in these experiences as long as it pleases you. Then,
when you desire, move to the next phase of the attunement.

The third phase of the attunement process is the *ending
period.* Here you re-activate your will in order to bring
yourself back to your ordinary consciousness.

**Step Seven. Return yourself to a clear awareness of
your human thoughts and emotions. Notice your
body and rejoice in it. Slowly and gently, with great
love for your personality, guide yourself back to
your ordinary awareness of yourself, physically,
mentally, emotionally. Create many thoughts and
feelings of all of the good that you have accom-**

plished during your attunement period.

After every attunement period, even ones during which you may have felt that you were too tense, or too worried, or too distracted, end your attunement by *reminding yourself of the truth.*

Step Eight. Say to yourself: "A great good and a great opening have taken place during my attunement, whether I was consciously aware of it or not. In my next attunement, I shall find even more joy, even more fulfillment."

Working in this way to attune more clearly to eternal realities, you are serving as a guide to yourself in your earth life. It is as if you are leading yourself into a jungle to observe the animals, to rejoice in the forest, and to love nature. As you make your way through the jungle, you are guiding yourself. You are choosing which path to take. You are controlling the process of discovery. However, when you come to the beautiful meadow where you will observe nature, your task of guiding yourself is ended. Now, you have only to sit, and to be fulfilled by the beauty of that which unfolds naturally and spontaneously before you, within you, and around you. When you are finished rejoicing in the beauty of the experience, then it is time to rise up and guide yourself home.

It is the same with your attunements to eternal realities. You must, with your will, prepare yourself, release earth distractions, and open your heart. Then, all else is guided by God, by your soul, and by your guiding-ones. When that experience of the eternal has filled you, you *choose* to end the attunement and you rise up again with your will to guide yourself back to your temporary home of earth awareness.

In your attunements, always know that you are simply bringing to your *conscious* awareness the magnificence of God that has *always* been living in you. You do not need to go forth to bring God into yourself. It is already living there. You do not need to transverse space that separates you from the eternal realities. Those realities live *within* you each moment of your human existence. You do not need to *create* goodness inside of you, for it is already there. All that you need to accomplish during your attunement period is *an adjustment of your conscious awareness* so that it is not so filled with earth preoccupations. You simply need to create some "space" in your human experience for the eternal realities that live within you to rise up into conscious awareness.

Attunement to eternal realities is a simple process, but it does require persistence, patience, and trust. It requires, most of all, a trust that these eternal forces of magnificence truly do live within you. If you can believe that this is true, then it will be quite simple for you to bring these eternal realities to your conscious awareness. During your attunement periods, the eternal forces will begin to fill your mind with thoughts of greater beauty, vastness, and magnificence. They will begin to fill your heart with greater feelings of love, majesty, fulfillment, and joy.

As you work with yourself each day to attune to the eternal realities, remind yourself:

"All that I need do in my attunement is to pull back the veil that has grown in my conscious awareness that temporarily prevents me from seeing, feeling, and living the eternal forces that are me, and the forces that are God, my soul, and my guiding-ones. I rejoice that I have chosen to become aware of the eternal realities. I rejoice that through my own free will I am creating the experience that allows me to bring the conscious awareness of God itself into my human life."

Each day, as you bring forth this attitude during your periods of attunement, you will begin to feel the eternal realities more clearly within your personality. Then, eventually, you can begin to bring those enlightened feelings into your day to day life. You can bring them into your relationships with others, into your desires and their fulfillments, and into all that you do as a human being. And, even if there do come periods of fear, confusion, doubt, or pain, you will have so deepened your capacity to feel the eternal realities within you that you will be able to experience those realities, even when you are temporarily challenged by your earth life. You will be able to *fully* live all of your earth experiences, whether they are pleasant or painful, with a sense of certainty within your being that these earth experiences do not alter that eternal force of love and magnificence that is expressing through your human personality.

As you continue to deepen your experience through your daily attunements, you will come to stand within your human personality as a great beacon of light that shines from the shore. Even when there are dense fogs and the light *appears* dim, you understand that it is still shining as brilliantly and as potently as it ever has. As you continue to fill your life with the light of love, you become the beacon of love and truth that can shine through the darkness that others have created about themselves by their own fear. *You become the example of the way in which fear is healed, and truth and love are brought forth from within the depths of the human personality. You become the example of how an eternal soul can be lived in a human personality in earth.*

As one seeking truth through deep attunements day after day, eventually, you will become a one *living* truth by the expression of your perfection in your personal life. As you do this, you will feel and understand that, indeed, you *are* the expression of God in earth. You *are* the reflection of that magnificence that has created you. And, at the same time, in the vastness of this great earth adventure, you are a *creator*. By *inwardly* creating your human experience in beauty and love, you become a creator of the beauty and love that unfolds *outwardly* as your *life* in the physical earth reality.

You are the seed planted by the master gardener. In coming forth to blossom and flower, you bless earth with your beauty. You also move toward that day in the future of earth in which *you* shall become the gardener, planting your seeds of perfection in new realms of existence. And those seeds will eventually sprout forth as beauty in new worlds.

To draw these particular teachings to a close for this time, we would say to you: as you go forth each day into earth to create your human life, always remind yourself that you are drawing upon an *infinite* reservoir of love and magnificence. You have total freedom to choose *how* you will bring those infinite forces into earth, how you will build them, how you will multiply them, and how you will rejoice in the beauty and love that come forth from your creation. You are free to use these forces to create your own personality fulfillment. If you do this while you love those about you, and while you rejoice in *their* fulfillment, then you will move toward the perfect earth experience that you have worked so many lifetimes to create. You will move toward the *completion* of yourself as a human being. You will move toward the *expansion* of yourself as an eternal soul.

All that exists in eternal realities *exists within you now.* You can go forth into this earth adventure to decide for yourself how much of that eternal reality will manifest in your earth expression as a human being. Thus, you stand with the universe in your hand. You stand with the freedom to manifest as much of God in the reality of earth as you wish to bring forth. In this sense then, you stand in earth as the *master* of the creative forces of God. You will decide for yourself: "How will these forces of God be used in earth? What shall earth become as a result of the way I choose to use the forces of God?"

As you live your earth adventure each day, look to *yourself* as the one who must choose what earth will become. And look to God itself as that from which you choose. With this attitude, and by going forth to love yourself and to love all those about you, you as a human being will create *in* earth, the perfection that you as a soul are *beyond* earth.

❖ ❖ ❖

In loving memory of my extraordinary

husband and soulmate, Ron Scolastico,

I wish you, Dear Reader, a joyful earth adventure,

filled with kindness, compassion and love.

Susan Scolastico
www.ronscolastico.com